FACING LIFE'S CHALLENGES

OTHER BOOKS BY AMY E. DEAN

Pleasant Dreams

Night Light

LifeGoals

Making Changes

Once Upon a Time

Letters to My Birthmother

Proud to Be

Peace of Mind

FACING LIFE'S CHALLENGES

*Daily Meditations
for Overcoming Depression,
Grief, and "The Blues"*

AMY E. DEAN

To Judy
love
Amy

Hay House, Inc.
Carson, CA

Published and distributed in the United States by:

Hay House, Inc., 1154 E. Dominguez St., P.O. Box 6204
Carson, CA 90749-6204
(800) 654-5126

Edited by: Jill Kramer
Designed by: Highpoint, Inc., Claremont, CA

The author of this book does not dispense medical advice or prescribe the use of any technique as a form of treatment for physical or medical problems without the advice of a physician, either directly or indirectly. The intent of the author is only to offer information of a general nature to help you in your quest for emotional well-being and good health. In the event you use any of the information in this book for yourself, which is your constitutional right, the author and the publisher assume no responsibility for your actions.

Library of Congress Cataloging-in-Publication Data

Dean, Amy.
    Facing life's challenges : daily meditations for overcoming depression, grief, and the blues / Amy E. Dean.
       p.   cm.
    ISBN 1-56170-145-9 (trade paper)
    1. Affirmations. 2. Attitude (Psychology) 3. Adjustment (Psychology) I. Title.
BF697.5.S47D42 1995   95-13930
158' . 12--dc20   CIP

ISBN 1-56170-145-9

99 98 97 96 95   5 4 3 2 1
First Printing, October 1995

Printed in the United States of America

To Pat Capozzi

(because you make me laugh)

INTRODUCTION

Do you have the right mental attitude to make life's difficulties work for you? If you do, then you can probably accept whatever comes your way as part of the natural ebb and flow of life. You *accept* that death, job loss, financial insecurity, addiction, and the end of a relationship, for example, are as much a part of life as birth, job promotions, salary advancement, recovery, and love's renewal. You *trust* that the unresolved will eventually be resolved; the sting of hurt will fade over time; the pain of tragedy will be offset by the joy of memory; the feelings of failure, rejection, and being lost will be replaced by success, acceptance, and discovery. And you *take action*—you do what you feel you need to do in order to facilitate changes in your circumstances, to encourage and nurture your personal growth, and to seek personal happiness and fulfillment.

But if you don't possess the right mental attitude to make life's difficulties work for you, then you may live each day or the majority of your days in quiet desperation or with chronic feelings of frustration, disappointment, sadness, and devastation because you're unable to recover from, or work through—even in some small way—the effects of some of life's harsh realities. You may find that you ask yourself and others questions such as: *"Why me?"* *"What did I ever do to deserve this?"* *"Why is life so unfair?"* *"Why can't I ever get a break?"* *"When will I finally be able to enjoy my life?"* and *"How long do I have to go through this?"*

When you don't have the right mental attitude to guide you through the uncharted waters and channels in the sea of life, you may feel like a sailboat stuck on a windless sea. You're frustrated by your inability to make progress and, consequently, unprepared to weather sudden squalls. You can be *hardy* at a time like this, when you're assailed by such stresses, or you can be *hardly*. When you're hardy, you feel somewhat in control of your life and your reactions to life's events, so you can be resilient and responsive. When you're hardly, you see yourself as having little control over what happens to you and, as a result, you may often experience depression.

Depression is a condition that varies greatly from person to person. Some individuals endure intense feelings of worthlessness, self-loathing, and mental paralysis continually; others experience symptoms ranging from frequent crying, chronic fatigue, anxiety, and irritability on a sporadic basis, but they are capable of feeling joy and optimism *some* of the time. Still others become depressed in response to traumatic events such as the death of a loved one, a prolonged period of unemployment, the break-up of a long-term relationship, and persistent health problems. And then there are those who may get depressed during certain life cycles such as pre-menstruation, the cold winter months, on the anniversary of a painful loss, during a slow time at work, or simply because a rainy Monday morning makes them feel "blue."

The best method for overcoming depression, grief, and "the blues" is to take responsibility for your own wellness. Study after study conducted on people who experience mild, as well as severe, forms of depression reveal that those who take responsibility for their own wellness achieve the highest levels of stability, health, control over their own lives, and overall happiness. By taking such responsibility, an investment is being made to ensure ongoing physical, emotional, and spiritual well-being. Responding positively and proactively during stressful life events can be a learned behavior that's developed and honed over time.

Facing Life's Challenges is designed to assist you if you are experiencing depression, are going through a grieving process, or are having a hard time shaking the blues. The 366 daily meditations in this book provide simple "mental conditioning" exercises that can help muster an optimistic attitude even when things are most difficult. They can also help you begin the process of "programming" positive thoughts into your mind, can suggest purposeful ways to effect change, and can encourage the use of mental empowerment to give you the strength to remain rational and active during times of adversity.

Through daily use, you may find that you're developing the right mental attitude to enable you to look objectively at yourself and your circumstances and accept the things that happen to you, trust that you can work through them, and take action that will give you a sense of control. Soon, you may find that you're no longer asking questions that stem from a base of helplessness and hopelessness. Rather, you may find that you're responding to life's challenges in affirmative ways, with such thoughts as:

"I can learn to accept life the way it is for me."
"I am in charge of my own thoughts and feelings."
"I have faith in the future, no matter what it holds for me."
"I am confident in my ability to cope."
"I have the courage to go on with my life."
"I know that I will have all I need to be happy and fulfilled."

You may choose to read each meditation on its corresponding date, at any one time during a particular day, or throughout the day, if need be. Or, you may choose to use the index to help you focus on those meditations that touch on a theme that's especially meaningful to you. Regardless of how you use the meditations in this book, keep in mind the advice given by Virgil Thomson at the age of 93: "Try a thing you haven't done three times. Once, to get over the fear of doing it. Twice, to learn how to do it. And a third time, to figure out whether you like it or not."

And remember: this book only offers options for facing life's challenges; what you do with this information will be up to YOU! The ability to choose is what will ultimately help you overcome depression, grief, and the blues. As Dr. Viktor Frankl, a Holocaust survivor who had everything and everyone in his life taken from him, said, "The last of the human freedoms [is] to choose one's attitude in any given set of circumstances, to choose one's way." What this means is that it's not what happens to you, but your reaction to what happens to you, that determines whether you'll feel miserable or marvelous.

So, let this book prepare you to gradually minimize the emotional lows and maximize the self-empowering highs in your life to help you effectively handle all of the challenges you face with strength, wisdom, and peace of mind!

ﾞﾟ　ﾞﾟ　ﾞﾟ

(**Please note:** *I have provided identifying information for some of the lesser-known sources of quotes on the daily meditation pages; however, many of the quotes are from individuals whose identity is unknown.*)

"Better do to no end, than do nothing."

— Robert Burton

TAKING RESPONSIBILITY

Robert Burton, a 17th-century scholar, wrote *The Anatomy of Melancholy*—an exercise in self-help—over 350 years ago to combat his own depression. The theme of his book presented a powerful challenge that has stood the test of time: *The only way to break the cycle of brooding thoughts is to act responsibly on one's behalf.* One way to do so is to start today to learn all you can about your mood disorder. Such knowledge can help you make decisions about your recovery, as well as enable you to decide how to combat such feelings in the future. You can learn more through published materials—books, audiocassettes, and magazine articles—or by talking with friends and family members who have gone through what you're now experiencing.

What you may discover from such self-education is that you may need to take responsibility for your feelings and release the blame that you've placed on everything and everyone else (your parents, your job, your health, your income, your friends, the cruel world, or even the weather) in your life. The difficult part of taking such responsibility is accepting that you own your feelings; the beneficial part is acknowledging that claiming such ownership empowers you to make positive changes that can free you from negative emotions.

So begin today, this first day of the new year, by resolving to keep the words of Elbert Hubbard in mind: "There is no failure except in no longer trying." Take responsibility for yourself and your feelings through self-education and by ceasing to blame, so you can begin to make responsible decisions for yourself.

🎉 🎉 🎉

I TAKE RESPONSIBILITY FOR MY OWN WELLNESS.

"Melancholy has ceased to be an individual phenomenon, an exception. It has become the class privilege of the wage earner, a mass state of mind that finds its cause wherever life is governed by production quotas."

— author Günter Grass

BUILDING A SUPPORT SYSTEM

When unemployment climbs, inflation rises, and the economy falls into yet another slump, economists often issue dire warnings about "recessionary psychology"—a pattern of cuts in consumer spending and investments that feed the downward spiral. But there's another, more profound kind of recessionary psychology that's measured by psychic, rather than economic, indicators. People change their behavior in the face of layoffs, cutbacks, or a drop in net worth. Some drown their troubles in alcohol. Others turn to snacks or rich food. Some become violent and abusive; others lethargic and hopeless. When the economy slumps, so does the national psyche.

During the Great Depression of the 1930s, everyone was in the same boat and knew that their fellow human beings were suffering equally. Due to this common bond, people as a whole were able to pull together in ways that aided themselves as well as the country. But as a result of the present-day disparity between the "haves" and the "have-nots," when the country suffers as a whole, the individual suffers, too. That's why it's important to build a strong support system that can help you through the tough times in your career or your financial situation. Today, make a list of three friends or relatives who can provide you with assistance when you're feeling down about these issues. Then add the names of two professionals who can offer you guidance to get you through these difficult times. Regard the individuals on this list as your personal support team—people who can help you make sound, objective decisions when you're not able to make them for yourself.

❧ ❧ ❧

I AM BUILDING A STRONG SUPPORT SYSTEM FOR PEACE OF MIND.

"An ice-packing plant in Chicago burned down years ago. This building had all the material inside capable of extinguishing the fire, but it was in unavailable form; it was frozen. You are the same way. You have all the material inside capable of putting out the fires in your life, but it is frozen by fear, doubt, anger, anxiety, and indecision."
— Dr. Allen Unruh, author of *Illness as a Teacher*

EMOTIONAL RESPONSIVENESS

There are healthy responses to emotional pain, as well as destructive responses. Most people have a tendency to react to trauma by denying, suppressing, or numbing their painful feelings. A common example of this phenomenon often follows the death of a loved one. Rather than openly grieve, the survivors may suppress their sad emotions because they feel they need to be strong for others or because they think they won't be able to handle those feelings.

But when you refuse to grieve, you prolong the healing process. You continue to have feelings of intense loss for a much longer period of time, are at a higher risk for developing physical illnesses, and are often prone to depression that is stronger than that of someone who openly expresses emotions.

How can you be more emotionally open following a loss? First, accept that it's normal to feel pain. Yes, it *does* hurt like hell to lose someone you love, but while you may not enjoy the pangs of sadness, it's healthy to admit that you cared so much. Next, you need to give yourself permission to express those emotions. Even though your mind may be telling you, "You shouldn't cry, you shouldn't be sad," you *need* to let your tears flow, and you *need* to feel melancholy. It will be good for you to cry on someone's shoulder—especially someone who will listen, care, and not be judgmental. Such natural responses to emotional pain can lead to healing and long-term recovery.

❧ ❧ ❧

I RESPOND TO THE PAIN OF LOSS BY EXPRESSING—NOT SUPPRESSING—MY GRIEF.

"You assume that the way you see things is the way they really are or the way they should be. But this is not the case. You see the world, not as it is, but as you are—or, as you are conditioned to see it."

— author Stephen R. Covey

SELF-OBSERVATION

Negative thoughts can play an important role in depression. Common thoughts include: "I'm no good," "No one understands me," "Life isn't fair," "I'm a failure," and other self-deprecating assessments. Oftentimes, these thoughts are combined with self-destructive behaviors. For example, if you think, *"I'm fat,"* then you may establish patterns of overeating that serve to confirm this label; if you think, *"I'm not a good lover,"* you may refrain from intimate involvements. Over time, negative thoughts can become so habitual that they warp your sense of reality, and you start to believe what you think. As a result, your depression will worsen. As Sally Kempton said, "It is hard to fight an enemy who has outposts in your head."

The best way to gain a clearer—and more realistic—understanding of yourself is to acknowledge that you are allowing your negative perceptions to supersede reality. So it's you, then, that needs to look at your life from a different perspective. The next time you have a negative thought, really listen to it. If you're communicating that thought to someone, hear what you're saying. If you're doing something that validates a negative thought, observe your actions. Objectively stand back and monitor your thoughts, words, and actions. What you may find is that simply being aware of a negative thought or feeling is all it takes to lessen its impact—and sometimes even dissolve it.

ధ ధ ధ

AS THE FIRST STEP IN LETTING GO OF NEGATIVE THINKING, I OBSERVE MYSELF.

"Sadness flies on the wings of the morning, and out of the heart of darkness comes the light."

— author Jean Giraudoux

POSITIVE ATTITUDE

A positive attitude doesn't pop into your mind by itself the minute you wake up in the morning. How you feel is a decision you need to make every day. If you find it hard to be upbeat, then you need to start each day in a more constructive way. Here are some suggestions for uplifting rise-and-shine activities:

- Wake up to your favorite radio station, not a shrill alarm. Allow yourself a few moments to slowly stretch, and then take several deep breaths.
- Think about one or more positive things you want to accomplish that day.
- Allow yourself enough time to get ready at a civilized—not a frantic—pace.
- Eat a healthful breakfast.
- Discuss interesting plans for the day with your partner, roommate, or children.
- Focus on some positive feature about the day, such as the weather, a hug from your child, or a nice wake-up cuddle from your pet.

Over time, you may feel so motivated when you wake up that you will add exercise to your morning routine, prepare a delicious lunch to take to work or school, or delay reading the morning paper or listening to the news so you won't be negatively affected by tragic stories or world problems.

ஃ ஃ ஃ

I DEVELOP A POSITIVE ATTITUDE AT THE BEGINNING OF EACH DAY.

Life is risky; we are all acrobats
Tiptoeing over one bridge or another.
To a tightrope walker
The rope is just like home.
Those who hold their bodies lightly
And their minds simply
May seem in danger
But they are safe.

— Chinese scrolls

RISK TAKING

Too often you may feel scared by what you want to do and might not be able to do, fearful about what others will think if you try something new, worried that the circumstances in your life will never change no matter how hard you try to change them, frightened that you'll never be able to realize your dreams. You may let these fears stand in your way, blocking your progress and thereby preventing you from taking risks that can help free you from feelings of despair. You may say yes when you really want to say no, you may stay stuck in the rut of your daily routine when you really want to try something new, you may behave in ways others have come to expect rather than push for acceptance of new behaviors.

But you're never going to feel different about yourself or your life if you don't try something you've never tried before. Life is a risk, but only to those who will take it. So what do you have to lose? Risk something today—take a different route to work, say no, ask for a raise, speak your mind. Try something. Try anything. Take the risk!

🎋 🎋 🎋

I TRY SOMETHING NEW AND BENEFIT FROM TAKING THIS RISK.

"Geez, if I could get through to you, kiddo, that depression is not sobbing and crying and giving vent, it is plain and simple reduction of feeling. Reduction, see? Of all feeling. People who keep stiff upper lips find that it's damn hard to smile."

— from *Ordinary People,* by Judith Guest

PLAY AND CREATIVITY

When you're depressed, you may feel like you're at the bottom of an emotional well—and incapable of summoning the strength to climb out. You may feel the need to lie down, curl up in a tight ball, and hope that you never wake up—that is, just totally put an end to your pain. As Dr. Carl Simonton observes: "When you're depressed, your whole body is depressed, and it translates to the cellular level."

Because the opposite of depression is expression, healing a depressed spirit requires raising the energy level. One way to do this is through play and creativity. What playful, creative things do you like to do or have you always wanted to do? Maybe you want to learn how to paint. Maybe you want to write poetry. Maybe you want to learn how to prepare vegetarian dishes. Maybe you want to make a quilt. Maybe you want to take up a sport such as golf or tennis.

Today, take the first step towards participating in a playful, creative endeavor. Buy or borrow a set of pastels and paper, and then experiment. Take a walk through the woods and create a poem about the experience. Visit a health food store and explore the cookbooks for a recipe you'd like to try. Sign up for a quilting class or lessons from a golf or tennis pro. Then let the fun you have and the creativity you express help you beat your depression!

🦋 🦋 🦋

I EXPLORE MY CREATIVITY SO THAT I AM MORE INVOLVED WITH LIFE.

JANUARY 8

"The little reed, bending to the force of the wind, soon stood upright again when the storm had passed over."

—Aesop

DEALING WITH CRISIS

In the Chinese language, the symbol for the word *crisis* denotes a duality—"a moment of danger and of opportunity." Through this symbol, the Chinese communicate that every crisis is both an enemy—a threat to your vital resources—as well as an ally, an experience that can help you feel challenged so you can make changes and grow.

The Greek meaning of the word *crisis* translates into "moment of judgment." When you face crisis, you make a judgment about whether to concentrate on the dangers or on the opportunities in the crisis. So the combined message of the Chinese and Greek meanings for *crisis* becomes: *There are dangers as well as opportunities in all of life's crises, but in any crisis you have the freedom to choose which you will view it as—a window of opportunity or a window with closed shutters.*

If you can feel challenged by any crisis that life tosses your way, then you'll be able to experience a sense of control over your reactions so you won't feel helpless, hopeless, and victimized. Just as a severe winter storm is often followed by brilliant sunshine and cloudless blue skies, so too do crises have their positive outcomes. Today, believe in the words of John Milton in his classic work, *Paradise Lost*: "The mind is its own place, and in itself / Can make a heav'n of hell, a hell of heav'n." Accept the challenge of a crisis by greeting it like a reed in the wind, bending through adversity, but always capable of standing upright once again.

୨ଈ ୨ଈ ୨ଈ

I AM FLEXIBLE DURING ADVERSE TIMES; I GO WITH THE FLOW OF LIFE.

JANUARY 9

"It's a rare person who goes through life without accumulating hurt feelings that can lead to anger and depression. When you consider that stress is the pressure of an unexpressed feeling, you realize how many feelings are being shunted into emotional overload every day of your life."

— Dr. David Viscott, psychiatrist

REMEMBERING THE PAST

Being depressed today doesn't necessarily mean that today is depressing. Most people who are depressed at this moment may have been depressed for years and not sought help for it. This may be a result of holding in negative feelings of hurt and anger whenever they occurred in the past or in having unresolved concerns over childhood issues. So, while dealing with the cause of your current depression can ease some of your present-day symptoms, it won't necessarily help you dig up the root feelings of the depression. The dynamics of this condition confirm this fact: First you're hurt, but you internalize the hurt instead of expressing it; your hurt turns into anger; your unexpressed anger is then directed inward as guilt; the energy used in this process of internalizing and redirection uses up your emotional reserves so you feel depressed.

Thus, the cure for depression is not to release the anger, but to release the original hurt from which the anger evolved. What this means is that rather than treat your current symptoms of depression, you can get the greatest help from searching for and then dealing with its root causes. To do so, work with a mental health professional who is trained to help you in the search, become involved in a support group that deals with childhood issues, or use meditation and journal writing as an aid in self-discovery.

I EXAMINE MY FEELINGS FROM THE PAST AND RELEASE THEM IN THE PRESENT SO I CAN ENJOY MY FUTURE.

"When I stick to a diet that is high in grains and vegetables, I feel better and my moods are more stable. Junk foods that are high in fat, sugar, and salt deepen my depression and make me more hyper."

— Mary Ellen Copeland, author of
The Depression Workbook

DIET AND NUTRITION

What you eat can affect how you feel. Caffeine and sugars speed you up, but then let you down. Dairy products can be hard to digest. Salty foods can make you feel bloated. Eating foods you're allergic or sensitive to can disrupt your digestive system or cause headaches, sinus problems, heartburn, or skin rashes. Yet, oftentimes the foods that make you feel the worst are the ones you crave the most. So while you may begin each morning trying to change your diet for the better, during the day you may give in to your cravings so you end up in the same "food mood" by the time evening comes around.

That's why a strict change in diet for a short period of time can be so important in making long-term changes. By giving yourself a chance to feel how a different diet can impact your moods, you can then become more sensitive to the food choices you make. A diet that's high in complex carbohydrates can increase your level of serotonin, a neurotransmitter that has an antidepressant effect. Interestingly enough, Prozac, a prescription antidepressant, chemically increases the level of serotonin in the brain. To nutritionally raise serotonin, you can eat foods such as whole grain breads, pasta, grains, potatoes, and vegetables.

Making dietary changes is not always easy. Your new diet may require more effort, but the positive results that you will see even after just two weeks may make this new way of eating much more appealing.

🦋 🦋 🦋

FOR TWO WEEKS, I FOLLOW A DIET THAT EMPHASIZES COMPLEX CARBOHYDRATES, AND I MONITOR HOW I FEEL.

"We must discover security within ourselves."
— author Boris Pasternak

HEALTHY LOVE

When pop idol Andy Gibb, the youngest brother of the singing group The Bee Gees, died in 1988 at the age of 30, those who knew him weren't surprised. In 1981, during his pinup-poster boy phase, he met actress Victoria Principal, whom Gibb regarded as his "very special lady." When the affair ended after 13 months, he was devastated.

"When we broke up," he told an interviewer on a national television show, "I gave up everything. I didn't care about life." Erratic behavior cost him a stint as co-host on a popular musical television show, and he was replaced in a Broadway production after missing 12 shows in 6 weeks. Throughout it all, Gibb blamed his problems on the breakup. Ironically, one of Andy Gibb's 1977 hits was "I Just Want to Be Your Everything," and that seems to be just what he expected from an intimate relationship—to have his woman be his everything. Marge Piercy described this kind of unhealthy love as, "Love says, mine. Love says, I could eat you up. Love says, stay as you are, be my own private thing, don't you dare have ideas I don't share."

In reality, there's no person in the world who can be your everything. Those you love can give you wonderful material and emotional gifts, but ultimately *you* have to be your everything. Losing a relationship only feels like it's the end of the world when you've given your world away. Today, resolve that when you love again, you'll share your love, and accept the love that's shared with you—but you'll give nothing more away.

❧ ❧ ❧

I CELEBRATE THE JOY AND PASSION OF HEALTHY LOVE.

"If you find your inner conversation running along negative lines, you have the power to change the subject, to think along different lines."

— Martha Smock

SOOTHING FEARFUL THINKING

Much of what you feel is caused by what you tell yourself, how you think, the ways in which you interpret situations, and your personal point of view. Many people begin in childhood to develop the habit of filling themselves with negative thoughts about themselves and the circumstances of their lives. One type of negative thinking involves fearful thoughts that plague you, go around and around in your head, and make you feel as if you have no choice but to think them.

For example, you may think such distorted, fearful thoughts as, *"My car is going to break down on a deserted highway," "I think I have cancer," "My depression is going to get so bad that I'll be locked up and drugged up for the rest of my life,"* and so on.

But what would happen if, the next time you had a fearful thought, you immediately asked yourself, "How true is that?" Sometimes, if you pause a moment to analyze what you're thinking and assess just how truthful such a thought is, you may realize that your fears are unfounded. You might then tell yourself, *"No, my car isn't going to break down because I keep up with maintenance and repairs," "No, I don't have cancer because I have a checkup every year,"* or *"No, my depression isn't going to get that bad because I'm aware of it and I'm taking steps to overcome it."* By replacing the irrational fears with responses that are grounded in reality, you can reprogram yourself so you begin to think differently—and less fearfully.

🍀 🍀 🍀

I CHANGE, OR EVEN ELIMINATE, FEARFUL THINKING THROUGH RE-EXAMINATION AND REALITY-CHECKING.

"I learned to live between steps. I never knew whether the next one would be my last, so I had to get everything I could out of that moment between picking up my foot and putting it down again. Every step felt like a whole new world."
— Ralph, a soldier, quoted by Barbara Brown Taylor

RECOVERING FROM LOSS

A professor who was invited to speak at a military base was met at the airport by a soldier named Ralph. As they headed towards the baggage claim area, Ralph kept disappearing and then reappearing—once he stopped to help an older woman with her luggage, another time he played with two cranky children until they began to smile, and still another time he gave someone directions. When the professor asked the soldier what was behind his selfless actions, he replied that when he had been in Vietnam he had been responsible for clearing minefields, and he had seen many of his comrades die in front of him. By taking small steps in his own life to help others, he was more able to deal with his memories.

Today it's not uncommon to have a number of friends die from AIDS-related illnesses, to have several family members succumb to cancer or some other disease, to serve in wars and conflicts where many soldiers in a unit are killed, and to witness—either directly or indirectly—surreal numbers of people dying in catastrophic disasters.

While recuperating from any loss is a slow and oftentimes painful process—and recovering from many losses is that much harder—those who allow themselves to grieve say that taking any action, any small step, provides some relief. So today, take a small step that helps you to appreciate the life around you and soothe the sense of loss within you.

❧ ❧ ❧

I TAKE A STEP TODAY THAT HELPS ME MOVE BEYOND MY LOSS AND GET BACK INTO LIFE.

"I have plumbed the depths of despair and have found them not bottomless."

— author Thomas Hardy

PERSEVERANCE

When you're going through tough times, has anyone ever said to you, "I know it's rough, but think about how much happier you'll be when this is all over"? Your quick retort may be, "That's easy for you to say!" To even try to link happiness or positive thinking with one of life's many trials may seem as frustrating as mixing oil and water.

Yet, sometimes significant personal happiness can stem from the greatest pain, sadness, loss, or depression. An alcoholic who hits bottom and then reaches out to Alcoholics Anonymous struggles with the physical addiction as well as the gradual thawing of frozen emotions. Nevertheless, the alcoholic eventually discovers supportive friends and a new way of life without the bottle. A grief-stricken mate may have to endure the painful demise of a relationship, but that person can reach out to friends who stay close throughout the time of need. Someone who's laid off from work may experience plummeting self-esteem and money woes, but he or she may change careers and find something more financially and emotionally rewarding.

A Sufi aphorism states: "When the heart weeps for what it has lost, the spirit laughs for what it has found." Rather than bemoan whatever difficult circumstances are in your life right now, rest assured that all will ultimately be well. Sometimes it takes reaching your lowest point to be able to reach your highest.

ॐ ॐ ॐ

I PERSEVERE THROUGH MY PAIN AND LEARN TO ACCEPT THE GOOD IN THE UNEXPECTED.

JANUARY 15

Sunday—Swam around bowl. Ate. Slept.
Monday—Swam around bowl. Ate. Slept.
Tuesday—Swam around bowl. Ate. Slept.
Wednesday—Swam around bowl. Ate. Slept.
Thursday—Swam around bowl. Ate. Slept.
Friday—Swam around bowl. Ate. Slept.
Saturday—Swam around bowl. Ate. Slept.

— "Diary of a Fish," by cartoonist Leigh Rubin

OVERCOMING BOREDOM

Your moods are not only caused by the way you look at life, but also by how you *live* your life. You may be a creature of habit—someone who does the same things in the same ways at the same time—and you may also find that you're bored living this way. You may be a people-pleaser—someone who places the concerns of others above your own wants and needs—and you may also realize that your choices make others happier than they make you. You may be someone who fears change, so you opt to stay in an unfulfilling relationship, an unrewarding career, or an isolated location.

Living life in these ways can lead to "the perpetual blues"—a loss of daily pleasure and joy; an indifference to the people, ideas, and events that once interested you; a sense of hopelessness that your situation won't change; and existential malaise, where you feel your existence is totally futile and without meaning. To stop singing the blues, learn another tune—one that's exciting, new, and interesting. Today, do something different from what you did yesterday. It doesn't have to be drastic—for example, if you usually read biographies, read a mystery. Very simple changes can really stimulate your mind!

🦋 🦋 🦋

I AM CHANGING THE SCENERY OF MY LIFE TODAY, AND I ENJOY IT.

"He (Kurt Cobain, lead singer of Nirvana) had made it big
but didn't feel good about himself, and that's what suicide
is all about. He had everything but self-worth."
— Margaret O'Neil, executive director of the
Boston office of The Samaritans

SUICIDAL THOUGHTS

Do you ever think about specific ways of killing yourself or hope
that you don't wake up in the morning? In the deep stages of
depression or grief, death may seem to be the only way out of an
intolerable situation, spiritual estrangement, or an isolated and love-
less existence.

There's been much speculation about the reasons for contemplating suicide. It can be used as a cry for help, be perceived as a
romantic gesture of self-renunciation, can come across as a spiteful
act of supreme vengeance, or simply be a response to self-hatred
and low self-worth. But the reality about suicide is that it's never a
tidy solution. Suicide tosses life aside like so much trash. It's not an
act of courage, but one of supreme selfishness. A suicide says, "The
gift of life is valueless because I could not deal with my problems
or ask for help in handling them."

Suicide doesn't always result in swift, painless, and sweet oblivion. Many times the attempt gets botched, resulting in pain, disfigurement, guilt, and humiliation. Or death comes days, weeks, or
even years later due to infections, permanent organ damage, or
painful corrective surgery.

Instead of deciding that the only way to relieve your misery is
through suicide, consider at this moment that there might be
another way. Don't abandon life—change it! Call a hotline, a therapist, or a trusted friend. Know that there *are* better ways to relieve
your pain.

🦋 🦋 🦋

I GIVE LIFE A CHANCE; I GIVE *ME* A CHANCE.

"When you worry, you go over the same ground endlessly and come out the same place you started."
— Harold B. Walker

FREEDOM FROM WORRY

When you're depressed, you rarely think about or analyze your life in rational or realistic ways; you tend to sulk, worry, and fret. You may even end up making yourself physically ill with your brooding. That's why an important aspect in overcoming depression is to let go of your need to worry. Think about worry in this way: If you were the sole inhabitant of a small island, then you would have a very limited and confined space in which to move. When you worry, you're like that island inhabitant. Your endless worrying keeps your mind confined to one set of thoughts. Even though you may believe that your worrying is helping you work towards a solution, in actuality all you're really doing is dwelling on the futility of the problem.

To free yourself from worry's constraints regarding any situation in your life, first ask yourself, "What can I do to change this situation?" Try to discover one, two, or more options for changing the situation. One of these choices can be as significant as seeking out a new job to combat the fear of being laid off, or as minor as reminding yourself not to think about the possibility of a layoff until it actually occurs. Then choose one of your options and put it into action. Soon you'll feel like you have enough wind in your sails to leave your remote island of worry so you can drift back to the mainland of life.

❧ ❧ ❧

I RELEASE MY WORRIES, AND I SET MYSELF FREE.

"In a real dark night of the soul, it is always three o'clock in the morning, day after day."
— F. Scott Fitzgerald, in *The Crack-Up*

WHAT'S YOUR MOOD?

Your moods are the most consistent determinants of the quality of your life. No matter what's going on, you can handle anything if your mood is upbeat. Some people seem blessed with a consistently positive outlook. They remain buoyant and optimistic even in the face of seemingly insurmountable odds. That's why a woman paralyzed in a car accident can recover and then go on to be a champion wheelchair athlete, why another can experience financial ruin and then start a successful business, or why a former drug addict can devote countless hours to counseling children about the virtues of staying clean.

Then there are people who, on the surface, seem to have all that life can offer, yet they are pessimistic and enveloped in dark moods most of the time. They live in misery, so depressed that they're blinded to all the good around them. These people do not use the trials of life as opportunities for growth, but as justifications for maintaining a sad, black, or blue mood.

Today, think about what the color of your mood is the majority of the time. Is it light, bright, and vibrant; or dark, dull, and somber? Then determine what the color of your mood is right now. Close your eyes and imagine that you are changing the color of your mood to a sunnier one than it is now. See yourself mixing this color in a large paint bucket. Visualize taking a brush and slowly painting yourself with it from head to toe. Then, see yourself wearing this fresh coat of "mood paint" today, and observe the different ways in which you respond to life.

ફ્ર ફ્ર ફ્ર

I DETERMINE MY MOODS TODAY; I DO NOT LET MY MOODS DETERMINE *ME*.

"Depression is your body's expression of emotional exhaustion. Your store of vitality is low because your body has been whipped by fear, frustration, despair, anger, anxiety. You have overdrawn on your emotional reserve; even so, your body will heal itself if you will allow it. This is nature's gift."

— Dr. Claire Weekes

EMOTIONAL RESERVES

Do you suffer from a habit of recurring depression rather than from a downward spiraling depression? If you do, you may find that you respond quickly and sensitively to mildly dispiriting environments (such as a darkened room on a gloomy day), to tragic news (plane crashes, animal abuse, or murder), and to those around you who are depressed (whom you may encounter on public transportation, in your office, or in your home). It may not be unusual for you to feel your spirits slowly sink in such situations. Yet, once your attention is distracted or you take steps to retreat from the oppressive person, place, or thing, you quickly overcome your depression.

If you tracked your emotional or energy level at the times you began to feel depressed, you might find that you're always emotionally drained or physically exhausted. And, because you don't like to feel any bout of depression coming on, the added strain of fear and apprehension over the approaching downswing further drains your emotions and energy, thus giving depression a green light.

However, if you keep your emotional reserves well stocked and remain physically strong on a daily basis, then you can give the red light to recurring depression. So, starting today, express your feelings, deal with the stresses in your life, eat well-balanced meals, exercise, and get plenty of rest!

ॐ ॐ ॐ

I SAVE UP FOR THE NEXT RAINY DAY IN MY LIFE BY LIVING WELL TODAY.

"Everyone is a prisoner of his own experiences. No one can eliminate prejudices—just recognize them."

— Edward R. Murrow

SELF-ACCEPTANCE

If you're a member of a minority group, then you may have to deal—on almost a daily basis—with prejudices, judgments, unkind remarks, stereotypes, and stigmas. You may find that you have to really fight to feel good about yourself no matter how society or others treat you. Yet the truth is, there will be times when you're going to feel abandoned, worthless, alone, and defeated in the face of constant defiance of who you are.

That's why it's important to keep in mind the words of an unknown philosopher, who said, "I am not a gold coin—not everyone is going to love me." You need to accept that you're never going to be unconditionally accepted by everyone, no matter what your color, ethnic background, religion, or sexuality. Even members of your own family may turn against you.

Today, on Dr. Martin Luther King's birthday, remind yourself that just as *you* don't necessarily show unconditional love and acceptance to everyone, so too may some people not show the same to you. Rather than feel depressed over who's not on your side or on those things that the minority group you belong to doesn't have, make it a goal to love and approve of yourself so that the acceptance of everyone else isn't necessary.

ॐ ॐ ॐ

I ACCEPT WHO I AM AND EMBRACE THIS TRUTH MORE THAN MY POPULARITY.

"If I had my life to live over, I would try to make more mistakes. I would relax. I would climb more mountains and swim more rivers. I would go barefoot earlier in the spring and stay that way later in the fall. I would have more dogs. I would ride more merry-go-rounds. I would pick more daisies. I would have more actual troubles and fewer imaginary ones."

— Don Herold

USING AFFIRMATIONS

You can often make dramatic changes in your life—even if you're depressed, grieving, or experiencing "the blues"—through the creation and repetition of positive affirmations. An affirmation is anything you think or say. Although the notion of a simple phrase repeated over and over again seems like a very simplistic solution to the enormity of the problems you may be going through, affirmations do have tremendous power to act as a positive force in your life.

To create the most effective affirmations, always use the present tense—for example: "I am safe and protected" or "I have a wonderful career that fulfills me." Always state your affirmation using the first person, "I," and be simple and brief. Also, do not use words such as "will" or "may" because that will keep your dream in the future instead of in the present. If you have a religious or spiritual belief, use it in your affirmation—for example: "I trust that my Higher Power watches over me." Create strong images of yourself.

After you compose one or more affirmations, practice them. Repeat them several times first thing in the morning and before going to sleep. Repeat them at any time during the day when you're able, such as during your commute to work. Repeat them when you're feeling down or negative. The more you repeat your affirmations, the sooner you will see their positive effects manifesting themselves in your life.

ɤə ɤə ɤə

I USE POSITIVE AFFIRMATIONS TO BRING ALL THAT IS GOOD INTO MY LIFE.

"Hope is like the sun, which, as we journey toward it, casts the shadow of our burden behind us."

— Samuel Smiles

BEING HOPEFUL

Climber Stacy Allison, the first American woman to reach the top of Mount Everest, tries to view all the challenges in her life as new heights to be scaled. She pushes herself to work hard and overcome obstacles, but such a positive and hopeful outlook took time to develop. In 1987, after an unsuccessful first attempt to climb Mount Everest, she experienced acute disappointment. Her self-worth suffered, and it was hard for her to motivate herself each day.

For a good part of your life—or even each day—you may feel similar disappointment and dejection. You may feel lost, uncomfortable, and blind to the good in yourself and the world around you. But just as such emotions changed for Stacy, so too can these feelings change for you.

Stacy admits that her first climbing failure turned out to be her greatest motivator. She says, "I had to fail to realize that self-worth isn't built upon one accomplishment. It's built through years of setting goals and reaching them." In fact, one year later, Stacy reached the summit of Everest.

Today, try to give to yourself rather than take away, to build yourself up rather than tear yourself down, to be kind to yourself rather than to be cruel. You can be comfortable with yourself and the world only when you see each day as a stepping stone to a greater challenge, a greater achievement, and a greater sense of self.

 youtube ya ya ya

I AM HOPEFUL ABOUT MYSELF AND ALL THAT HAPPENS TODAY.

"Like many people in personal turmoil, she rose late, didn't dress other than to cloak herself in her dressing gown, and she fell asleep easily throughout the day."

— Carol Bly

GETTING IN MOTION

When you're depressed, grieving, or feeling "under the weather," you may want to withdraw from all activity. You just stay in bed or curl up on the living room couch. You let the phone ring. You ignore obligations. But, as John Ciardi says, "The day will happen whether or not you get up." So it's important to get involved in the day rather than wish it away.

There *are* things you can do when you feel a lack of motivation, though. You can eat healthfully, for starters. But stay away from sweets and snack foods, and get the basic protein, vitamins, and minerals into your body. With proper nourishment—even from one good, balanced meal a day—you can acquire more energy and clearer thinking.

Second, take a shower or bath so you can feel clean on the outside, even if you feel muddy on the inside. Brush your teeth. Comb your hair. Shave or put on makeup, even if you're not going out. Wear clean clothes. Such simple grooming rituals can become an important element in helping restore your dignity and self-esteem.

Finally, get in motion! Physical activity is an extremely important part of recovery from depression. Exercise keeps the muscles toned, the blood moving, and pumps oxygen to the brain for sharper concentration. You don't have to run a marathon or pump iron to get moving. Simply take a walk. Walk to the store, to the park, or even just around your apartment complex or yard. Walk at least ten minutes every day, and you'll be taking the necessary steps to help you feel better.

ᵛᵃ ᵛᵃ ᵛᵃ

I LET MOTION OVERRIDE MY MENTAL PARALYSIS SO I PARTICIPATE IN *TODAY*.

My baby's left my lily pad,
my legs were both deep-fried,
I eat flies all day and when I'm gone
they'll stick me in formaldehyde...oh,
I got the greeeeeeens, I got
the greens real baaaaaad...

> — A frog singing the blues,
> in a Gary Larson cartoon

PERSONAL TIME

One of the best ways to stop singing "the blues" is to take a mental health break, where you focus your mental energy on something new, different, and out of the ordinary—or perhaps even focus on the simple and routine in your life in a way that allows you to see your life, yourself, and your goals more objectively or creatively.

Think of today as a "mental health day." It's a day in which you can do whatever renews your mental energy—that drive and focus that helps you go after what you really want. You don't have to be physically sick to take a day off from responsibility once in a while. Spend it on whatever renews you mentally, whether it's browsing for antiques or just lying on the beach.

Or, if you can't afford an entire day, sometimes quiet moments alone doing five minutes of deep abdominal breathing can help. So can good, old-fashioned daydreaming. Let your mind reflect on whatever pleasant, quiet, and beautiful scene you like. Picture yourself engaging in whatever activity you most enjoy. By doing so, you're letting your mind "escape" from its sometimes "blue"-tinted outlook so you can see the rainbow colors of the world.

🐸 🐸 🐸

I TAKE TIME TO CREATE A PEACEFUL SPACE AND PLACE IN MY MIND SO THAT I BOOST MY MENTAL ENERGY.

"It is impressive to see a person who has been battered by life in many ways, who is torn by a variety of unsolved problems, yet who is still fighting, still struggling, still striving to find the path to a more fulfilling existence, moved by the wisdom in knowing, 'I am more than my problems.'"

— author Nathaniel Branden

GRIEF SUPPORT

Children who survive difficult childhoods learn to disengage from the painful aspects of their family life by a survival strategy called "strategic detachment." They somehow know that the way things are for them at that moment is not the only way things can be for them or will always be for them, and that someday they will find their way to a better, more enjoyable life. While this knowledge doesn't spare them suffering at the time, it allows them to avoid being destroyed by it.

You can use strategic detachment as you grieve the loss of your loved one, a job change, retirement, relocation, or the end of a relationship. One way to do so is to find someone with whom you can participate in a grief recovery partnership. You may resist at first. You may feel that no one really understands the pain you're in. But no matter how convinced you might be that no one can understand or help, the support of others or even one other person can help you through your painful time.

A grief recovery partner can help you realize that there is life beyond your loss, and that someday you will find your way to it. Choose someone you know who has been through what you're enduring. Then share how you feel. Let your partner show you that you need not be a prisoner to your losses of yesterday, but can be free to choose how you feel today.

ॐ ॐ ॐ

I AM COMMITTED TO WORKING THROUGH MY GRIEF WITH THE HELP OF ANOTHER.

"Sometimes it seemed to him that his life was delicate as a dandelion. One little puff from any direction, and it was blown to bits."
— from *Bridge to Terabithia,* by Katherine Paterson

RISING ABOVE ADVERSITY

During her 30-year career, talk-show host Sally Jessy Raphaël has been fired 18 times. Every time this has happened, however, she has focused on something she *could* do. When no mainland radio stations would hire her—they thought women couldn't attract an audience—she moved to Puerto Rico, became fluent in Spanish, and proved them wrong. To sell her hit radio program, she pitched her idea time and time again to several network executives until it sold. Now she's the Emmy award-winning host of her own television show, reaching eight million viewers daily.

As long as you're stuck in a depression that's a response to failure, mistakes, or defeat, you'll stay depressed. You'll only be able to focus on what you believe you didn't do well, the job you lost, the book that got rejected, the business that failed, the relationship that ended. That's why looking for the advantage in any disadvantage is the best way to prevent defeat-induced depression.

But what should you do to prevent the onset of such a depression or, if you're already in the midst of a such a condition, to help lift yourself out of it? Engaging in an interesting hobby, changing your scenery, or becoming involved in a service-type endeavor (such as volunteering at a nursing home) are the kinds of things you might try to rise above the difficulties in your life. Today, enjoy a favorite pastime, take a different route to work, or relax for an hour with a cup of tea and a good book. Activities such as these can strengthen your mind and make it harder for the winds of adversity to blow your confidence, pride, and determination to bits.

ॐ ॐ ॐ

I USE ADVERSITY TO SPUR ME ON TO GREATER ACHIEVEMENTS.

"The effect of my excess weight is diminishing to nothing. About three years ago, I decided I was going to stop feeling inferior, stop talking about it, wear attractive clothes, and go swimming in a lovely $60 suit."
— A woman involved a study of depression recovery

WEIGHT CONTROL

Nearly half of the people who participated in a depression study reported that they were significantly overweight and blamed this on the binging or lethargy that accompanied their mood swings. For many, food is sometimes the only panacea for oppressive feelings. But besides being unhealthy, excess weight makes you feel self-conscious and unattractive, thereby lowering your self-esteem and further complicating your ability to overcome depression.

If you've decided that your weight is a problem that needs to be addressed, either for reasons related to your health or to help you enhance your self-worth, now is the time to begin to do something about it. Right now, determine how many pounds you'd like to lose. Then decide how long you're going to give yourself to lose those pounds. Remember, it's never healthy to lose more than two pounds a week, and weight loss rarely progresses evenly, no matter how careful you are about what you eat. So be easy on yourself as you set your goals.

To support your weight-loss efforts, you can consult with a doctor or health professional, join a support group, or assemble resources such as low-fat cookbooks. If you succumb to temptation, don't give up. Just get back on the diet as soon as possible and stick to it! And don't forget to give yourself a pat on the back for every good day you have.

ஃ ஃ ஃ

I AM PATIENT AND PROUD OF THE HARD WORK I DO TO CONTROL MY WEIGHT.

"All miseries derive from not being able to sit quietly in a room alone."

— Blaise Pascal

INDEPENDENT THINKING

One of the best ways to enhance your self-esteem is by exercising your ability to think for yourself when it may not be easy or popular to do so, when it may be frightening, or when you have feelings of uncertainty, doubt, and insecurity. You may not enjoy being alienated from the thinking and beliefs of those around you, especially those whom you admire the most or those whose love and acceptance dearly matter to you. But from this strengthening of self-esteem—this ability to direct your own thoughts and feelings—comes the development of independent thinking, where you're comfortable with your values, convictions, and beliefs.

When you behave in ways that conflict with your intuitive feelings about what's appropriate for you, or when you revise your needs because of others, you lose face, which puts you at war with yourself. If this behavior becomes habitual, you begin to mistrust and disrespect yourself more and more, which can result in a fear of being with yourself—for when you're alone, you have no choice but to listen to your inner self.

So begin now to be with yourself—to decide what it is you think, feel, need, or believe at this particular moment of your existence. Just because someone tells you to "get over it" or to "see the light" doesn't mean that your way of thinking or the actions you are taking are wrong. Think independently, and you'll begin to develop confidence in yourself, in your opinions, and in your ability to know what's right.

இ இ இ

I AM PROUD OF WHO I AM BECAUSE I'M WILLING TO THINK FOR MYSELF.

"Analysts keep having to pick away at the scab that the patient tries to form between himself and the analyst to cover his wounds. [The analyst] keeps the surface raw, so that the wound will heal properly."

— Janet Malcolm

SEEKING PROFESSIONAL HELP

There are certainly times when you're experiencing depression when you might consider going to a doctor or therapist:

- if your symptoms are unrelated to a recent trauma such as a death, job loss, or divorce;
- if your symptoms have lasted for more than two weeks;
- if you've had dramatic changes in your appetite—either eating too much or too little;
- if you're experiencing sleep problems, either insomnia or sleeping excessively;
- if you're crying uncontrollably; and
- if you're contemplating committing suicide or harming other people.

If you're experiencing one or more of these symptoms, then contact a psychiatrist, psychologist, therapist, or other health-care professional. Be honest with whomever you contact. Answer all questions. Offer information that can provide further enlightenment about your thoughts, feelings, and behaviors. And don't be afraid that you'll shock this person. There's nothing you can confess, do, or say that a member of the helping profession hasn't seen or heard before. Help the person you've chosen to help *you*—that's the best way to heal yourself!

❧ ❧ ❧

I PROVIDE A HELPING PROFESSIONAL WITH INFORMATION THAT WILL HELP *ME*.

"You can clutch the past so tightly to your chest that it leaves your arms too full to embrace the present."

— Jan Glidewell

LETTING GO OF THE PAST

Do you have an "energy drain" in your life—a person or circumstance from the past that is negatively affecting your current existence? Perhaps it's an ex-lover who broke your heart, an error you made on a report that cost you a promotion, an opportunity you passed up, or a friend you refused to forgive who later died. Constantly dwelling on this person or circumstance can make you feel unhappy, exhausted, out of touch, and imbalanced as you transfer your time and energy away from today and back to the past.

Such energy drains are like the barnacles that cling to the hulls of ships. Over time, they can drag you down and make you feel more and more depressed. So no matter how successful, happy, or satisfied you may become in your life, such an energy drain can distract you and thus prevent you from moving full-speed ahead in the present.

The next time you find yourself reflecting on your energy drain, say aloud: "It's over and done with. There's nothing more I can do about it now that will change the person or the outcome. It's time to move on and concentrate on today!" Then focus your time and energy on yourself or on a person or circumstance that is a positive presence in your life right now.

ℬ ℬ ℬ

I FOCUS ON THE POSITIVE ASPECTS OF MY CURRENT LIFE AND LET GO OF THE PAST.

"The greatest regrets I heard were not from those who had taken a risk and lost. Invariably, they felt proud for having dared, and even educated in defeat. The real regret, bordering on mourning, came from those who hadn't taken chances they'd wanted to take and now felt it was too late."
— Ralph Keyes, author of *Chancing It: Why We Take Risks*

CHALLENGING BOUNDARIES

Are you in a comfort zone? Jobs, family relationships, even small things like the route you take to work or favorite seats at the movies are all components of the particular comfort zone that you may be in. There's nothing wrong with comfort zones—not until they hinder you from doing or achieving what you can and want to do. Just as comfort zones define your world, so too can their borders limit you and prevent you from finding out what's beyond them.

This wasn't the case with premed student Roger Bannister. He had been informed, through professional literature of the time, that nobody could run a mile in under four minutes. The body simply couldn't take the stress, the researchers said. Bannister thought differently and, in 1954, he shattered the four-minute barrier. In the two years following his achievement, over a dozen people ran the mile in under four minutes. They learned that there was no *physical* obstacle; the obstacle was entirely mental.

Four-minute miles aren't limited to sports. Think of the all the barriers you erect in your life that prevent you from achieving all you can. Perhaps you stop yourself short; perhaps you sell yourself short. Today, test the limits of your comfort zone by taking baby steps out of it. If you want to become more social, for example, don't throw a huge party. Just make contact with one friend by phone or letter. Gain confidence from this small step...then take another.

ஜ ஜ ஜ

I EASE MYSELF OUT OF MY COMFORT ZONE BY TAKING SMALL, SLOW STEPS.

*"It was just too emotionally painful. It would just remind me
of how much I lost. And I thought, How can I get it down.
I'm so weak I can barely stand up, and I have no balance
because I can't see."*

— David S. Wolfe

PHYSICAL WELLNESS

In 1991, dancer and choreographer David S. Wolfe stopped working
because AIDS had robbed him not only of his stamina, but also of
his sight. "I can't do this anymore. I am very sick," he said. But in
1992 Boston dancer Jeffrey Pike began nagging him to create another dance. Working like Beethoven after his deafness, David
created "A Simple Story," an autobiographical dance piece that pre-
miered in 1993. David said the work was his response to the
question he was often asked when people found out he had AIDS:
"Why don't you kill yourself?"

Suffering from a terminal or chronic illness can be physically
wearing as well as emotionally draining. You may often contemplate
suicide, consider not taking life-saving medication, or become
careless in how you take care of yourself in the hopes that such
things will accelerate your death or alleviate your pain.

Rather than focus on the effects of your current condition on
your life and the way you feel, consider instead what coping
strategies might help you. The effort you direct toward improving
your physical condition, the beneficial changes you make in your
lifestyle as a result of your condition, and the positive thoughts you
generate, can enhance your overall well-being and help stabilize depression about your condition.

Although David Wolfe gave up on himself in 1991, through
knowledge of his craft, a supportive friend, and a goal, "A Simple
Story" enriched his life and brought him great pride until his
death in 1994.

❧ ❧ ❧

I IMPLEMENT POSITIVE CHANGES IN MY LIFE FOR PHYSICAL
AND EMOTIONAL WELL-BEING.

"But one day when I was sitting and feeling like a motherless child, which I was, it came to me that feeling of being part of everything, not separate at all. I knew that if I cut a tree, my arm would bleed."

— author Alice Walker

CONNECTING TO LIFE

One day, on the famous "bullet train" from Kyoto to Tokyo, a commotion occurred among the passengers. They all rushed to one side of the train just in time to see thick clouds suddenly part, revealing the beauty and majesty of Mount Fuji. Passengers exclaimed and took pictures until, just as suddenly, the clouds once again hid the mountain from view. But the incident changed the climate on the train car for the rest of the journey. People who had been strangers or who had shied from human contact were now chatting together like close friends. Those who had been sleeping now opened their eyes and marveled at the green lushness of the rice fields they were passing. Many commented on the beauty that had touched them and, miraculously, had united them for a brief time.

Today, be aware of the simple truth that you belong. You're an essential part of the world—of humanity, of nature, of the pulse of life that beats through everyone and everything. So you can choose to seek that connection that makes you part of a powerful and magnificent universe.

Today, let the clouds of sadness, self-doubt, self-pity, remorse, helplessness, guilt, and fear part for just an instant—just long enough for you to see the miracles that these negative feelings keep hidden from you. Maybe it's a glorious sunset or a breathtaking snowfall. Or maybe it's contact with a new friend. Push away the clouds, and you'll be surprised what you'll discover on the horizon.

ॐ ॐ ॐ

I TRUST THAT I AM PART OF EVERYONE AND EVERYTHING AROUND ME.

"It isn't the mountain that wears you out—it's the grain of sand in your shoe."

— Robert Service

CREATING YOUR MINDSET

It's only natural to feel momentary pangs of unhappiness when faced with the obstacles of everyday life. But many people elevate that degree of unhappiness into a way of life. That's why your current mood of misery may be directly related to the way you look at your world. You may stubbornly cling to personal dissatisfaction and despair, almost as if you've made suffering an essential part of your identity. When this mindset is part of your personality, you sincerely believe that it's necessary, essential, and proper to complain, moan, and sulk when you don't get what you want. So you make yourself miserable over every little thing—while viewing the whole of your life as a constant struggle.

The goal of recovery from such a negative mindset is to create a new, constructive image of yourself and your life. To do so, you need to drown out the noise of your habitual negativity and saturate your mind with positive thoughts. Purchase a prerecorded tape filled with inspirational messages, ask a friend to create such a tape for you or, if you feel inspired, make this tape yourself. Every night before you go to sleep, turn on this tape and fall asleep to the positive thoughts. When you wake up in the morning, turn on the tape and listen to it. Focus on a few of your favorite messages and repeat them aloud or write them on slips of paper and post them where you're sure to see them—perhaps on the bathroom mirror. Do this night and day for two weeks, then notice how your negative thoughts are shifting from gloom and doom to hope and happiness.

№ № №

I REPROGRAM MY MINDSET TO BE MORE PLEASANT AND POSITIVE.

"Life is partly what we make it, and partly what it is made by the friends whom we choose."

— Tehyi Hseih

SUPPORTIVE HOME LIFE

Do you know that you can "catch" depression from others? A study of 96 pairs of college roommates found that among those of the same sex, mild forms of depression—characterized by sadness, tiredness, irritability, and motivation problems—were contagious. The sample included roommates who had chosen each other, as well as those randomly assigned to share a living space. All were tested initially for depression; three weeks later, they were retested. Over the course of the study, roommates of depressed students became more depressed themselves. So, living with someone who's chronically depressed can be depressing in and of itself. As Russell Baker observed: "Misery no longer loves company. Nowadays it insists upon it."

But while those suffering with depressive moods can have a negative impact on those who come into direct contact with them, they can also have a positive influence. Most negative responses to depression are a result of household members refusing to learn about depression or to take part in treatment and recovery. But many people who suffer with this condition report that they're able to develop mutual understanding, become closer to, and communicate better with their household members as they overcome their morose feelings. The key to such a positive influence is the support they receive. So, choose to associate with friends and family members who are willing to educate themselves about your depression, listen to you, be available when needed, and offer you encouragement. You'll find that it's easier to deal with your own depression when you're supported by those around you.

૪૨ ૪૨ ૪૨

I HELP MYSELF THROUGH THE SUPPORT OF OTHERS.

"Hiding leads nowhere except to more hiding."
— Margaret A. Robinson

COMMUNICATING FEELINGS

When you're depressed, "blue," or grieving over a loss, do you try to hide how you feel from others? If you're like most people who experience such moods, you'd rather try to hide, deny, or cover up your despair rather than talk about it. The reason for this phenomenon is that most people are more comfortable focusing on their bodies than on their emotions or psychological symptoms. Physical pain is more understandable and, therefore, more acceptable, so if you're not in physical pain, then you tend not to talk about "mental pain." Or you may feel ashamed to let others see that you're weak, guilty about the mess you feel your life is in, or afraid you'll be rejected. Then again, you might fear that people will think you're crazy. You might even convince yourself that suffering in silence is better than the anger, lectures, disapproval, or condemnation you may receive from others if they are privy to how you feel.

But an important aspect of overcoming depressive moods is to give voice to how you feel. Seeking help from a counselor, doctor, caring family member, intimate partner, or loving friend not only helps you feel less alone, but also lets you know that your reasons for wanting to hide how you feel are, in reality, quite common. Depression is now 10 times more prevalent than it was half a century ago—about 20 percent of Americans will suffer from an episode of major depression in their lifetime.

As Emily Kimbrough said, "...we all stumble, every one of us. That's why it's a comfort to go hand in hand." So, give voice to your depression today. In being heard, you're being cured.

🦋 🦋 🦋

I COMMUNICATE MY FEELINGS OPENLY AND HONESTLY.

FEBRUARY 6

"My mother thought it would make us feel better to know animals had no soul and thus their deaths were not to be taken seriously. But it didn't help and when I think of some of the animals I have known, I wonder. The only really 'soulful' eyes in the world belong to the dog or cat who sits on your lap or at your feet commiserating when you cry."
— columnist Liz Smith

GRIEVING FOR A PET

When your pet passes away, it can be as emotionally devastating as losing your best friend. Although some unenlightened people may call them "dumb animals," pets are actually friends, confidants, advisors, teachers, comforters, and the only living creatures that consistently give unconditional love. You know how your dog never fails to wag her tail and jump around in ecstasy when you walk in the door—how many close friends greet you in such a way? Or, think about how your cat always sits on your lap and instinctively rubs his head against yours when you're upset— how many intimate partners would nonjudgmentally empathize with you when you're sobbing aloud? Your pet always accepts your bad moods and irritable temper with total trust and love—how many family members would respond so forgivingly?

That's why the process of grieving applies as much to a pet as it does to a human being. Well-meaning people who tell you that getting a new pet will make you feel better believe that replacing your beloved "child" will make your loss easier to deal with. But, in reality, you need to work through your feelings and bring closure to the grieving process before you can be open to loving a new pet.

Today, give yourself time to grieve the loss of your beloved friend. Flip through a photo album and reminisce about the times you shared together. Let the spirit of your pet remain forever in your heart.

ॐ ॐ ॐ

I GIVE MYSELF THE TIME AND SPACE TO GRIEVE THE LOSS OF MY BELOVED PET.

"God asks no man whether he will accept life. That is not the choice. You must take it. The only choice is how."
— clergyman Henry Ward Beecher

SPIRITUAL HEALING

One of the often-overlooked methods for overcoming depression is based upon spirituality, or a belief in something greater than yourself. Some people call what they believe in a Higher Power, God, Goddess, an Angel, or a Universal Guide. But no matter what the designation, rarely is such a spiritual resource consulted during times of depression. People would much rather believe in the resources provided by therapy, medication, changes in diet, exercise, light therapy, and revised ways of thinking, than turning to a spiritual source for healing. That may be the case because these people blame this spiritual source for their plight, they dislike the feelings of powerlessness that they attribute to the worship or belief in a higher power, or because they've simply lost faith that anything exists beyond that which they can see in the material world.

Yet, while you're powerless over many things, such as the actions and beliefs of others, and the forces of nature—you still have control over your own life. That means that you can choose to follow a course of action that can lead you to greater strength, hope, security, and serenity. A path to such a course is provided by the simple, yet meaningful Serenity Prayer: *"God, grant me the serenity to accept the things I cannot change, courage to change the things I can, and the wisdom to know the difference."* Beginning each day and closing each night with this prayer can provide you with a different, more spiritual perspective.

ॐ ॐ ॐ

I USE PRAYER WHEN I WISH TO SPIRITUALLY HEAL MYSELF.

"Iron rusts from disuse, water loses its purity from stagnation...even so does inaction sap the vigors of the mind."
— Leonardo da Vinci

TAKING ACTION

One of the symptoms of depression is mental dullness. You may find that your thinking seems slow and cumbersome, as if you were trying to find your way out of a thick fog. New and creative ideas not only evade you, but even the most exciting notions don't seem to interest you. You have poor concentration and trouble making decisions. Like a dull knife that tries to slice through a fresh tomato, your thinking loses its edge.

Percy Knauth, who wrote about his own depression in his memoir, *A Season in Hell*, said that the only way to clear the fog and emerge from a conscious coma is to act. "Do something, anything," wrote Knauth. "It really doesn't matter what, as long as it is a positive action." For Knauth, this type of behavior involved three simple activities that he performed every day:

- He got out of bed.
- He made some coffee.
- Then he made the bed.

Even though such actions may seem trivial, they showed Knauth that he was still able to accomplish something. Small successes can slowly lead to greater accomplishments. So today, get out of bed. Turn off the TV. Accept an invitation to go out to dinner or see a movie. Do *something!* Simple acts can clear the mind and gradually entice you back into the thick of things, where you'll no doubt find things that interest you and give you pleasure.

❧ ❧ ❧

I OVERCOME MENTAL NUMBNESS THROUGH PHYSICAL ACTION.

"Depression is a very common disorder that can have a very varied presentation. Often when people go to see their primary care doctor because they feel there's something wrong with them, they're not thinking about depression. They say, 'Well, doc, I just don't feel myself. It's hard to get going. How's my blood doing?'"

— Dr. Lloyd Sederer, psychiatrist

RECOGNIZING SYMPTOMS

For decades, psychiatrists have stressed that insomnia, loss of appetite, feelings of anxiety, fatigue, and other physical symptoms are hallmarks that help identify classic depression. But new data from a national depression screening test demonstrates that previous emphasis on the physical signs of depression has been misplaced. Currently, the most frequent markers for a diagnosis of depression are five *psychic* (of the mind) rather than *somatic* (of the body) signs:

1. difficulty performing commonplace activities,
2. lack of enjoyment in everything one does,
3. feelings of hopelessness about the future,
4. difficulty making decisions, and
5. feeling worthless and unneeded.

The value of these new findings is that they get across the message, both to the person suffering from depression and those trained in the helping profession, that psychic symptoms of depression need to be recognized in conjunction with physical symptoms. If you have any of these five symptoms for two weeks or longer, contact your physician or a psychiatrist. After identifying your symptoms, you're ready to start resolving them through group or individual counseling.

❧ ❧ ❧

I IDENTIFY MY SYMPTOMS AND THEN ENLIST THE SUPPORT, COUNSEL, ADVICE, AND UNDERSTANDING OF A PROFESSIONAL.

"There are times in everyone's life when something constructive is born out of adversity. There are times when things seem so bad that you've got to grasp your fate by the shoulders and shake it....In times of stress and adversity, it's always best to keep busy, to plow your anger and your energy into something quite positive."

— Lee Iacocca

CHANNELING ANGER

In his autobiography, corporate head Lee Iacocca recounts the crushing experience of his dismissal from the Ford Motor Company and how he channeled his intense anger at his loss into a positive force for his career and for his entire life. Can you form a similar alliance with your anger and let it be a partner when the world you love turns upside down? Can you keep in mind Nietzsche's incantation: "That which does not kill me, makes me stronger"?

Anger is one of the steps in the recovery from any loss. Anyone who grieves knows that it's common to hold others responsible for whatever real or perceived tragedy has occurred: "I'd be okay if only so-and-so hadn't done such-and-such to me. Now look at me—I'm a mess—and all because of what was done to me!" It's okay to feel this anger, but then you need to release it—to move on with your life. If you just sit and stew, you're like a time bomb that gets more and more ticked off, not only at the person and the situation, but also at other unrelated people or things. Soon you're angry at the world, and this anger affects all of your attitudes and actions.

When you make other people responsible for creating your feelings, then you also make them responsible for "curing" your feelings. Either way, it's a lose-lose situation. Today, release your anger by turning your attention to a different focus. Start a new book, take a walk in the woods, or rent a video. Sow your seeds of anger and then plow over them by taking positive action.

❧ ❧ ❧

I RECONSTRUCT MY ANGER AND BUILD A MORE POSITIVE OUTLOOK.

"Much unhappiness results from an inability to remember the nice things that happen to us."

—W. N. Rieger

FINDING JOYFUL MEMORIES

The feeling of being "down in the dumps" may come over you at the beginning of the week (particularly on a Monday), when you haven't had enough sleep, when you're hungry, when the day creeps by slowly, and when you feel more "off" than "on." It's not that you're in the midst of a debilitating depression or that a tremendous tragedy has occurred in your life; it's just that you can't seem to shake your "blue" feeling. As a result, you sink even deeper into gloom, doom, and a victim mentality.

Everyone has days like this, where it's a struggle to put on a happy face, walk with a bounce in your step, and feel your usual confidence. It can be easier to wallow in your funk rather than try to lift yourself out of it. But if you take emotional "time-outs" periodically and mentally revisit special places you've been to and wonderful friends you've interacted with, you'll be able to re-experience feelings of joy and happiness so you can revitalize your sense of well-being in the present.

Just as you can mentally review the past, you can also reflect on the good that's part of your life at this moment. Be grateful for the blessings that are in your life today, and you'll find that your spirits can rise far above your doldrums.

ༀ ༀ ༀ

I REVIEW THE PAST AND VIEW THE PRESENT IN WAYS THAT BRING JOY BACK INTO MY LIFE.

"...to share confidences is universal. We confirm our reality
by sharing."

— author Barbara Grizzuti Harrison

BREAKING THE SILENCE

The 25-year-old daughter of a famous film star killed herself, and then, one year later, his wife also committed suicide. How did this husband and father deal with his losses? He hired powerful attorneys to pressure those who knew the truth behind the deaths to sign documents declaring that they would never speak publicly about the suicides.

Many people feel that there's a stigma attached to the symptoms or diagnosis of depression. In our current culture, it seems that it's more socially acceptable to admit to a problem with drugs or alcohol or to confess to a past criminal record than to admit to any type of mental illness. Shame and guilt are two of the biggest silencers, as well as a need to protect family members, a fear of recrimination, losing face with others, and so on.

If we look at the good that has resulted from chemical dependency declarations by Betty Ford, Elizabeth Taylor, Liza Minnelli, and many other celebrities, we can see that their honesty inspired others who suffer from drug and alcohol addiction to obtain necessary treatment. Imagine what would happen if depression could be similarly acknowledged and accepted as a disorder that affects millions. As one depression sufferer declared: "I lost 20 years of my life before my depression was diagnosed and treated. My whole outlook has changed now."

You no longer have to suffer silently with your depression. Break your silence today by talking to at least one trusted person about how you feel. You're not only helping yourself, but you could be helping someone else, as well!

≈ ≈ ≈

I TALK ABOUT MY FEELINGS OF DEPRESSION WITH A TRUSTED INDIVIDUAL.

"Rough weather makes good timber."

—Appalachian adage

SURVIVING THE TRIALS OF LIFE

The above adage is popular among the mountain people in southern Appalachia. To them it symbolizes how the trees on the top of the mountain are forced to withstand the elements. Storms, winds, and seasonal changes impact the trees, which are unprotected. Only the strongest survive. In fact, the trees that do survive provide the finest quality timber and are used for buildings that require the most durable and sturdy construction.

The lesson inherent in the adage also applies to people. For, you're like the tree that stands at the top of a mountain. You're unprotected from the traumas and tragedies of everyday life. To survive the force of life's difficulties—the end of a relationship, death, financial difficulties, job loss, major illnesses, and so on—you must be like the strongest trees or you'll perish. You wither away and die when you let life's adversities devastate and disable you; you survive when you develop an inner strength and resilience that enable you to use crisis and disappointment constructively, by effecting fulfillment and insight.

You can feel positive about your life in fair, as well as rough, weather. Today, recognize that traumas in life are as inevitable as storms on a mountaintop. Brace yourself for them, hold firm to your position, and never let them dislodge you. Standing up to life's harsh realities rather than letting them uproot you can help you recover from them more quickly and enable you to accept the fact that each event shapes the peaks and valleys in your life.

🦋 🦋 🦋

I AM A SURVIVOR WHO WITHSTANDS ALL OF THE DIFFICULTIES IN LIFE WITH STRENGTH AND DIGNITY.

"Love is the water of life—receive it in thy heart and soul."
— Rumi

LOVE AND SELF-LOVE

Today you can give the gift of love to yourself in many ways. As you heal and recover, recognize that change can sometimes seem chaotic, confusing, and frightening. Seek the support of others who can love and reassure you during this time. Ask people who have been through treatment for depression, have lost a loved one, or who know all about "the blues" and are further along in their healing process if they would be available to take telephone calls from you or would talk to you about their own experiences. Sometimes nothing is quite so reassuring as hearing someone say, "I know exactly how you feel because I felt that way, too. Here's what I did to get through it." Ask trusted friends or family members for their help with specific tasks or responsibilities that overwhelm you right now. You may even want to ask your boss if it's possible to have your workload lightened for a while. People may so no to your requests, but in asking them, you're giving them a chance to say yes.

Then, be gentle with yourself as you give yourself love and reassurance. As Dr. Theodore Isaac Rubin said, "Compassion for myself is the most powerful healer of them all." Just as you ask others for support, ask yourself, too. Postpone major decisions if you can. Declare a truce in your war on yourself. Remember that mistakes will happen. Give yourself the time you need to heal. Be active when you can; sit quietly and comfortably when you can't. Keep in mind the words of Confucius: "It does not matter how slowly you go so long as you do not stop." Praise yourself not only for your courage to change, risk, and grow, but also for all the little victories you make on the path of healing.

ça ça ça

I ACCEPT THE LOVING ACTS BESTOWED UPON ME BY OTHERS AS WELL AS BY MYSELF.

"Once upon a time, two frogs fell into a bucket of cream. The first frog, seeing that there was no way to get any footing in the white liquid, accepted his fate and drowned. The second frog didn't like that approach. He started thrashing around in the cream and doing whatever he could to stay afloat. After a while, all of his churning turned the cream into butter, and he was able to hop out."

— parable of "The Two Frogs," by creativity consultant Roger Von Oech

CREATIVE RISK-TAKING

Whenever you try something and then fail, what's your next step? Do you try again, or do you give up? All growth in life springs from the tension between limits and drive. Sometimes you take a risk and succeed, and sometimes you take a risk and fail. It's what you do after a failure that determines how you limit your life. As Rollo May writes in his book, *The Courage to Create*, "The creative act arises out of the struggle of human beings with and against that which limits them."

In any attempt, sometimes things will work to your advantage and sometimes to your disadvantage. You can be like the frog that believes it can't do anything about its situation and give up. Or you can be like the frog that believes that there's got to be another way and strives to find it. You need to actively struggle to find the best approach to reach any of your goals. And when you fail, you need to try again. And again. And again.

How can you do this? Be creative. Invent new ways of doing things, change old attitudes, revise former behaviors, try out new paths. Each attempt stretches your limits and allows you more room in which to experiment and grow. The wider the territory of your existence, the greater is your freedom to explore. And the more you can explore, the less likely you are to meekly accept any failure and drown in the sorrows of your defeat.

🐸 🐸 🐸

I BECOME A CREATIVE RISK-TAKER EACH TIME I TRY TO FIND A WAY TO ATTAIN MY GOALS.

"Anybody who is anybody seems to be getting a lift—by plastic surgery these days. It's the new world craze that combines the satisfactions of psychoanalysis, massage, and a trip to the beauty salon."

— Eugenia Sheppard

CULTIVATING INNER BEAUTY

Are you depressed about your outer appearance? Do you feel that if you were stronger, prettier, handsomer, or thinner, you would be a more acceptable, worthwhile human being? Do you spend lots of time compulsively dieting, exercising, or grooming yourself, but look in the mirror and never like what you see? Do you spend more time fantasizing about how you'd like to appear than in accepting how you really do appear?

Worrying excessively about your physical image keeps your focus on the surface of things in life. While modern life emphasizes the superficial side of things—what you do, where you live, how much money you make, and how you look—these accouterments really mean nothing. That's because the surface never stays the same. Weight is gained and lost, with or without a diet. Wrinkles and gray hair happen in the young as well as the middle-aged. Blemishes erupt and heal. Muscle tone changes; strength weakens.

It's not what you look like but who you are that gives your life its meaning and purpose. Dieting, exercising, grooming, and even plastic surgery are things you may do to try to feel better about who you are on the outside, but they aren't who you are on the inside. Take time today to pay closer attention to who you are as a friend, lover, co-worker, family member, or parent. Stop worrying about your physical image, just for today.

ℰ ℰ ℰ

I CULTIVATE MY INNER BEAUTY BY FOCUSING ON WHO I AM AS A WHOLE PERSON.

"Needing people too much can cause problems. Other people become the key to our happiness....The magic is in others, not us, we believe. The good feelings are in them, not us. The less good stuff we find in ourselves, the more we seek it in others. They have it all; we have nothing. Our existence is not important."

— from *Co-Dependent No More,* by Melody Beattie

HEALTHY DEPENDENCY

Orbiting your life around another person, according to Melody Beattie, goes hand-in-hand with co-dependency. The source of such co-dependency often springs from your own emotional insecurity—a feeling that you're so worthless, so inadequate, so insignificant, and so weak as a human being that you need another to make you a more competent and confident person. As long as you're in the company of this person, you feel good about yourself and your life. But the instant this person goes away or wants to take time for himself or herself, you feel lost, alone, abandoned, worthless, and depressed. While part of your healing and recovery from depression, grieving, or "the blues" involves enlisting the support of others, this doesn't mean that others will support you emotionally, physically, and spiritually every step of the way. You still need to stand on your own and, for the most part, stand alone.

There are important benefits you can reap from needing others in a healthy dependency. You can share experiences, suggestions, and information with one another. You can learn that you're not the only one who has ever been depressed or who has ever lost a loved one—and that you can recover from your depression and work through your grief. You can be comforted by touch—through hugs—as well as by discussion. But most important, you can both be supportive of each other's commitment to your own healing and your own healthy independence.

ﮮ ﮮ ﮮ

I SEEK OUT THE HELP OF OTHERS AS I REMAIN COMMITTED TO HEALING MYSELF.

"When I was at the height of everything, I was having a hard time. I felt like I was on this snowball that kept rolling downhill. It kept getting bigger and bigger and faster and faster, and I didn't know how to slow it down. I was afraid that if I tried to slow it down at all, it would stop."

— Kathy Mattea

SETTING PRIORITIES

Today country singer Kathy Mattea cares less about pleasing the marketplace than about making music she'd like to hear. Yet, this wasn't always the case, for she was so driven, so focused on pleasing her fans and business handlers that she ignored the pressure she was putting on herself. In 1992, her voice gave out and she had to undergo vocal surgery. Instead of being devastated by her experience, however, she learned something about herself. For the first time in years, she discovered that she wasn't as unhappy as she had thought she was.

"I had a mission—to get through this vocal surgery," she explained. "I had a lot of time to think about priorities. I came away from that knowing that not all of my emotional happiness is tied up in whether or not this works. I can be valuable and productive and happy whether it's [my career] going great guns or not."

Today, take the pressure off yourself to have to worry about everything, have to "do" for everyone, have to be available for anyone, have to fix everything, and have to be successful at everything you do. Try not to push yourself to do things that are too risky, too far out of your character, or which you do to satisfy the desires of others. Set your own priorities, and you'll discover that you're a much happier and more relaxed person.

🍃 🍃 🍃

I PICK AND CHOOSE THE THINGS I LIKE TO DO IN MY LIFE SO THAT I TRULY ENJOY THEM.

"Many times I am trying very hard to put my life back together and people don't recognize that. Telling me to 'get my act together' or to 'buck up' makes it even more difficult to cope. I feel more hopeless than even before. That is one of the worst things someone can do for me."

— Participant in a depression study

COMMUNICATING YOUR NEEDS

When you're depressed, here are some of the things that you might not want other people to do:

- blame you for the depression,
- abandon or avoid you,
- tell you to get your act together,
- tell you to cheer up or "smile,"
- give you sympathy,
- pressure you to go out,
- do everything for you,
- make fun of you or humiliate you, and
- call you names, or attach labels to you ("lazy," "whacked out," "crazy," "mad," etc.).

It's important that you communicate to those around you how you would like to be treated when you're depressed. You may want to ask people to allow you more time to complete tasks, to ask if you need to talk, to remind you that you've felt this way before, to include you in activities but also to give you space, to listen without trying to have answers, to remind you not to be so hard on yourself, to be patient yet firm with you, and to reassure you in understanding and caring ways.

You'll be surprised by how well people respond to you when you honestly communicate with them!

ॐ ॐ ॐ

I LET PEOPLE KNOW HOW I WANT TO BE TREATED SO THAT THEY CAN HELP ME.

"Hope is the feeling you have that the feeling you have isn't permanent."

— author Jean Kerr

SPIRITUAL HOPE

Visitors to the Fiji Islands learn about a strange custom among its native people known as "Calling to the Dead." A mourner climbs high up into a tree or scales a cliff and, after calling out the name of the deceased, cries out, "Come back! Come back!" The cry is made even more heartrending by the echoes that reverberate in "reply."

When you're feeling physically, emotionally, or spiritually low or are filled with grief, you may be convinced that your situation won't improve—and will probably get worse. Because the present is so unbearable, you may think that the future holds more of the same. You may even blame God or your understanding of a god for your present condition. You may cry out, "Why did You do this to me?" or "Why don't You help me?"

Estrangement from a Higher Power can leave you with an intense spiritual emptiness. But even though you may feel as if you stand alone and are exposed to the elements of a cruel, heartless world that have been personally directed at you by some all-powerful, unkind Being, that's just not the case. Every event in your life has been experienced by millions of others. You're not the recipient of a vengeful act that's been inflicted upon you from above.

Rather than dwell in hopelessness, reach out hopefully. Cry out your pain, beat your hands against your chest, let your tears fall, get on your knees, or simply close your eyes and silently ask for spiritual guidance. You will get an answer.

ℬ ℬ ℬ

I PRAY WITH HOPE AND FAITH, AND I KNOW MY PRAYERS ARE HEARD.

"Eeyore, the old grey Donkey, stood by the side of the stream, and looked at himself in the water. 'Pathetic,' he said. 'That's what it is. Pathetic.'"
— from *Winnie the Pooh,* by A.A. Milne

MORNING ATTITUDE

Do you have the Eeyore Attitude? The Eeyore Attitude enables you to find something bad, something tragic, something hurtful, something impossible, something overwhelming, something unfair, and something wrong in every person and every thing. The Eeyore Attitude is a garden that's sown with disgust, cultivated by complaint, enriched by pessimism, and harvested by hopelessness. The Eeyore Attitude gets in the way of things like wisdom and happiness and pretty much prevents any sort of real accomplishment in life. The Eeyore Attitude is, by its very nature, humorless and not much fun to experience.

When the day starts for Eeyore and he's greeted by a cheery "Good morning" from his friends Pooh and Piglet, his gloomy response is always "Good morning—if it *is* a good morning. Which I doubt." Yet Pooh and Piglet never see the world in this way. When Pooh starts his day, the first thing he wonders is what's for breakfast. When Piglet starts his day, he wonders what exciting thing is going to happen. Both Pooh and Piglet have a noticeably different attitude from Eeyore—an attitude of happy serenity. This attitude enables them to enjoy the simple things in life and spontaneously find joy and humor in everyone and everything.

This morning, think about the attitude you wish to cultivate. You can be a grumpy Eeyore, wallowing in a joyless and terribly depressing world, or you can be a peaceful Pooh or Piglet, content and calm throughout the day. Which do you choose?

🍃 🍃 🍃

I LOOK AT MYSELF IN THE MIRROR THIS MORNING AND SAY, "VERY GOOD. THAT'S WHAT I AM. VERY GOOD."

"They were so strong in their beliefs that there came a time when it hardly mattered what exactly those beliefs were; they all fused into a single stubbornness."

— author Louise Erdrich

REVAMPING DISTORTED THINKING

A depressed mind is encouraged by beliefs that result from distorted ways of thinking. Polarized thinking is one style. This distortion involves perceiving everything at the extremes, as either black or white, right or wrong, good or bad—with nothing in-between. Polarized thinking perpetuates mood swings, for it encourages you to think either that things are all great or all horrible—there's no middle ground.

A thought formed from polarized thinking could be: "I couldn't pay all my bills this month without borrowing money from my partner. I'm a failure and a freeloader." The distorted perception that evolves from this thinking is that your self-worth and who you are in your relationship are defined by your ability to pay your bills. But a more rational, logical response to this polarized thought might be: "I've had a bad month, but that's because the economy's been bad and business is off. There was a time when my partner couldn't pay all the bills and I helped out then, when things were going well for me. I've had better months in the past, and I'll have better months in the future."

Think of a recent example of such polarized thinking. Write down what you thought on a piece of paper. Identify the distorted perception in your example. How did you feel at the time? Did such feelings cause a conflict with others in your life? Then write a rational comeback to replace your distorted perception. Do this exercise as often as you need to, and you may find that you're able to see shades of gray where previously there had been only black or white.

છે છે છે

I BECOME MORE AWARE OF THE DISTORTIONS IN MY THINKING, SO I MODIFY MY VIEWS FOR MY OWN *GOOD*.

*"The positive emotions are no less a physiological factor on
the upside than are the negative emotions on the downside."*
— author Norman Cousins

MIND-BODY HEALING

If you're not in touch with how your mind can affect your body,
you may be suffering from "phantom" aches and pains and not realize that these are a result of your morose feelings and your depression. There's a lot to be said for the mind-body connection
when recognizing and treating depression. Depression is often
veiled by physical complaints and confused with a variety of
physical illnesses. It may be masked by, or co-exist with, other illnesses. For example, a person with diabetes may also be suffering
from a separate biochemical depression. Because depression can
cause a drop in neurotransmitter levels—by decreasing saliva-
tion, slowing down gastrointestinal activity, and causing dry
mouth, stomachaches, gas, and constipation—it can bring on
symptoms for which no cause can be found. Common physical
symptoms of depression include nausea, chest pains, low blood
pressure, headaches, backache, and muscle spasms.

Yet, even if you're depressed, you can "heal" your physical
symptoms by sending your body positive, affirming messages
from your mind, as well as by performing gentle healing on your
body. Ask a friend to give you a massage, and while he or she is
doing so, think positive thoughts such as, "I will allow every muscle in my body to experience the pleasure of this massage." Or you
can do gentle, deep breathing as you think, "I inhale peace and
serenity and let my stomach tension go with each breath I exhale."

ॐ ॐ ॐ

I SEND MY BODY RELAXING, HEALING MESSAGES SO I RELIEVE
MY PHYSICAL ACHES AND PAINS.

"You can fulfill the expectations of others, yet fail your own. You can win every honor, yet feel you have accomplished nothing; you can be adored by millions, yet wake up each morning with a sickening sense of emptiness."

— author Nathaniel Branden

BUILDING SELF-ESTEEM

Because you're human, you're also a social being—someone who depends upon receiving some measure of your self-esteem from others. But the acclaim, admiration, approval, or acceptance of others doesn't create your self-esteem. To link how you feel about yourself to the opinion of others is to give up your power.

Self-esteem, according to Nathaniel Branden, is what you think and feel about yourself, not what someone else thinks or feels about you. While how you're viewed by your family, friends, coworkers, intimate partner, and acquaintances may be important to you, such outlooks can't influence whether you have a love, a hate, or a love-hate relationship with yourself.

The most effective way to develop your self-esteem is to learn to think for yourself. One way to do so is to eliminate thinking in terms of "should"—for example, "I *should* follow my partner's advice" or "I *should* never feel jealous." *Should*-thinking forces you to operate from a rigid set of indisputable rules created by everyone else. So when your behavior doesn't conform to those rules, your self-esteem suffers.

Today, eliminate the word *should* from your spoken words as well as your thoughts. Then allow yourself to experience who you are and what you do from your own perspective.

❧ ❧ ❧

I AM MORE OCCUPIED WITH WHAT *I* THINK AND FEEL THAN PREOCCUPIED WITH WHAT *OTHERS* THINK AND FEEL.

"As children, we all experience helplessness, but as adults we are no longer helpless. You can allow yourself to be at the mercy of events, circumstances and of other people—or you can take charge of your life."

— author Julia M. Busch

RELEASING THE PAST

Are you one of those people who isn't happy unless you're miserable? You may have started feeling "blue" years ago in response to an emotional hurt or disappointment—when your lover left you, after you lost a valuable friendship, when you gained weight, or when you discovered you didn't have the stamina you had when you were 20. Over time, you may have fine-tuned your blue feelings into "forever-blue" feelings. so today you don't know how to feel any other way.

Being emotionally hurt is a natural response to the events of life, but *remaining* emotionally hurt is a choice. If you're currently suffering as a result of an old hurt, it's because you choose to do so. If that choice makes you happy, then continue to follow that path. But if you're tired of feeling despondent, then it's time to make another choice.

Today, look at your past hurt as something that's repairable, then set your mind to doing the necessary repairs. If the hurt is a result of a love you lost, then make yourself available to love again. If the hurt is due to something that your parents "did" to you as a child, then let them know how you feel...and then forgive them. If the hurt is due to changes in your body, then take steps to feel more comfortable with your appearance and stamina. If you can't make these efforts on your own, seek help from others. Remember, holding on to past emotional pain keeps you isolated and negative; releasing these hurts restores your connection to yourself and to life.

 youngsters youngsters youngsters

I TAKE CHARGE OF MY LIFE NOW BY RELEASING MY PAST HURTS.

FEBRUARY 26

*"I wish there were windows to my soul, so that you could
see some of my feelings."*

— Artemus Ward

EXPRESSING FEELINGS

Wouldn't it be wonderful if people could see your feelings? All you'd have to do is walk into a room and someone would say, "I see you're feeling sad right now. Let me help you. Talk to me. Tell me why you feel the way you do." Such sensitivity and encouragement could make you feel more inclined to share feelings that you might otherwise feel too hesitant, reluctant, ashamed, or embarrassed to open up about.

You may have grown up expecting people to be mind-readers. Without voicing your feelings or asking for help, you may have believed that people should be able to see how you felt. When they didn't, you may have become hurt, angry, or depressed. You may have moved into adulthood with the same expectations, believing your intimate partner, roommate, co-workers, friends, and family members ought to be able to automatically divine your emotions.

Today you may not recognize the impact that such high expectations have had upon your ability to express your emotions. In fact, until someone points this out, you may not recognize how silent you've become, how much you suppress your feelings, and just how unrealistic your standards for others' behavior are.

Unless you verbalize your emotions, they'll never be heard. And unless you ask for help, you'll never get assistance. Today, tell someone how you feel. Ask for help if you need it. The people in your life have ears to listen and arms to hold you, but they're not mind-readers. They can be there for you, but only if you choose to open the windows of your soul.

ॐ ॐ ॐ

I EXPRESS MY EMOTIONS FREELY, WITHOUT WAITING FOR SOMEONE TO ASK ME HOW I FEEL.

"I think there's something new about our age that amplifies our personal problems, that wears away our protective psychic skins until we feel flayed by each new bit of bad news."

— author Linda Weltner

TUNING INTO GOOD NEWS

Let's face it. The world doesn't feel safe and secure. Terrorism, dictatorships, shady political maneuverings, and unspeakable suffering dominate headlines. The country doesn't feel safe and secure. Government officials and those in positions of authority abuse trust, and random acts of violence defy explanation. The place where we live doesn't feel safe and secure. Children are kidnaped, crime is on the rise, and neighbors are sometimes not who they appear to be. Is it any wonder, then, that the strength you need to live on a day-to-day basis is so depleted by terrible news and rising fears that your spirit often feels broken, you feel physically drained and exhausted, and your mental outlook is dominated by depression and anxiety about the future?

There seems to be a widespread lack of appreciation for the good things in life—not because such things don't exist anymore—but because natural disasters, crimes against humanity, and the suffering of the world is what sells newspapers, increases television ratings, enables books to achieve bestselling status, and lends notoriety to horrific criminals and their nefarious deeds.

Yet, you can restore your appreciation for the good in life and reduce your feelings of depression by turning your attention away from newspapers, radio, and television. Focus instead on activities that bring you pleasure. Play your favorite music while you sew, cook a new dish, reread a favorite novel, or pore over your photo album. Filling your mind with such comforting activities can repair your mental outlook.

ﭼ ﭼ ﭼ

I TUNE OUT THE BAD NEWS OF THE WORLD AND TUNE INTO THE GOOD.

"So I can't sink down and let the time of my real being take me, for if I try and for a moment can see no direction, cannot tell where I am going, I am filled with panic, scared of emptiness. I must be doing something...."

— author Joanna Field

SLOWING DOWN

When you experience anxiety and depression, you may find that you have incredible bursts of energy coupled with a fear of dealing with your feelings. These emotions cause you to fill each minute of the day and night with projects. The first sign of such high-energy surges may be an inability to either get or stay asleep at night. As you lie in bed, your mind may be racing, shifting you into overdrive and making it impossible to lie still. Soon you're up and running—making lists, planning what you're going to do the next day, writing notes for yourself—basically taking on too much.

There are ways to alleviate or even eliminate such episodic energy surges. Physically, you can channel your need to be in motion into vigorous exercise, gardening, yoga, or dancing to your favorite music. Avoid caffeine and sugar, maintain a balance of rest and activity, and eat a diet high in complex carbohydrates. Emotionally, you can stop making lists, strive to understand why you're doing what you're doing, and focus on living one day at a time—or even one minute at a time. You can also go to a support group, talk about how you feel with an understanding peer or counselor, arrange to have friends around, and try to shift from overdrive into neutral. Finally, on a spiritual level, you can use prayer, relaxation tapes, and meditation to help you get in touch with your calmer, more peaceful side.

❧ ❧ ❧

I STAY CALM AND FOCUSED AS I MOVE INTO A MORE COMFORTABLE PACE OF LIVING.

"My dear mother, sisters and brother comforted me, but their comfort only increased my sorrow and poured more oil on the fire, so that the flames grew ever higher."
— Gluckel of Hamelin

DEALING WITH DEATH

Dealing with the death of a loved one can be made more difficult by the attempts at reassurance made by others. For example: "Now you know he/she wouldn't have wanted you to feel this way" is a guilt-inducing statement often expressed by well-meaning friends to help you handle your grief. "You should be grateful you had him/her for so long" denies that you can feel anger and resentment over losing precious moments with your loved one. "Don't feel bad" tells you to suppress or bury your feelings. "On Saturday we'll get you a new dog" assumes that you can simply replace and forget about your trusted friend. And "It's God's will" or "God never gives you more than you can handle" rarely provides the comfort you truly need—that of validation, identification, and understanding that you're not the only person who has ever gone through what you're enduring.

What such inappropriate or ineffective responses to grief show us is that most people are ill prepared to offer soothing, comforting words during times of distress. In fact, it's often much easier for people to deal with minor accidents or even major surgery than it is to deal with the grief caused by death. People often don't know what to say, how to say it, or when to say it.

But, since it's only natural and even quite healthy to seek solace from others when you're mourning someone's death, you need to carefully select whom you choose to provide that comfort. Anyone who has lost a loved one in the recent past might be an ideal sounding board for your emotions or your grief. Seek out this person, and then be open to accepting words of understanding and empathy.

❧ ❧ ❧

I MOURN MY LOSS WITH SOMEONE WHO TRULY UNDERSTANDS.

"It's hard to take yourself too seriously when you look at the world from outer space."

— Thomas "Ken" Mattingly II

REGAINING PERSPECTIVE

Are you someone who believes that there's a right way to squeeze the tube of toothpaste or to hang a roll of toilet paper? Do you rush to the train station each weekday morning so you can park in "your" spot? Do you become irritable when your socks aren't folded the way you want them? Is your day ruined if the restaurant where you eat lunch is out of your "usual"? If such things matter to you, then you're taking life much too seriously.

To live—to really be alive—means that you allow yourself to flow with the people and events around you. You don't confine yourself to any rigid picture of who you are, what ought to happen, or how things should be done. You don't take yourself or anything else too seriously, and you certainly don't give too much power to the little things in life.

Today, strive to keep the little things in perspective. It doesn't matter how the toothpaste gets out of the tube, as long as it ends up on the brush. It doesn't matter where you park, for you'll still be able to ride the train. It doesn't matter how your socks are folded because that's not how you're going to wear them. And it's okay to try a different lunch from time to time.

Apollo XVI astronaut Ken Mattingly II was able to see his world from a much different perspective in outer space. Today, imagine that you can see the immensity of the universe—all the people and places in the world—so you can view this particular day and how you respond to it in context.

ço ço ço

I RELAX IN MY OWN SMALL WORLD BY REMEMBERING THAT I'M PART OF A MUCH BIGGER WORLD.

"By suffering comes wisdom."
— Aeschylus

GROWING PAINS

You may have heard the expression "No pain, no gain" used in connection with sports or athletic endeavors. But have you ever thought of applying the same expression to the learning, growth, and positive change that can come out of your mood swings? Dr. Claire Weekes defines depression as "your body's expression of emotional exhaustion." She explains that because your vitality is low and your emotional reserves have become overdrawn, your body begins to experience an emotional downswing. But, she adds, "Your body will heal itself if you will allow it. This is nature's gift." And this is the gain that can come after the pain.

When you're in the midst of depression, grief, or "the blues," you can remain in your pain by sitting around the house and watching the day pass by, or you can try to fill each empty hour as best you can. You can gain from your pain by getting outdoors, where your depressed spirit can benefit greatly from the stimulation provided by an outside environment. The brightness of the day, the expanse of the sky above you, the smells of the outside world, the sounds of humanity and nature, the absence of limiting walls, your ability to move around, and being able to breathe deeply of the fresh air all help to keep your spirits raised and your troubles in proportion.

Sit outside on your porch or balcony, take a walk around the neighborhood, or go for a drive in the country. While such activities may not make your pain disappear, they can help repair your body and restore your soul. And, in the end, a simple change of scenery can help you lift yourself out of other mood swings or even prevent the onset of subsequent depression.

ﻬ ﻬ ﻬ

I GROW FROM MY PAIN BY BEING WILLING TO MAKE SIMPLE CHANGES IN MY LIFE.

"They that will not be counseled, cannot be helped. If you do not hear reason, she will rap you on the knuckles."
— Benjamin Franklin

BENEFICIAL COUNSELING

Therapy is one tool you can use to help you work through a particularly trying or discomfiting time in your life. But even though you suspect that therapy may be helpful, you may be reluctant to seek help—even fearful about making the initial telephone call. You may offer excuses such as: "I don't have time," "I don't know if my insurance will cover it," "I think parking will be a problem," "I just need to work things out for myself," or "I don't want to have to go on medication for the rest of my life."

Yet, you can benefit from working with a counselor trained in psychotherapy, behavior therapy, or cognitive therapy. When you're feeling utterly discouraged, a therapist can offer you a sense of realistic hope. This type of professional won't advise you (as your friends or relatives might) to "snap out of it" or "to get on with your life." Instead, a therapist can help you honestly face and deal with your feelings in a noncritical and nonjudgmental way.

A therapist can also assist you in seeing that you have options and help you evaluate these areas so you can make a choice. A therapist may prescribe "activity therapy"—simple activities such as grocery shopping or taking a short walk every day—to help you start moving in a more positive direction. A therapist can also teach you assertive skills for dealing with everyday situations so you can learn to ask for help and stand up for yourself.

But the only way you can explore the benefits of counseling is to pick up the telephone and make an appointment for an initial evaluation. After all, what do you have to lose?

🍃 🍃 🍃

I AM OPEN-MINDED ENOUGH TO GIVE COUNSELING A TRY.

"Our weak and negative states leave us open to 'take on' outside prevailing conditions....We are shaken with the wind and float with the current because we present the negative."

— Henry Wood

OUTSIDE INFLUENCES

Mind reading and personalization are two forms of negative, distorted thinking that make you feel as if your moods are always at the mercy of the moods and actions of others. With mind reading, you base assumptions and conclusions about the actions of others on your "psychic ability" to look into these people's thoughts. So if your co-worker doesn't invite you to lunch, you think she hates you, or if your partner yawns when you're talking about your day, you know he's bored with you and ready to leave the relationship.

When your thinking is distorted by personalization, you interpret everything around you in ways that reflect on you and your self-worth. Personalization can be a double-edge sword, for when everyone around you is happy and relaxed, then you interpret this as a response to what a good person you are. But when those around you are angry, grumpy, or withdrawn, then you interpret this as a response to how awful you are.

Your life can be so much more enjoyable—and you can enjoy yourself much more—when you aren't drowning in your distorted perceptions of everyone else's frame of mind. You don't have to absorb the moods of others or get caught up in their responses to the events in their own lives. How other people respond and behave is out of your control; how you respond and behave is all that needs to concern you.

❧ ❧ ❧

I PROTECT MYSELF FROM THE INFLUENCES OF OTHERS BY RESPONDING TO REALITY AND RATIONALITY.

"One thing that comes out of myths is that at the bottom of the abyss comes the voice of salvation. The black moment is the moment when the real message of transformation is going to come. At the darkest moment comes the light."
— author Joseph Campbell

CONFRONTING SUICIDAL THOUGHTS

The reality of depression is that it does end; it does not go on forever. Millions of people who have experienced depressive episodes can confirm this fact. But the tragedy of depression is that thousands of people have ended their lives through suicide. Many people feel that ending their lives is the only way to put an end to the intolerable feelings of despair. The pain and blackness they feel inside are so overwhelming that suicide is viewed as the only option.

Even though you may be in such a state of profound and hopeless depression, there is always hope. Most suicidal thoughts are not just triggered by the actual depression, but also by your response to other influences: low self-esteem, loneliness, guilt, bad memories—particularly those associated with childhood abuse—seasonal triggers, fatigue, and even reactions to certain foods or smells—perfumes, household cleaners, or products used in painting.

To help you identify the basis of your suicidal thoughts, complete this statement on a separate sheet of paper: "I feel suicidal because _____." If there is more than one reason, list them all. Then, next to each reason, finish this statement, "What I need to do to work through this feeling of _____ is to _____." Think of at least one action that can help you deal with each emotion, then try it. Working yourself out of your desperation can help your negative feelings diminish considerably!

ॐ ॐ ॐ

I FOCUS ON THE LIGHT AT THE END OF THE TUNNEL SO I CAN FIND MY WAY OUT TO THE OTHER SIDE.

"Life is a series of moments. To live each one is to succeed."
— serigraph artist Corita Kent

TALKING OUT YOUR GRIEF

What makes you forget your sadness or loneliness after the loss of a loved one? Being with family or friends? Spending more time at work? Reading a book? Walking on the beach? Listening to a beautiful piece of music? Watching your favorite old movie?

Finding moments of serenity and happiness when your world is in turmoil and your heart is broken can be difficult. Trying to ignore the emptiness of your home, to suppress endless tears, or to resume your daily routine can be almost impossible right after your loss. It may seem as if you spend every minute focused on what you don't have anymore.

The teachings of *Tao* counsel to "Be still and discover your inner peace." How can you do this when your inner peace has been shattered? One way is to think about the little things you shared together that you now miss. Maybe it was the way you'd read portions of the Sunday newspaper out loud to each other or how you'd give special nicknames to your pets. Now imagine that you can tell your loved one how, in looking back, such moments make you feel. You might say out loud, "I really loved it when you'd read our favorite comic strip on Sunday morning and use different voices for the characters. It made me laugh, and it set the right mood for spending the day together." Feel the inner peace that comes from the acknowledgment and communication of this special moment together, then return to the present moment, secure in having expressed how you really felt. Allow yourself to do this as often as you need to as you mourn your loss.

🎗 🎗 🎗

I "TALK" OPENLY WITH MY LOVED ONE SO I CAN OVERCOME MY FEELINGS OF GRIEF.

> *"When you fall in a river, you're no longer a fisherman; you're a swimmer."*
>
> — *Field and Stream* writer Gene Hill

ENCOURAGING SELF-TALK

Psychologist Carl Jung, in *Mysterium Coniunctionis* (*The Mysterious, Mystical Union*) points out that "in myths the hero is the one who conquers the dragon, not the one who is devoured by it. And yet both have to deal with the same dragon." So why, then, isn't the victim also a hero?

Too often you may visually lock yourself into an image that's less than who you really are. But in doing so, you allow yourself to become what you think. You think you're a failure, so you set impossible goals that will make you fail. You think you're not good with numbers, so you don't prepare a household budget or balance your checkbook. You think people don't like you, so you cancel social invitations and isolate yourself from others. You think you don't have the energy to do anything, so you sit in front of the television and do nothing. With such thinking, if you think you're a fisherman and then fall into the river, you will probably drown.

Such thoughts can become self-fulfilling prophecies. Even though they may accurately reflect how you feel, they are not constructive. So how can you make the most out of the strengths and abilities you feel you have? Engage in constructive self-talk that conservatively measures an amount of inner strength you could have. For example, you may feel you're not good with numbers, but you can say, "I can research what car will give me the most for my money." This positive approach assesses what you can work with and what you can do in a way that helps you repair your damaged self-esteem—so you can become a swimmer when you need to be one!

ɣa ɣa ɣa

I USE CONSTRUCTIVE SELF-TALK IN ORDER TO ENCOURAGE MYSELF.

MARCH 8

"When I look back on all these worries, I remember the story of the old man who said on his deathbed that he had had a lot of trouble in his life, most of which never happened."
— Winston Churchill

USING RELAXATION

Sir Winston Churchill was tormented with depression throughout his life. But his wife said that after the failed Dardanelles Expedition in 1915, he "was filled with such a black depression that I felt he would never recover." Yet, Churchill managed to overcome his depression to be a powerful world leader and masterful decision-maker who guided his country through extremely tumultuous times.

Many well-known men and women have succeeded in life in spite of debilitating depression. And many not-so-well-known millions have conquered this condition in ways that have enabled them to function much better. One way in which they have done so is by using relaxation techniques that help to minimize the focus on obsessive worrying, which can create moods of despair.

To learn how to calm yourself, you can take a relaxation or meditation course. Look for courses in the community calendar section of your daily newspaper, or check with your local hospital or mental health hotline. You can rent an instructional video, or you can listen to audio relaxation tapes that combine natural sounds and music with the spoken word or which simply feature the sounds of nature, such as the ocean or bird calls. Or, you can read self-help books that offer guidance in a variety of relaxation procedures. Whatever technique you decide to use, be sure to practice it daily so that these skills will be available to you when you need them most.

ৡ ৡ ৡ

I USE RELAXATION TECHNIQUES TO STABILIZE MY MOODS AND EASE MY DEPRESSION.

"I think women typically tend to accommodate to the expectations of others, and to build a lot of their self-esteem on those expectations."

— Judy Jordan

WOMEN AND DEPRESSION

Judy Jordan, a psychologist who heads the Women's Treatment Program at McLean Hospital in Massachusetts, has worked with women who are depressed, and she concludes that women can be different from men with respect to their propensity towards depression. While both men and women may suffer equally from this condition, there is a growing recognition that depression can appear differently in men and women and that these differences can impact responses to treatment.

However, this is not to say that today's research still supports the outdated and erroneous stereotypical premise that women seem to be more vulnerable than men to depression because their depression is thought to be a result of oppressive social roles or hormones. What this does say, however, is that women need to be aware of their depressive episodes and to treat them as such, rather than fall into the trap of blaming them on any number of "female issues"—childbirth, puberty, menstrual cycles, children leaving home, menopause, and so on. Likewise, a man who loves and cares for a woman who is suffering from depression needs to learn that her emotional downswings are just as valid as his. Supporting the steps that are taken towards alleviating depressive feelings are far more important than trying to seek a reason that is designed to minimize—or even invalidate—a woman's very real feelings.

❧ ❧ ❧

I RECOGNIZE THAT WOMEN AS WELL AS MEN ARE AFFECTED BY DEPRESSION AND THAT APPROPRIATE TREATMENT DOES EXIST.

"The greatest thing in life is not where you are, but the direction in which you are moving."

— Oliver Wendell Holmes

FOLLOWING YOUR DESTINY

When your purpose in life is blocked, you may experience depression, irritation, anxiety, or frustration. On the other hand, if you're living in accord with your real desires, then you experience joy, completeness, meaning, and satisfaction. If you find that you're unhappy with your situation or that you complain a lot, chances are that you aren't giving yourself an opportunity to fulfill your purpose.

What is a purpose in life, and how can you find it? Just as a salmon, by its very nature, must swim upstream, so too does each human being follow a similarly powerful inner calling, which can be "voiced" through your desires, your feelings, what you want out of life, and your learning experiences, recreational choices, hobbies, social life, and the community activities in which you're involved. Such things reflect who you are and how you express yourself. When you "listen" to the experiences that make you feel the most alive, then you're more willing to seek them out and let them lead you towards greater wealth, health, and happiness.

Today, spend less time pursuing those activities that cause you unhappiness and pain, and set aside more time to do those things that really empower you. Your life will be wonderful if you allow it to progress in ways that help you fulfill your purpose in life!

❧ ❧ ❧

I AM WILLING TO LISTEN TO MY INNER VOICE SO THAT I CAN FULFILL MY PURPOSE IN LIFE.

"A handful of patience is worth more than a bushel of brains."

— Dutch proverb

DEVELOPING PATIENCE

You will find that you will receive the most benefits from your healing and recovery if you exercise patience. Just as Rome wasn't built in a day, the ceiling of the Sistine Chapel was the result of years of work, barns built centuries ago still stand firm, and the finest and most brilliant gems are the result of hours of study, cutting, and polishing, so too is your healing and recovery the result of thorough and persistent attention.

For example, if you're in a recovery program such as Alcoholics Anonymous, you learn from your very first meeting that putting away the bottle won't instantly solve all of your problems. You hear the life stories of others who talk about the years and years they spent on their recovery, taken one day at a time. You read the 12 Steps and begin to recognize that the personal work and growth involved will never be accomplished in 12 days.

But, to paraphrase a familiar quote, "Good things can come to those who take their time." To heal and recover from anything—a business failure, a financial setback, a divorce, the death of a child, or an illness—requires long hours and dedication. Today, try working on a part of your recovery without setting a deadline or expecting a quick outcome. Eliminating a time frame and any specific expectations can help you progress in ways that will have a long-lasting and beneficial effect on your life.

ॐ ॐ ॐ

I HEAL AND RECOVER PATIENTLY, KNOWING THAT THE END RESULT WILL BE WORTH MY EFFORTS.

"There is perhaps no more effective way to relieve psychic pain than to be in contact with another human being who understands what you are going through and can communicate such understandings to you."

— Frederic Flach, in *Resilience*

SUPPORTIVE PEOPLE AND GROUPS

There are many people who care about how you feel. But sometimes it may be hard for you to identify these individuals because you may always turn to those whose help and support you want, but who never seem to give it to you. Continuing to believe that those people will eventually come around and respond to you in the ways you desire may keep you stuck in your negative feelings—and prevent you from reaching out to those who *can* support you.

Take a moment to think about the people you already know who can help you, such as:

- empathetic friends;
- a doctor, teacher, or counselor;
- a priest, rabbi, minister, or spiritual healer; and/or
- family members.

There are also a number of national organizations that can provide you with immediate support at the local level, including the National Depressive and Manic Depressive Association, which has about 250 support groups across America. You may reach them at (312) 642-0049. There may also be state and local government agencies that can provide help. Look under listings for Mental Health Agencies, as well as Mayor's Hotlines in your phone book. Even though you may not personally know the people who work for these organizations, they are dedicated to helping people like you and can give you the support you need!

❧ ❧ ❧

I PICK UP THE PHONE AND SEEK THE HELP I NEED.

"The problems of alcoholism and drug abuse have strong links to depression. The search for highs may often begin as a flight from lows."

— Dr. Nathan Kline

DRUGS AND ALCOHOL

Do you use alcohol or mind-altering drugs as a form of self-medication that provides temporary relief from the lows you feel? You may not want to admit this, nor do you want to be told that you're only making your depression worse by continuing to using these substances. And, you may not want to deal with what you may have already realized: while alcohol and drugs may momentarily soothe your pain, even small amounts can cause depression or intensify existing bad feelings. So why continue to engage in a lifestyle that degrades your mind and body and makes you feel well below par most of the time?

If you admit today that alcohol and/or drugs play an important role in keeping you depressed, miserable, and unhappy, and if you set a goal to eradicate them from your life so that you can take better care of yourself, what you may discover over time is that you have increased energy, better mental concentration, and a greater sense of well-being. In fact, without alcohol and/or drugs to fuel your depression, distort your thoughts, and rule your moods, you may become the person you've always wanted to be—someone you admire and respect.

You don't have to be an alcoholic to have a problem with alcohol; you don't have to be a drug addict to have a problem with drugs. But you may find Alcoholics Anonymous or Narcotics Anonymous meetings helpful in attaining your goal to be abstinent.

ชอ ชอ ชอ

I AM DRUG AND ALCOHOL FREE, AND I ENHANCE THE QUALITY OF MY LIFE.

"They got scared when they started feeling good, just because it was so unfamiliar. Like chronic prisoners facing release from their cells."

— author Lisa Alther

CREATING A NEW VISION

Could you start the day in a good mood—with hope, joy, serenity, and a positive outlook—and maintain that mood throughout the day? If you're someone who can't enjoy what you've worked hard to attain, and remain unhappy and depressed when you're surrounded by love, comfort, and success, then you're probably someone who isn't able to start and end the day in a good mood. For you, misery may be normal, so all you can do is find ways to maintain that miserable state.

But when you wallow in your misery, you're using your chronic depression as a rationale for not feeling better, as well as an excuse for not being a fully functioning, responsible person. You use your symptoms to evoke sympathy and reassurance from those around you. You focus on your inadequacies and weaknesses so you lower your own expectations of yourself; therefore, you don't have to perform and achieve. And you have a built-in justification for taking a "time-out" from life and its stressful situations.

Yet, your perspective on life sets the tone for your existence. You can look at your life and feel an oppressive negativity, or you can create a new vision of yourself and your life. Imagine what the "healed you" would be like. Write ten positive descriptions about this "new you," such as "I am confident," "I am lovable," "I am admired," and so on. Then, for the next two weeks, read your "new you" list aloud to help make your vision a reality.

ද්‍ය ද්‍ය ද්‍ය

I CREATE A NEW VISION OF MYSELF THAT GIVES ME A MORE HOPEFUL AND POSITIVE OUTLOOK ON LIFE.

"If the only tool you have is a hammer, you tend to see every problem as a nail."

— psychologist Abraham Maslow

TOOLS OF LIVING

Dr. Murray Banks, a professor who blends psychology and mental health with entertainment, tells this story of two little boys who were playing in the surf one day. Along came a huge wave that suddenly toppled both of them. One little boy regained his footing and ran back to the beach to his mother, crying and begging to go home. The other little boy scrambled to his feet, took a deep breath, laughed, and raced back into the surf. One learned to see the ocean as an enemy that would do the same thing time and time again, with the same result; the other enjoyed the unexpected event and was ready and willing to experience the next one.

What's your reaction when you're knocked down by one of the blows of life? If you're someone who expects the worst, then you probably respond in the same way each time—you fearfully flee from troubles, problems, or worries. To you, life is like one big overwhelming wave that topples you. But if you're someone who embraces life and all it has to offer, then you know how to deal with each wave, no matter how big or small or how weak or powerful. You believe that life is manageable and enjoyable because you know how to handle whatever comes your way.

It's not so much what life *does* to you, but what you do in response that determines your character, your destiny, and your happiness. As Arnold Bennett said, "Your mind is a sacred enclosure into which nothing harmful can enter except by your permission." Today, rather than run from the waves in your life, think of them as tools that you can learn from.

ɤð ɤð ɤð

I TRY OUT NEW "TOOLS" TO HANDLE THE PROBLEMS IN MY LIFE.

"The desire of perfection is the worst disease that ever afflicted the human mind."

— Louis de Fontanes

QUEST FOR PERFECTION

Although your morose feelings or depression may not be continuous, what may be constant is your desire for perfection. Perhaps you have a compulsive style of living in which you can't leave the house in the morning without the beds made or the dishes in the sink washed and put away. Maybe you follow a structured daily routine which, if interrupted in any way, throws you into fits of anguish and tension. Perhaps you find it extremely unsettling to have one hair on your head out of place or a wrinkle on your clothing. Or perhaps you pressure yourself to perform perfectly in many areas—to be a perfect parent, a perfect son or daughter, a perfect lover, a perfect employee, or to have a perfect body and keep a perfect house.

But whenever you strive for perfection, you'll find that you will fail, because it's simply not possible to be absolutely perfect. As a result, you may often feel dissatisfied with your accomplishments and limit the opportunities in which you feel good about yourself. Eventually you get caught on a circular wheel in which you struggle for perfection, don't attain it, get down on yourself, struggle again for perfection, don't attain it, get even more down on yourself, and so on.

The only way to cease your quest for perfection is to tell yourself as often as necessary that nothing and no one can ever be perfect. Instead of attempting to do the impossible, strive instead to do what *is* possible—that is, to simply do your best.

ॐ ॐ ॐ

I KNOW THAT SIMPLY DOING MY BEST IS THE MOST "PERFECT" WAY TO LIVE.

"The only thing that ever sat its way to success was a hen."
— Sarah Brown

CREATING DAILY ACTIVITIES

When you're depressed or grieving, you may spend a whole day or many days literally doing nothing. Even the smallest and most familiar task can feel overwhelming. But such inactivity and lack of accomplishment may deepen your depression, keep you mired in your grief, and lower your self-esteem.

To break this cycle and to feel better, you might consider the following: When planning your daily schedule, make a list of the things you have to do—preparing a meal, showering, or washing dishes—and the things you want to do, such as taking the dog for a walk, talking to a friend, or watching a movie. Select at least one chore from each list that you want to accomplish. If that one activity seems too overwhelming, break it up into smaller tasks. For example, preparing a meal may involve driving to the supermarket, shopping for food, and unpacking the groceries, as well as preparing and cooking the meal. You might only be able to shop for the food, but that's okay. You've still accomplished something, and for that you need to give yourself credit.

Remember, there's no rule for what you need to do in any given day. Some days you may be full of energy and able to complete many tasks. Other days you may not do as much, and still other days you won't get anything done. But by paying close attention to anything you do, you can give yourself credit in ways that can create positive feelings, as well as build your self-esteem.

కా కా కా

I MAKE A LIST OF THE THINGS I'D LIKE TO DO TODAY AND GIVE MYSELF CREDIT FOR ALL I ACCOMPLISH.

"Hope is definitely not the same thing as optimism. It's not the conviction that something will turn out well, but the certainty that something makes sense, regardless of how it turns out. It is this hope, above all, that gives us strength to live and to continually try new things, even in conditions that seem hopeless."

— Czech president Vaclav Havel

STRENGTH IN GRIEF

What does it mean to lose a loved one, to get AIDS, to be raped, to become disabled, or to be molested as a child? If your answers are based on negative reactions and filled with fear, then your healing and recovery from any of these life traumas will be difficult. If you believe you're a helpless victim or that life is scary, then you're more likely to remain anxious, depressed, and angry than if you believe that you have a sense of control over your life and that there are always silver linings behind every life trauma.

Author/healer Joan Borysenko, Ph.D., in her book *Fire in the Soul*, tells the story of her teenage son, who lost a young friend in a tragic car accident. During the first few hours after the tragedy, many teenagers gathered at her home to grieve together. One after another, they repeatedly asked, "Why did he have to die? Why? Why?"

One young woman finally responded, "Don't even ask that question. It doesn't have an answer that we could possibly understand." While others were responding to the tragedy in helpless, subjective, and negative ways, she was the only one who maintained a semblance of control and objectivity.

Rather than fold in any time of crisis, remember that you have the innate capacity to recover from problems. You can learn from these trials and emerge from them stronger and more compassionate as a result.

ॐ ॐ ॐ

I TAP INTO THE RESERVOIR OF STRENGTH WITHIN MY SOUL SO THAT I VIEW EACH SITUATION IN A POSITIVE WAY.

"I was devastated. I couldn't imagine life without Raytheon. All of a sudden, my life was just gone. When you lose your job, you ask yourself, 'Who am I?'"

— Amy Lowell

SURVIVING JOB LOSS

For eight years, Amy Lowell made bombs at Raytheon, a large defense firm. She started the job two years out of high school, working her way up to earn $14 an hour. With overtime, she sometimes pulled in close to $40,000 a year. Amy felt proud to work for this firm because of the role played by Raytheon's Patriot Missiles in the Gulf War. But with the end of the war and the nation's military complex in retreat, Amy was laid off. She was just one of millions of Americans displaced by a labor market in flux who had to deal with the stigma and financial insecurity inherent in being unemployed.

How can *you* get through the anguish, shame, and lack of self-esteem that occurs after a job loss? First, remind yourself that it wasn't you or your job performance that took your job away, but rather, external forces. Second, reach out for emotional support from family members and friends who have gone through, or who are currently enduring, a similar situation. Third, make contact with as many business connections as you can, including high school and college buddies, bosses and co-workers at former jobs, and names that you find on business cards. Fourth, be flexible enough to consider taking a job in another field, accepting a position that pays less, or going back to school to retrain in a different area.

Make finding a job your new job! With persistence and a positive attitude, you *will* attain your goal of meaningful employment.

🌿 🌿 🌿

I AM ENTHUSIASTIC, MOTIVATED, AND ENCOURAGED AS I SEARCH FOR A NEW JOB.

"This reminds me of 1954 and the way we treated and discussed mental illness. It is time to end these outdated stereotypes and talk about medical realities."

— Tipper Gore

ACCEPTING DEPRESSION

While some forms of depression have a biochemical basis and require medical treatment, most types result from emotional factors. But no matter the type, depression is quite common. In fact, one in five women and one in ten men can expect to develop a depressive or a manic-depressive episode sometime during the course of their lives. Those statistics translate to well over 30 million people in the USA.

As a result, it's important that treatment options for depression be readily recognized and openly discussed. Effective medical treatment can relieve or even totally eliminate the symptoms in over 80 percent of those who experience biological depression. Antidepressant medications can be effective for some, as can various forms of psychotherapy and alternative self-help methods, such as hypnosis and relaxation techniques.

But one of the most effective treatments for any form of depression is a supportive family and friend network that will be behind you and be a part of your healing and recovery process as you go through your difficulty. With caring, concern, and communication, the outdated perception of depression as a mental disease can be modified so that it is regarded as a fairly normal psychological response to biochemistry or the stresses of life.

яа яа яа

I ACCEPT DEPRESSION AS A NATURAL AND HUMAN RESPONSE IN MYSELF AS WELL AS IN OTHERS.

"Take time by the forelock. Now or never. You must live in the present, launch yourself on every wave, find your eternity in each moment. Fools stand on their island opportunities and look toward another land. There is no other land; there is no other life but this."

— Henry David Thoreau

BREAKING OLD RULES

The journals of Henry David Thoreau include compelling essays on the importance of living in the present moment. Yet, you'll never be able to seize the moment if you're governed by old rules and negative beliefs that may have been pounded into as you were growing up with respect to who you are and how you're supposed to live your life. Such rules might include:

- I must never make mistakes.
- I must never be angry.
- I must never put myself first.
- I must hold back my tears.
- I must excel in everything I do.

When you live by these kinds of self-defeating affirmations from your past, you set the stage for depressive and gloomy moods in the present. Because you accept these rules, you don't stop to explore other options; instead, you just continue to try to measure up to these unrealistic, unproductive standards for behavior.

Right now, make a list of at least ten "family rules" that impact you today. Then pick one of the rules you'd like to change. List all the ways in which this rule is unreasonable and destructive, and think up a new rule for yourself. Then start living by your new rule!

❦ ❦ ❦

I RELEASE NEGATIVE BELIEFS OF THE PAST AND LIVE BY NEW, PRODUCTIVE RULES.

"Suppose I wake up feeling sad. Instead of letting this sadness touch me and put me in contact with what is happening in my life, I may concentrate on how it punctures my self-image of being a together, successful person....When I judge sadness negatively and cut myself off from it, it becomes frozen, losing its tender quality that connects me to life."

— author John Welwood

"INFORMATIONAL" FEELINGS

Feelings such as anger, sadness, fear, and disappointment aren't a problem if you let them inform you about your responses to events or changes in your life, such as interpersonal losses, existential losses, illnesses, or anything else that causes you stress on a prolonged basis.

An interpersonal loss—the loss of a loved one—includes loss through death, marital separation and divorce, children moving away from home, and being rejected by a friend or lover. An existential loss forces you to face difficult questions about the meaning of your life, your mortality, and your basic satisfaction with life. It can be triggered by the sudden death of a casual acquaintance who's your age or by the realization that you may never be able to buy your "dream house."

Some life events deal a blow to your self-esteem—you fail to receive a promotion or flunk an exam. Illnesses can create serious emotional distress through chronic pain. And prolonged stress can make you feel overwhelmed and incapable of coping effectively.

Today, listen to all of your feelings. Remember that they're there for a reason. Then, explore the current events and changes in your life so you can better understand why you feel the way you do.

☙ ☙ ☙

I MAKE CONNECTIONS BETWEEN MY LIFE AND MY FEELINGS.

"If anyone had told me then that by the time I was forty-three, I would be crippled and George would have cancer and my beloved family would have begun to die, I would have cried out, 'Oh no! I could never stand the pain!' But if anyone had told me that, in the presence of these realities, I would find myself, without warning, pierced by joy, I would have been stunned speechless, certain that my informant was either perverse or outright mad."

— Nancy Mairs

HOLDING ON TO HAPPINESS

What level of happiness do you think you could feel if you found out today that you would have to live the rest of your life without your partner? Do you think you could still feel joy if you couldn't work in the job that means everything to you? Would you be able to feel confident and have a marked sense of self-esteem if you lost the use of your legs and had to be confined to a wheelchair?

In 1987, journalist and author Nancy Mairs wrote an article on happiness that included the above quotation. Although afflicted with multiple sclerosis, as well as dealing with many other traumatic events, she wrote about the bliss she felt when attending her daughter's graduation. In her article, she also offered an uplifting and inspirational message for her daughter and all of her peers: to open up to the experience of discovering great joy and happiness in their own lives, to encourage growth and empowerment, and to embrace life's challenges and view them as gifts—gifts that allow for even greater fulfillment

So, do you think *you* can be happy, joyful, and confident no matter what life places in your path? Know that the extent to which you can be content has little to do with what "happens" to you. Happiness depends more upon your ability to find pleasure in life, no matter what your circumstances.

❧ ❧ ❧

I ADJUST TO THE TRAUMAS IN MY LIFE IN WAYS THAT CONTRIBUTE TO MY HAPPINESS.

"The mind ought sometimes to be diverted that it may return to better thinking."

— Phaedrus

POSITIVE SELF-TALK

It can be startling to tune in to what's going on in your mind at any given moment. The inner dialogue that takes place can sometimes be like a nonstop talk radio station, filled with your constant rehashing of past memories; imagined conversations you conduct with those you fear, dislike, or whom you seek to please; an endless assessment of your feelings; your highly critical judgments of yourself; and your doubts and regrets. While some of your inner dialogue can be interesting, most of it is mindless brain chatter that serves to cut you down.

How often do you give yourself advice, support, encouragement, or praise during your self-talk? Most people tend to rely on others for such things. Yet being dependent on others to recognize and reward you when you need to hear positive and soothing sentiments can make you feel disappointed when such words aren't forthcoming. And waiting for the encouraging words of others can prevent you from exercising your own voice and becoming a resource of inner strength.

Today, take a refreshing and sorely needed break from your negative internal dialogue. Use positive self-talk—and do it out loud. To feel more comfortable with self-talk, first get used to the sound of your voice. "Discuss" a topic with yourself for at least two minutes every day. Over time, you'll find that the two minutes pass quickly, and you'll feel more comfortable with this process. As William Steig wrote in his classic children's book, *Abel's Island*: "Abel began talking to himself. He had done it before, but only internally. Now he spoke out loud, and the sound of his own voice vibrating in his body felt vital."

૪૦ ૪૦ ૪૦

I LEARN TO TRUST MY VOICE, RELY ON IT, AND FEEL BETTER ABOUT MYSELF BECAUSE OF IT.

"It is impossible for a man to despair who remembers that his Helper is omnipotent."

— Jeremy Taylor

HEALING THROUGH PRAYER

If, at any time today, you feel hopeless, morose, powerless, fearful, anxious, confused, lonely, or suicidal, remind yourself that no matter how you feel, there's a Higher Power who's there for you and who understands what you're going through. Whether you're at home alone, at work, caught up in a stressful daily pace, in an abusive or unsafe environment, facing a difficult decision, or in the company of those with whom you feel uncomfortable, your Higher Power is always there to protect and care for you. And because there's always a loving and comforting spiritual presence around you, you're safe and secure at all times.

As you may read these words about the presence and protection of a Higher Power, it may be hard for you to release your apprehensions, doubts, and concerns. If that's how you feel, then you might find prayer beneficial. Prayer is the personal and private dialogue you have with your Higher Power. Through this conscious contact, you allow yourself to become more willing to receive reassurance and peace from a spiritual source. Prayer is your connection to your Higher Power's wisdom and love.

Today, pray to your Higher Power. Rather than dwelling on the fears that gnaw at you, focus on the help and guidance you can receive from your spiritual source. A simple prayer is: *"Higher Power, I turn to you in my despair for your care. I ask you to free me from my feelings of fear, anxiety, and sadness so I can feel trust, serenity, and happiness. Please protect me from any self-destructive tendencies I may have. I believe that there's nothing I can experience—no situation, place, or person—that can harm me as long as I open myself up to your love and guidance."*

❧ ❧ ❧

I TURN TO A HIGHER POWER AND PRAY FOR PEACE AND PROTECTION.

"We never know, believe me, when we have succeeded best."
— Miguel de Unamumo y Jugo

HANDLING REGRET

Regret is an inescapable part of life. For every choice you make, you give up a host of other options, leaving you open to feelings of regret. The degree of pain accompanying feelings of regret is closely related to the amount of self-blame you feel, which can lead to depression in the present and impact your ability to make positive decisions in the future. Thus, coming to terms effectively with your regrets requires not self-blame, but self-compassion. That doesn't mean excusing yourself for past actions, but assessing the past more realistically so you're able to see your successes rather than your failures, your achievements rather than your limitations.

While you can't change an event that's already happened, the one thing you can control is your attitude and reaction to it in the present. Even if you think you made a very bad decision in the past, that doesn't mean that you're a bad person or that you're destined to continue on the same unproductive path forever. Use your regret to understand what you did that you didn't like, then hope to do better next time.

One way to do so is to reframe your perspective in order to view the situation in a new and more positive light in the present. For example, you might regret not spending time with your father prior to his death; now you believe that you're a worthless daughter or son and constantly bemoan all the things you didn't get to do with him. You can take that experience and reframe it, though, concentrating on the precious time you *did* spend with your father and using this memory as the impetus to spend more time with your surviving parent or other family members whom you cherish.

ঙ ঙ ঙ

I CONVERT MY REGRET INTO A POSITIVE TOOL TO MAKE EFFECTIVE LIFE CHOICES IN THE PRESENT.

"There are no victims, only volunteers."

— Anonymous

CHALLENGING DISTORTED THINKING

Do losses and disappointments always result in despondent moods or depression? The answer is no. Most losses do lead to feelings of sadness, but there are important differences between sorrowful feelings and those of true depression. The former is a natural response to a painful life event that gives an accurate perception of the situation and which can lead to eventual healing. The latter is a distorted response that results in increased pain.

Imagine that you've been laid off from work. A realistic response to this all-too-common life event is that you may be in for tough times, will probably have to cut down on your living expenses, and might have a hard time locating a new job. A distorted response is that you'll lose your house, your family will starve to death, and no one will ever want to hire you. Realistic thinking allows you to feel the appropriate emotional response to your situation, but places it in its proper perspective so you can then take positive action. Distorted thinking escalates your emotional response and creates such a hopeless, bleak picture of your future that you become psychologically paralyzed and can do nothing to alleviate your situation.

While the reality may be that it will be difficult to find a new job, it won't be impossible. Today, reject the victim status that you have adopted as a result of your distorted thinking. Refrain from jumping to conclusions in the absence of substantial evidence. Stop making broad, sweeping statements about yourself and your situation. Challenge the distortions in your thinking. See the losses and disappointments in your life for what they really are!

ია ია ია

I CHOOSE REALISTIC THINKING AS MY PATH TO HEALING AND RECOVERY.

"In addition to my other numerous acquaintances, I have one more intimate confidante....My depression is the most faithful mistress I have known—no wonder, then, that I return the love."

— Danish philosopher Sören Kierkegaard

STAYING ACTIVE AND SOCIALIZING

When people experience grief, depression, or "the blues," a common reaction is to withdraw and slow down the pace of their lives. They limit their social and recreational activities, refuse opportunities for interaction with others, and physically shut down. Some withdrawal is appropriate and normal. However, a prolonged retreat can set the stage for trouble. If you start avoiding people, they may respond by avoiding you. If you remain inactive for too long, you may cut yourself off from positive experiences. The result can be increased social isolation, profound loneliness, alienation, and sadness—and a downward emotional spiral that can make you and your depression best friends.

That's why it's important to set limits on how much time you choose to stay away from others. Decide right now not to allow for more than a week. During that time period, set a goal to get mobilized. Think about the steps you can take to get past the roadblocks you've created through your inertia and isolation. Tell yourself that you'll take action by the end of your time period. Then, don't wait until you feel motivated to do something or call someone; if you wait to feel motivated, you may be waiting a long time. You just need to get moving. Even going out and walking around your house once or twice can energize you and give you the boost you need to back away from your depression—and move towards others.

❧ ❧ ❧

I TAKE ACTION TODAY THAT WILL BRING ME IN CONTACT WITH OTHERS.

"There is no sadder sight than a young pessimist."
— Mark Twain

REJECTING SUICIDE

On February 11, 1963, poet Sylvia Plath put her head in a gas oven in her London apartment as her two children, for whom she had left glasses of milk and a plate of bread and butter, slept in a nearby bedroom. Before her death, few had ever heard of the 30-year-old American expatriate. But with the posthumous publication of *Ariel*, the volume of poetry she had written in the last months of her life, and the 1971 publication of *The Bell Jar* in America, she became wildly popular. But, in fact, it's more the details of her suicide rather than the brilliance of her writing that have afforded her a cult status in the decades since her death and have made her into an enduring legend— "a literary James Dean," remarked one writer.

Suicide is often depicted as a swift, painless, and uncomplicated answer to life's problems. An extreme solution, to be sure, but many young people view this step as an awesome and perhaps courageous step into the void. What more people need to realize is that suicide doesn't always bring about sweet oblivion. The attempt sometimes gets botched, and the would-be suicide suffers pain and disfigurement, or the attempt is successful and what's left behind is a legacy of immeasurable grief and confusion. Even if you believe you've left your affairs in order by paying all your bills, compiling detailed funeral instructions, or composing a lengthy note to explain your reasons behind your decision to end your life, what such things really do is create more chaos.

No matter what your age, you're far too young to kill yourself. You need to understand that suicide is forever and has long-lasting effects on all those who know you—your friends, your children, your partner, your parents, and many, many others.

🐚 🐚 🐚

I LOOK AT THE LONG-RANGE EFFECTS OF SUICIDE AND REALIZE THAT IT'S NOT THE ANSWER.

"It is a crisis that few in the emergency room are equipped to handle. Concerned friends have just arrived with a frightened man in his 20s. He is not bleeding. Nothing's broken. Yet he cannot stop crying, and his companions are worried he might kill himself."

— an article in *Time* magazine, by Christine Gorman

CHOOSING LIFE

You may have suicidal thoughts, but you may also have thoughts that tell you that you really don't want to kill yourself. What you want is not death, but a cessation to the pain in your life. It's very common to think about suicide, for such thoughts and feelings are, in fact, a symptom of depression. But remember, depression is a very treatable condition; thus, suicidal thoughts and feelings can be temporary. You may benefit from treatment provided by a mental health professional. There's also a lot you can do to gain control over your depression on your own. To begin, keep in mind the words of P.D. James in *Death of an Expert Witness*: "It was not...that she was unaware of the frayed and ragged edges of life. She would merely iron them out with a firm hand and neatly hem them down."

Today, you can begin to repair the ragged edges of your life. How? By choosing life! Say aloud affirmations that confirm this choice:

- Today I desire to live.
- I discover value and meaning in my life by the long-term goals I set.
- I feel good about myself by recognizing the small steps I take to heal and recover.
- I experience my feelings and accept that they're part of life.
- I talk to someone and know that communication is what connects me to others.
- I see the humor in life by laughing at a joke or comic strip.

Use these affirmations and three others you create to strengthen your desire to live.

❧ ❧ ❧

I HOLD ON TO THE DESIRE TO LIVE BY CREATING POSITIVE, LIFE-AFFIRMING THOUGHTS.

"The seven steps to stagnation: We've never done it that way; we're not ready for that; we are doing all right without trying that; we tried it once before; we don't have money for that; it's not our job; and, something like that can't work."

— Unknown

MAKING CHANGES

Dr. Patrick Thomas Malone, medical director of Mental Health Services at Northside Hospital in Atlanta, has invented the term *selficide* to describe a state of being where a person is stuck, unable to learn and grow from life's experiences. Common characteristics of people who are "selficiders" include: the feeling that life is boring, not being able to enjoy intimate relationships, being out of touch with themselves, and not being able to find satisfaction in their world or anything in it. In sum, a selficider is a stagnater.

To visualize how to change your feelings of selficide to feelings of contentment and pleasure, Dr. Malone suggests that you reflect on this analogy: When babies first begin to explore their world, they crawl. But when they learn to walk, they stop crawling. When you're happy in your world, you walk from event to event, but when you're unhappy with yourself and your world, you resort to crawling. You react in old ways instead of responding in new ones because you let your mood be your motivator.

You can end stagnation by being willing to dismiss the old ways you have of doing things. Be ready to respond in new ways that will express *wants* rather than *shoulds,* and *hopes* rather than *regrets.* As Karl Jaspers said, "It is true that the whole world will not change if I change. But the change in myself is the premise of the greater change."

❧ ❧ ❧

I DISMISS MY OLD WAYS OF DOING THINGS AND RESPOND TO LIFE IN NEW, POSITIVE WAYS.

"So long as we believe we are only human, we are going to experience pain, suffering, tears, disease, and death."
— Donald Curtis

STOPPING NEGATIVE THOUGHTS

It's true that you—as well as all human beings—will, at various times in your life, experience sadness, grief, disappointment, and despair. That's because you care—about your family, your friends, your job, your pet. When you lose a loved one, when your marriage falls apart, or when you lose your job, it's normal to feel "blue."

But you don't have to always feel down in the dumps. Even though it's human to have morose feelings, it's not normal to experience them all the time. That's why it's important to release the powerful hold that negative thinking may have on your psyche. Thought stopping is a simple way to eradicate inappropriate thoughts so that you can eliminate the feelings that go along with them.

To begin, on a piece of paper write down a negative thought, such as: "I feel stupid, so therefore I must be stupid." Then ask yourself the following questions:

- Is this thought realistic?
- Is this thought productive?
- How does this thought make me feel?
- Does this thought interfere with my life?

Based on your answers to the questions, it will be clear whether you would benefit from eliminating the thought. Then whenever that negative thought comes up, immediately replace it with a positive affirmation, such as: "I'm a smart, capable person." You may have to repeat your affirmation continually, as stopping a thought takes time and patience. But you'll gradually notice that your negative thought recurs less and less.

❧ ❧ ❧

I SUBSTITUTE A POSITIVE THOUGHT FOR A NEGATIVE ONE.

"I'm looking out a large window and I see about forty dog-wood and maple and oak and locust trees and the light is on some of the leaves and it's so beautiful. Sometimes I'm overcome with gratitude at such sights and feel that each of us has a responsibility for being alive...."

— author Maya Angelou

NOTICING NATURAL WONDERS

How often do you take time to notice the wonders of the natural world—the rainbow after a rainstorm, the birds frolicking around your bird feeder, or the silvery brilliance of a full moon? How often do you go out of your way to discover a new path through the woods or a less traveled route to work? How often do you allow time in your schedule to quietly connect with nature in some small way—by getting up early to sit in a park and watch the sunrise slowly awaken the city, or by peering up at a star-filled evening sky?

When you're in the midst of grief, feeling down, or caught in the web of depression, you can easily forget that there's a natural world around you that's teeming with wonders. But those wonders won't come to you; you have to take time to notice *them*.

Today, no matter how you feel, take time to notice the beauty that surrounds you. Pack a bag lunch for work so you can eat outside and feel the sun on your face. Or schedule a walk with a friend in the early evening that will take you to a place you've never been before. By becoming more aware of the world around you, you can become more alive. As author Alice Walker wrote: "Life is better than death, I believe, if only because it is less boring, and because it has fresh peaches in it."

ยัง ยัง ยัง

I PAY ATTENTION TO THE NATURAL BEAUTY AND WONDER OF THE WORLD.

"What's wrong with trying? Trying is lying."
— author Emrika Padus

TRYING VERSUS DOING

If you don't believe that trying is lying, try to turn the page of this book. Did you? If you did, then you didn't *try* to do it—you *did* it. That's the trouble with trying, because when you say you'll try to do something, you're really not telling the truth. You either can or cannot do something. Trying is a convenient way out; it just reinforces your negative thought that what you're setting out to do may be futile. Trying confirms your limitations, inabilities, and shortcomings and becomes a self-defeating affirmation. Thus, trying gives you permission not to do things you might benefit from.

Do you remember the classic children's story, *The Little Engine That Could*? Because it wasn't as big as the other engines, the little engine didn't think it could pull its heavy load up the steep incline on the track. So it began its attempt by saying, "I think I can, I think I can." In effect, the little engine conveyed that it was trying to pull its load, while all the time it still believed it probably couldn't. But once the engine reframed its thinking into a more positive outlook, it realized that it was as strong and powerful as the other engines. Then it said, "I know I can, I know I can." In essence, the little engine stopped trying and simply did what it set out to do.

Today, pay close attention to the language you use when you set out to make changes, take risks, or interact with new people, places, or things. Every time you begin a sentence with "I'll try," begin again. Instead, say, "I can" or "I'm capable of." Then don't try—just do it!

ॐ ॐ ॐ

I ASSURE MY SUCCESS BY *DOING*, NOT *TRYING*.

"Dark nights of the soul are extended periods of dwelling at the threshold when it seems as if we can no longer trust the very ground we stand on, when there is nothing familiar left to hold on to that can give us comfort."
— author/healer Joan Borysenko, Ph.D.

GROWING OUT OF CRISIS

Psychiatrist Victor Frankl, in his book, *Man's Search for Meaning*, addressed life in the Nazi death camps during the Holocaust. He observed that some people succumbed to the epidemics that swept through the camp, some died at the hands of the brutal Nazis, and some met their fate in the fiery ovens. Yet others who were able to find some meaning in their suffering were more likely to hold on to life. Frankl himself survived four death camps before liberation. Frankl and others like him used their crisis as a way to transform their suffering. In fact, it was in the camps that Frankl conceived of logotherapy, a system of psychological growth and healing based on the apprehension of meaning.

If you have a strong belief that your suffering is a component of growth, then your "dark night" experiences can lead you to healing that you may never have dreamed possible. This is evidenced on an almost daily basis by the millions who use 12-step recovery programs. Their "dark night" experiences of addiction helped to guide them from being out of touch with a Higher Power to one in which the reality of that Power is not only a force for their recovery but also a renewal of hope and personal growth.

Today, trust and believe that your "dark night" is really a prelude to the dawning of a guiding light that can lead you to a more meaningful and rewarding life.

🦋 🦋 🦋

I TRUST THAT MY SUFFERING IS A NECESSARY PREPARATION FOR POSITIVE CHANGE AND GROWTH.

"Energy is higher in the spring, and people feel more independent and less depressed, but it's when people are starting to come out of deep depression that they're at highest risk of committing suicide. That's when they may feel empowered to take control of their life—by ending it."
— Margaret O'Neil

SUICIDE SUPPORT SYSTEM

Margaret O'Neil, executive director of the Boston office of The Samaritans, the national suicide prevention organization, says that in the spring, the number of calls she receives increases by 25 percent. She attributes this phenomenon to the fact that in the winter, most people are forced inside and can't benefit from the healthiness that comes from being outside; thus, people with depression feel closer to other people in the winter because everyone seems to be down. But in the spring, when most people start to feel better, those who are depressed sometimes find that their despondent feelings worsen.

Today, set up your own suicide support system. Make a list of the people you like and trust the most, with whom you're most comfortable, and who understand what you're going through. Your support system can include stable and understanding family members, your therapist or doctor, or a staff member at an emergency hotline. Choose at least five people who are most accessible—you should never expect just one person to be available at all times. Select people in your suicide support system who know you so well that they may even be able to spot your mood swings before you do so they can assist you in taking preventive actions. Write their names and telephone numbers on slips of paper, then keep the lists in your pocketbook or wallet, by your bed, in your living room, in your car, and at work.

🦋 🦋 🦋

I CONTACT SOMEONE ON MY SUICIDE SUPPORT TEAM IF I'M FEELING DESPONDENT.

"What makes people despair is that they try to find a universal meaning to the whole of life..."

— author Anaïs Nin

ENJOYING LIFE'S ADVENTURES

The only universal meaning to life that holds true for everyone is that no one's ever going to get out of it alive. So rather than waste your time and energy today trying to understand why you're here, where you're going, or why you have to face the trials you do, perhaps the best approach to life is simply to relax and savor it for as long as you can.

Would you appreciate your life more if you added a meaningful challenge that would bring adventure, rather than adversity, to your life? Then sign up for a white-water rafting expedition or a rock-climbing course. Would you enjoy your life more if you were able to be more playful and less serious? Then buy a bag of peanuts and go to the park and feed the squirrels. Would your life be more meaningful if you had more opportunities to get in touch with yourself? Then look at your calendar and plan to spend a weekend at home alone or make reservations at a peaceful country inn. Would you find pleasure in spending more time with others instead of isolating yourself? Then plan a dinner party or set aside time to visit friends.

The enjoyment of life can involve many different factors. But, most importantly, it can involve the realization that you're part of something more immense than yourself.

❧ ❧ ❧

I VIEW LIFE AS AN ENJOYABLE ADVENTURE.

"...people with depression are blamed for being weak in character, for not being able to 'just snap out of it.' [The] message is simple: The brain is part of the body...willpower alone just won't fix it."

— from an article by Kay Harvey on
"Battling Depression's Stigma"

EXAMINING GENETIC INFLUENCES

Even though many of the world's greatest painters, writers, musicians, and gifted artists have suffered from depression, this condition affects more than just those who have creative energy. Depression is not just "all in your mind." You may have inherited genetic factors that make you especially vulnerable to it. Out of all the brothers, sisters, parents, and children of a depressed person, approximately 20 to 25 percent run the risk of having the disease themselves. Although depression does occur more frequently in particular families than in the population as a whole, it can sometimes skip generations or vary in intensity from one generation to another—or even from one person to another. And it has been found that about 25 percent of the daughters of mothers with depressive illnesses will develop some form of depression themselves.

What all this means is that if you suffer from depression, you might want to examine your family history with a professional who can help you evaluate the biological impact of your own depression. Prior to meeting with the professional, find out the medical and emotional backgrounds of parents, grandparents, aunts, uncles, and siblings. Ask, "Is there any history of suicide, depression, anxiety, psychiatric treatment, eating disorders, alcoholism, or drug abuse?" This exploration can yield valuable information. So, learn whatever you can, share this information with someone trained to interpret your findings, then focus on your own healing and recovery.

🌿 🌿 🌿

I EXAMINE MY FAMILY BACKGROUND TO LEARN MORE ABOUT MYSELF.

"Life only demands from you the strength you possess. Only one feat is possible—not to run away."
— Swedish statesman Dag Hammarskjöld

GROWING PAINS

You might feel that there's a great deal of pain and sadness in life. But when you try to avoid coming to grips with the heartaches and disappointments in life, your suffering and struggle are often multiplied. As psychologist and author R. D. Laing wrote: "There is a great deal of pain in life, and perhaps the only pain that can be avoided is the pain that comes from trying to avoid pain."

To resist the pain and challenge of trauma is to travel a personally dangerous and harmful path. Resistance to dealing with trauma can lead to an emotional or physical breakdown, rob you of a meaningful life, damage your relationship with others, and prevent you from making progress. What this means is that there are going to be difficult times in your life in which you simply have to accept things the way they are—even if this involves going through pain. When you're feeling absolutely powerless over a situation, know that it will change, although not necessarily in the way you anticipate or in the time frame you would like.

While it may be difficult—if not impossible—to see how anything good can come out of the suffering you have to endure, and while you may complain about how unfair life is, there will always be growth that results from pain. Just as the body can heal physical wounds, so too can you heal your emotional ones. You just have to give it time.

❦ ❦ ❦

I GROW AS A HUMAN BEING AS I GO THROUGH MY PAIN.

"If you eat sugar, the yeast in your body ferments the sugar into alcohol and alcohol-like substances. Your body is acting as a brewery."

— author Dr. Wayne London

ENDING THE SUGAR BLUES

The number-one food culprit for those who suffer from "the blues" and depression is sugar. Many describe the white powder as a "mood-altering substance" and advise eliminating it from your diet. Some nutritionists claim that if you start the day eating sugar-based products, you continue eating sugar throughout the day; like an addict, the more you eat, the more you crave. Medical doctors are becoming more aware that excess yeast in the system can cause or worsen mood instability, depression, inability to concentrate, and mental fogginess. Other descriptions of the effects sugar can have on the mind and body include mood elevation, hyperactivity, fatigue, increased pulse rate, anxiety, phobias, mood instability, depression, headaches, and irritability.

In his book, *Back to Basics*, Dr. Wayne London advises avoiding or severely limiting your intake of simple carbohydrates such as sugar, corn sweeteners, honey, and maple syrup. As a way of determining what sugar's impact is on you, eliminate all sugar from your diet for two weeks. Pay attention to the labels on the foods you eat so you can avoid sugar-based additives. Closely monitor how you feel by keeping a daily journal in which you list your most uncomfortable physical and emotional symptoms and detail whether they're aggravated, alleviated, or unchanged as a result of your sugarless diet. If you notice positive changes, think about permanently adopting a no-sugar or low-sugar diet.

ৠ ৠ ৠ

I EVALUATE THE EFFECTS OF SUGAR ON MY MIND AND BODY AND TAKE APPROPRIATE ACTION.

"So every faithful heart shall pray to Thee in the hour of anxiety, when great floods threaten. Thou art a refuge to me from distress so that it cannot touch me; Thou dost guard me in salvation beyond all reach of harm."

— Psalm 32

EFFECTIVE PRAYERS

The great teachers of religion and spirituality advise not to pray for the cessation of pain, but for the courage to endure whatever suffering occurs on the path to harmony and healing. Praying to be a whole person rather than asking that your sickness be healed is an example of this type of spiritually healing prayer. So is asking to remain open so that "Thy will be done" in any given situation rather than making specific requests. While praying in this way may be foreign to you, here are some prayers to get you started. Substitute Higher Power or any other designation so you're completely comfortable with the language of each prayer.

- *Lord, I pray not for tranquility, not that my tribulations may cease; I pray for Thy Spirit and Thy love that Thou grant me strength and grace to overcome adversity.* (Savonarola)
- *Bring this life into harmony with Divine purpose....May this life come into harmony with God's Will. May you so live that all who meet you will be uplifted, that all who bless you will be blessed, that all who serve you will receive the greatest satisfaction. If any should attempt to harm you, may they contact your thought of God and be healed.* (Peace Pilgrim)
- *Let me not pray to be sheltered from dangers but to be fearless in facing them. Let me not beg for the stilling of my pain but for the heart to conquer it.* (Rabindranath Tagore)

ॐ ॐ ॐ

I PRAY FOR ATTUNEMENT WITH A HIGHER POWER IN MY LIFE.

"We either make ourselves miserable, or we make ourselves strong. The amount of work is the same."
— from a book by Carlos Castaneda

RELEASING MISERY

"Woe is me!" may be your familiar cry; it may be something you've bemoaned long and hard to yourself. But you may not even be aware of how much energy you've expended feeling miserable—by discussing it, analyzing it, and living and reliving it. If a close friend who has known about your affiliation with misery over the years asked you right now, "Are you depressed?," how would you respond? The sad part of being so wrapped up in your misery may be that you don't even how that misery may influence your moods.

Many people think that in order to qualify as depressed, their symptoms have to be severe: extreme pessimism, despondency, and negativity. Yet depression can exist without the presence of such factors. Some symptoms may be so subtle that you're not even aware of them, such as a misery-based outlook. Think about comments you make, such as "I just can't get going in the morning because I've really got nothing to get up for anyway," "I don't like my job but I can't do anything about it," or "I don't know what I want to do with my life, so I'm just going to do nothing."

You don't have to wallow in misery. You have choices, and one of those involves releasing your grip on the misery that you hold today. Reach out to grasp on to a positive, strength-giving activity. Do something good for yourself or another human being...and see how good this positive action can make you feel.

❧ ❧ ❧

I LET GO OF MY MISERY SO I CAN HOLD ON TO SOMETHING MORE POSITIVE.

"People disturb us. They sap our vitality from us...they pile upon us their conditions of fear and their atmosphere of despondency. In such cases we must regain our poise by the realization of the power that is ever within us. Find your center."

— Horatio W. Dresser

RESTORING YOUR CENTER

Are you an uncentered person? You are if your life is structured around pleasing others. You are if you often feel caught in conflicting commitments. You are if you don't know, at any given moment, what you need and what you want to do. You are if you can't separate choices based on your wants or needs from those made out of guilt and obligation to those in your world. You are if you can't detach from the problems, conflicts, and negative energies of others.

Detaching from others can restore your center and enable you to focus more on yourself than on others. Detaching doesn't mean you can't enjoy your work, your family, your relationship, or your commitment to a cause. Rather, detachment means that you don't have to *identify* with any of them. Detaching doesn't mean giving up, but rather opening yourself up to your center—your source of peace. To do so, you need to affirm your right to choose for yourself, to feel for yourself, to think for yourself, and to act for yourself. Affirmations to help restore your center are:

- I have a job, but I am not my job.
- I have a family, but I am not my family.
- I have a relationship, but I am not my relationship.
- I have a cause, but I am not my cause.

Today, enjoy the blessings that are a *part* of your life, but not *all* of your life.

ৡ৹ ৡ৹ ৡ৹

I OPEN MYSELF UP TO MY CENTER—MY SOURCE OF PEACE.

"I refuse as I age to deny my years. When asked at 30, I'll be 30. When the question comes up at 45, I'll take 45. For what year could I subtract? The one in which my son or daughter was born? Or the year I first fell in love? How about one less favorable? Like the year I came down with pneumonia. Or one of those grief-filled years spent saying good-by to someone close?... No, I think I'll keep them all, the good years, the bad and even the not so memorable."

— Sheila B. Cabrera

GROWING OLDER, GROWING BETTER

For some, it can be very depressing to grow older. As you age, you may find that you're not as strong, agile, attractive, lean, or as motivated as you were in your twenties or thirties. Although you may want to live a long and meaningful life, you may have difficulty dealing with your emotional and physical changes and fear the infirmities or disabilities that may come with advancing age.

But there's a difference between aging and getting old. Aging encompasses all the biological changes that naturally occur over time—hearing loss or decreased hormone activity, for example. Getting old, on the other hand, is a social and personal concept. In a society that has a strong prejudice and apathy towards its elderly population, it's only natural to pick up on some of that stigma yourself. Your image of being a "wise old woman or man" may often be at odds with the majority who feel that once you hit 40, you're past your prime.

Yet the decades after 40 can be rich and fulfilling—a time when you can truly enjoy your life and also make valuable contributions. You can learn new skills, travel, and live out long-delayed dreams. But you can only do this if you view the second half of your life as one filled with promise and potential.

❧ ❧ ❧

I ENJOY MY LATER YEARS AND MAKE THE MOST OF THIS PRECIOUS SEASON OF MY LIFE.

"When I'm happy I feel like crying, but when I'm sad I don't feel like laughing. I think it's better to be happy. Then you get two feelings for the price of one."

— Lily Tomlin as Edith Ann

HEALING THROUGH HUMOR

Many others besides Edith Ann have observed that there's a strong laughing/crying connection that can provide a cathartic cleansing, release stress and tension, help to diminish pain, and improve one's perspective and outlook on life's difficult and trying situations. But when you're depressed, laughing may simply not be a concept you can understand. As a result, you may find it hard to see the humor in life—to laugh, to joke, or to be playful.

Author Allen Klein, whose wife Ellen died after a long illness, remarks in his book, *The Healing Power of Humor,* that his wife showed him how to laugh during her terminal illness. He observed that the humor took them away from their troubles, if only for a few moments, and made them easier to bear. He surmised that "...if humor helped relieve some of the distressful times associated with the death, dying, and grieving processes, then surely it was of value in such less life-threatening upsets and losses like failing an exam, burning the dinner, or being fired."

To begin to add humor to your life, tape a photo in which you're laughing on your bathroom mirror. If you can't find an actual photo, then draw the picture. Look at it each day and night. Try to remember why you were laughing at the time the photo was taken. Mimic your facial expression in the mirror as you laugh out loud. It's okay to force such laughter at first. Then say out loud, "I will look for laughter in my life each day and learn to take things a little less seriously."

જ જ જ

I LAUGH AND CRY AND BENEFIT EQUALLY FROM BOTH EMOTIONS.

"Money doesn't always bring happiness. People with ten million dollars are no happier than people with nine million dollars."

— Hobart Brown

ENRICHING YOUR LIFE

You may think you'd have fewer "blue moods" if you had more of the "green stuff." There's nothing intrinsically wrong with a desire to have money or to make more money—until it begins to affect how you feel about yourself and your life. Think about what your life would be like if you had everything you wanted—all the clothing, cars, furniture, jewelry, and other material goods that money can buy. How would you feel?

Most people would say, "I'd feel great! I'd have all the things I ever wanted." But think of those who have achieved great success and found themselves with millions of dollars. You read and hear about such people often—about their divorces, their run-ins with the law, their addictions to drugs and alcohol, their ruined careers, and assorted other difficulties. Money may have gotten them what they wanted, but it certainly didn't give them what they needed—self-esteem, acceptance, and love.

Today, list your nonmaterial needs on a piece of paper. Then circle the one that's most important to you. Perhaps it's growing closer to your children, dealing with difficult childhood issues, or taking better care of yourself. Then take steps to meet this need by spending time with your kids, beginning counseling, or joining a health club. It's the fulfillment of your needs that will bring you the happiness that money can't buy.

જી જી જી

I KNOW THAT MY LIFE IS MORE ENRICHED BY MEETING MY PERSONAL NEEDS THAN MY MATERIAL NEEDS.

"To be depressed was to be 'in Saturn,' and a person chronically disposed to melancholy was known as a 'child of Saturn.'"

— Thomas Moore, from *Care of the Soul*

DEPRESSION IN GIRLS

A number of social inequities spur female depression at a very early age. While the relative rate of depression in preteen boys and girls is roughly equal, by late adolescence it nearly doubles for females, with teenage girls attempting suicide far more than boys of the same age. Those who have studied adolescent depression in girls conclude that during the teenage years, they begin to lose their identities, hate their bodies for not being the "slim fit" models that match the images they see in fashion magazines and TV commercials, and start to realize that boys and men receive more attention and opportunities.

If you're a parent who suffers from depression, your daughter may also suffer from a disturbance that closely resembles this condition—or which may turn into depression later in life. Some warning signs to pay attention to are:

- a decrease in academic performance;
- social isolation;
- a loss of interest in sports, hobbies, and other activities;
- unusual physical complaints that have no medical cause;
- marked moodiness; and
- abuse of drugs and alcohol.

If you observe any of these behaviors, seek the advice of a child psychiatrist.

ᏪᏪ ᏪᏪ ᏪᏪ

I PAY CLOSE ATTENTION TO MY CHILD'S MOOD SWINGS.

"Nothing is interesting if you're not interested."
— author Helen MacInnes

INTERESTED ATTITUDES

For many, the word *normal* connotes boring and ordinary. So if you're not in the midst of a devastating life crisis, reveling in juicy gossip about the catastrophes of others, or about to embark on some opportunity of a lifetime, then you may be totally disinterested in the routines and people, places, and things around you. As a result, you may find it hard to motivate yourself and to suppress your boredom-induced "blue mood."

But there's a law in psychology that says if you form a picture in your mind of what you'd like your life to be—and if you keep that picture there long enough—you can move in the direction you're visualizing. If you think thoughts in which you're happy and interested in yourself and your life, then you will act as if those things are so; conversely, if you think sad and indifferent thoughts, you will act as if they are so. What you expect profoundly influences what you get.

There are people who are always interested in everyone with whom they come in contact, enjoy the old as well as the new routines in their lives, and actively seek to create ways in which they can change all facets of their lives. They don't need to buy a new car every two years because they're bored with the old one, escape old relationships for the excitement of new ones every few months, or live from high point to high point like an excitement junkie. Instead, they positively program themselves so they can appreciate and enjoy their lives as they are now.

ఈ ఈ ఈ

I KNOW THAT IT'S HOW I LOOK AT MY LIFE THAT EITHER MAKES IT INTERESTING OR DULL.

"Grief is the agony of an instant; the indulgence of grief the blunder of a life."

— Benjamin Disraeli

SHORT-TERM SELF-PITY

Self-pity is an emotion that you're entitled to feel whenever you go through one of life's trials, which may encompass the death of a loved one, the loss of a job, or a financial setback. But engaging in self-pity for any extended period of time or allowing this feeling to dominate the grieving process can have serious consequences.

When you're in the throes of self-pity, you have a limited perspective. All you can see is your loss and how it affects you. Yet, you may not have been the only person touched by the loss, so too much self-pity can cut you off from supportive people who can share your grief—or can even damage your relationship with them. Self-pity can sometimes exacerbate the loss in ways that make it seem far worse than it is. Self-pity can focus your energy on the problem rather than the solution, keeping you stuck in a negative cycle in which recovery and healing become impossible. And self-pity can offer you a convenient excuse to do nothing so you're not able to get past the point of crisis, nor do you have the willingness to take action to help yourself.

Willingness to let go of your self-pity is all it takes to process your hardship in effective ways. Although you may stand still from time to time as you grieve, you'll be able to make progress if you release the need to feel sorry for yourself.

❧ ❧ ❧

I ALLOW MYSELF TO INDULGE IN SELF-PITY FOR A SHORT TIME, BUT THEN I MOVE FORWARD WITH MY LIFE.

"Life is in the breath. He who half breathes, half lives."
— Ancient proverb

DEEP BREATHING

You may live for years and years and never give breathing a second thought. But if you're not breathing optimally, you're not getting the most out of the process in ways that can make you feel less stressed, stabilize your mood swings, make you feel more mentally relaxed, alleviate depression, and create a greater sense of overall well-being.

Resolve today to practice deep breathing on a regular basis. To begin, lie down with your knees bent and your spine straight. Place one hand on your abdomen and one on your chest. Inhale slowly and deeply through your nose into your abdomen to push up your hand as much as is comfortable. Your chest should move only slightly. Exhale slowly, then repeat this procedure a few times.

When you become accustomed to abdominal breathing, you can then begin deep breathing by inhaling through your nose and exhaling through your mouth. Make a low, relaxing noise or sighing sound as you gently push out the air. Continue taking long, slow, deep breaths that raise and lower your abdomen in this manner. It's best to do this deep breathing for five to ten minutes every day or even twice a day. As you become used to proper deep breathing, you can practice it whenever and wherever you happen to be—in a grocery line, in your car, at a business meeting, before a job interview, or when you're feeling down about yourself.

ℬ ℬ ℬ

I USE RELAXING DEEP BREATHING TO STABILIZE MY MOODS.

"Let us not go over the old ground; let us rather prepare for what is to come."

— Cicero

LIVING IN THE NOW

Do you often wake up in the morning with an "emotional hangover"—an inability to let go of some past event that caused you pain, suffering, heartache, humiliation, regret, or other negative feeling? Maybe you can't stop thinking about a presentation you gave at work a few days ago that didn't go well. Perhaps you awaken crying over an ex-lover who left you months ago. Maybe you wake up feeling angry at a friend who still hasn't paid you back money borrowed last year. Or perhaps you arise with anxious feelings over the childhood abuse you endured. Unless you let go of such feelings, they'll be with you all day, dragging you down physically and emotionally and making you feel out of touch with life in the same way a drug-induced hangover would.

Today is a new day—a chance for a new beginning. Today is a golden opportunity to let go of the past, to put aside unrealized expectations, to forget about yesterday's disappointments, to stop mourning losses. Today is the day to be open to new ideas, new events, new people. Today is the time to concentrate on the present.

While your feelings from the past may still creep into your mind at various times today, you need to react to such intrusions immediately. Let them know they aren't welcome in your world today. Then begin again to look at today as a new day. You can do this at any time—morning, noon, or night. Always begin anew; in that way, you'll always be ready for what's to come instead of remaining stuck in what's already gone.

ᕉ ᕉ ᕉ

I SEE THIS DAY AS A CHANCE TO WALK ON A NEW PATH OF LIFE.

"Never let us be discouraged with ourselves."
— François de S. Fénelon

TREATING YOURSELF WELL

Do you know how to be good to yourself? When you're feeling down, it's easy to say, "I'm always going to feel like this. I'm never going to get better." So instead of taking actions that can change your negative outlook and help you feel better about yourself, you remain discouraged and stuck.

One thing you can do to feel better is to employ the common rules of good health—practices based on things you may already know, but don't always follow. If you feel a little shaky, you can cut back on caffeine and sugar. You can eat three meals a day that consist of low-fat, high-fiber foods such as salads, fruit, chicken, and brown rice. You can get some exercise; even 20 minutes of walking a day—that can make all the difference in the world. Also, you can adhere to regular sleep schedules so you start each day well rested.

You can also benefit from relaxation to ease stress and tension. You can cancel obligations that aren't imperative and cut back on the amount of activities you do for others. Take time to soak in a hot bath, listen to your favorite music, read a book, or feel the spring sun on your face. While such activities may seem simple, they can help head off or lessen the effects of a mild depression.

Healing your despondent moods involves more than simply bringing them under control. It also includes being good to yourself in basic ways that can result in ongoing, positive results. Then you can say, "Every day, in every way, I'm feeling better and better about myself."

&a &a &a

I TREAT MYSELF WELL, AND I BENEFIT FROM MY EFFORTS.

"Sorrow makes us all children again, destroys all differences of intellect. The wisest knows nothing."
— Ralph Waldo Emerson

CHILDHOOD EXPERIENCES

Current life events can sometimes trigger grief or depression that's based upon an emotionally powerful childhood experience. You may have "lost" a parent due to death, divorce, or marital separation, a serious illness that required long periods of hospitalization, or a job that required this parent to be away from home for extended periods of time. Or, your parent may have had problems with drugs or alcohol that interfered with the formation of an intimate bond between you. So when you lose a loved one now, as an adult—through death, the end of a relationship, or a geographical separation—you may not only feel the current upset, but also the traumatic loss from the past. Present-day difficulties often bring up the memories of unhealed wounds from one's childhood.

A number of other early-life experiences may have significant consequences when triggered by present-day events. The emotional trauma of physical and sexual abuse can profoundly affect today's relationships and erode your basic feelings of stability, trust, and security. Overprotective parenting can lead you to be extremely dependent on others to the point of co-dependency; when these individuals leave your life, you may believe that you can't function without them.

You can overcome such deep and painful wounds of the past through the help of 12-step support groups, professional treatment, and even self-help books. If you can't afford private psychotherapy, lower-cost treatment is available in community mental health centers.

❧ ❧ ❧

I HEAL MY WOUNDS FROM THE PAST BY DEALING WITH MY CURRENT ISSUES.

"Life does not accommodate you, it shatters you. It is meant to, and it couldn't do it better. Every seed destroys its container or else there would be no fruition."
— author Florida Scott-Maxwell

SELF-NURTURING

At certain times in your life, you may experience emotionally or physically draining situations. Perhaps you dislike your job so much that you feel tired and run down all the time. Maybe your relationship makes you so unhappy that you can't seem to concentrate on anything else. Or, it may be that your son or daughter has an alcohol or drug problem, and you're worried sick about it.

Imagine that whatever situation you're in is like a house plant that's root-bound—it's grown so big that it's tightly confined to its small pot. Obviously you need to repot the plant in order for it to flourish and grow. The longer you let the plant go without attention, the more of a risk you run of its withering and dying from lack of nourishment and space.

You need to identify the "plants" that need to be repotted in your life—the situations that cause you physical and emotional distress. Then, explore resources that can lead you to larger pots and richer potting soil—the tools you need to ease your distress. Such tools include making an appointment with a career counselor to discuss a job that's right for you, asking your partner to openly discuss issues in your relationship, and attending Al-Anon meetings to learn more about living with addictions. Starting today, think of things to do to alleviate the pain or distress caused by a circumstance or important person in your life.

❧ ❧ ❧

I AM A SELF-NURTURER WHO MAKES GROWTH A PRIORITY.

APRIL 24

"The only courage that matters is the kind that gets you from one moment to the next."

— Mignon McLaughlin

ONE DAY AT A TIME

Do you choose to do nothing when it comes to certain tasks because you just assume that you would fail? For example, you might say, "What's the good of quitting smoking today if I have to do it every day for the rest of my life?" "How can I be happy today when the same problems will be there tomorrow—and the next day, and the next day?" or "I can't change who I am or how I look at life; that's just the way I am and the way I'll always be."

You can only make changes, try new activities, set goals, and get through life with a courageous commitment when you decide not to scale a majestic mountain peak, but simply to walk up the mountain path one step at a time, one day at a time.

You don't have to worry about what's going to happen tomorrow or next month or next year if you don't want to. Just work on what you have to do *today!* To help you build your self-confidence, here are some thoughts to inspire you:

- *Nothing will ever be attempted if all possible objections must be first overcome.* (Samuel Johnson)
- *You never really lose until you quit trying.* (Mike Ditka)
- *We don't know who we are until we see what we can do.* (Martha Grimes)
- *Courage is doing what you're afraid to do. There can be no courage unless you're scared.* (Eddie Rickenbacker)

ℱℱ ℱℱ ℱℱ

I LIVE MY LIFE ONE DAY AT A TIME; I LET TOMORROW HAPPEN AS IT COMES.

"When God is doing something wonderful, He begins with a difficulty. But when He is going to do something very wonderful, He begins with an impossibility."

— Unknown

CHALLENGING IMPOSSIBILITIES

How many times have you experienced despondent moods or depression over the immensity of a goal or project that has faced you? Maybe it was the desire to lose several pounds or to work through the end of a relationship with a therapist. Perhaps it was doing something you felt was far beyond your capabilities, like enrolling in graduate school or moving to a new apartment or house. Or maybe it was taking a risk that tapped into one of your biggest fears, such as getting on an airplane to visit a family member in a different part of the country.

Feeling overwhelmed and lacking confidence at the start of a project is a common occurrence. Your mind may be screaming at you to run away and just forget what you're about to do, or it may just be telling you that you won't be able to do it anyway. That's when you need to say to yourself, "Maybe I'm experiencing such a strong emotional response to what I'm about to do because I don't know how I'll handle my success." You may be facing one of the greatest adventures of your life, getting ready to make your wildest dreams come true, or beginning the process of turning your life around.

From now on, tell yourself that "nothing is impossible." Instead of being overwhelmed by what's facing you, be challenged. Break up your projects or tasks into small, manageable steps. Tackle them one at a time—and you'll make the impossible *possible!*

இ இ இ

I DO WHATEVER I SET MY MIND TO DO.

"I also had nightmares. Somehow all the feelings I didn't feel when each thing had actually happened to me I did feel when I slept."

— Andrea Dworkin

HELPFUL DREAMING

Dreams are the messages you send yourself about the people, places, and things in your daily life for which you may have intense, often unexpressed feelings. When certain situations in your life impact on you, you may numb yourself so you don't feel the pain, fear, hurt, anger, tension, or sadness that such things evoke. During your waking hours, this numbing process may be quite successful. But while you're sleeping, your dreams acknowledge and resurrect these feelings so that you have to confront them.

Within your dreams, there may be scenes from the day's events that made you feel anxious or tense. You may view a collage of images that convey how "blue" you feel about yourself. Or, you may get to re-experience feelings that you shared with someone you loved—and lost.

Although your dreams may sometimes turn into frightening nightmares, it's important to recognize that they're simply outlets for feelings that you're not consciously expressing. Tonight, when a dream rouses you from your sleep or touches your emotions in ways that you find difficult to handle, keep in mind that dreams are your gentle, emotional guides. If you're honest with yourself, you can probably figure out what the dream is about. By understanding it, you may learn what feelings you've suppressed—and need to express—in your waking moments.

ﾃ ﾃ ﾃ

I STRIVE TO UNDERSTAND THE UNDERLYING MEANING OF MY DREAMS.

"I was never taught that my choice of words would have anything to do with what I would experience in life. No one taught me that my thoughts were creative, or that they could literally shape my life. Nobody taught me that what I gave out in the form of words would return to me as experiences."

— Louise L. Hay

POSITIVE THINKING

Author, publisher, and metaphysical lecturer and teacher Louise Hay recommends that you imagine that your thoughts are like drops of water. As you repeat thoughts over and over to yourself on a daily basis, you may first notice a small stain on the carpet on which you're standing. Later on, you may notice a much larger stain. A short time later, you may find you're in the middle of a small puddle, then a pond, and—as your "thought-drops" continue—that you're in a lake and then in an ocean. The question she asks you is: "What kind of ocean are you creating with your thoughts? Is it one that is polluted and toxic, or one that invites you to enjoy its refreshing waters?"

The way you think can influence how you feel about yourself. When you wake up in the morning, do you affirm to yourself, "It's going to be a great day," or do you grumble, "I know I'm just going to screw things up again"? What are your last thoughts before you go to sleep: "I'm proud of the things I accomplished and how I feel about myself," or "I'm just a failure"? Are your thoughts powerful, healing, and positive, or are they negative, irrational, and degrading? What you think is important, because your mind makes no judgments; it accepts everything you say and think and returns to you what you declare is true.

Today, instead of thinking, "I'm not worth anything," replace this thought with a more positive one, such as, "I have a great deal of value."

🎐 🎐 🎐

I THINK POSITIVELY BECAUSE I KNOW THAT MY THOUGHTS CREATE MY LIFE.

"Except for our higher order of minds, we are like the little moles under the earth carrying out blindly the work of digging, thinking our own dark passage-ways constitute all there is to the world."
— from *Spring Came on Forever*, by Bess Streeter Aldrich

THE ART OF CREATIVE HEALING

At the onset of a bout of depression, there is often a chain re-action of distortions in thinking that trigger distortions in actions. Like a single spade of earth that begins a hole, one thought leads to another and another, generating more misery and pessimism. Additional digging is then done to enlarge the hole—actions that keep depression alive and interfere with emotional healing. Soon you've dug yourself into a deep, dark chasm. You're surrounded by darkness and isolated from the ebb and flow of life on the surface. In this location, you have tunnel vision—you can only look at a small part of any situation, to the exclusion of everything else.

To emerge from this hole of your existence, you need to be willing to look at more than just the same old dirt walls. You need to step away from your hole so you can look at the "big picture" of life. Like a visitor to an art museum, you won't be able to appreciate the beauty and meaning of any painting by standing a foot away from it. You must stand at a distance so you can see how the artist has brought all the elements of creativity together to complete the entire work.

Today, use your creativity to focus on something other than your depression. Knit, draw, write, sculpt, or sew. Play a musical instrument or begin taking lessons. Start a stamp or coin collection. Visit a museum and learn as much as you can about the exhibits. By doing so, you'll be able to escape from the hole of your depression to see that there's much more to life.

🍃 🍃 🍃

I HEAL DEPRESSION THROUGH CREATIVE PURSUITS.

"I only went out for a walk, and finally concluded to stay out till sundown, for going out, I found, was really going in."
— naturalist John Muir

NATURAL CONNECTION

When your mind and spirit are troubled, going out into nature can help you smooth out the rough edges of your life, enlarge the tight passageways of your journey, and reconnect with everything and everyone that's in your world. Recognizing your connection with nature can expand your vision, as well as give you a more profound sense of who you are.

There are many ways to commune with nature, from camping and hiking to working in your garden. The best way to begin this process is to put down this book and go outside. Take a slow, meditative walk through nature. Feel the earth beneath your feet, soft and yielding as it prepares for spring and summer growth. Savor the warmth of the sun on your skin. Be conscious of how the wind caresses your body. Smell the fragrance of the trees and earth. Hear the rustling of the leaves beneath your feet and the snap of an occasional twig. Look closely at the plants around you, noticing the varieties and the different shades of green. See and hear the birds, squirrels, and other creatures around you. Feel how the rhythms of your body interact with the natural rhythms around you.

Then, when you're ready, slowly return the way you came. Remain in the present, re-experiencing all the sights you've just seen, and also noticing those you missed the first time. Then say out loud, "I am one with the sun. I am one with the trees. I am one with the wind. I am one with the birds. I am one with nature. I am one with myself."

🍃 🍃 🍃

I CONNECT WITH THE INNER ME WHEN I COMMUNE WITH NATURE.

"May you live as long as you want to. May you want to as long as you live."

— Celtic toast

DECIDING TO LIVE

Today, give yourself a powerful message that helps you not only to reaffirm your decision to live, but also to live life as fully and meaningfully as you can at this moment. Start by deciding that you don't want to die and will not, under any circumstances, take your own life. In fact, don't even allow yourself to consider dying as a possibility. Contemplating suicide, for someone who's depressed, often becomes a habit. You feel bad, so you think, Well, I'll just end it all so I don't have to feel this way anymore. Although you might not actually take this drastic step, habitual negative thinking prevents you from noticing and appreciating the people you love and the good things that happen to you.

Take control of your life today by eliminating your habitually suicidal thinking. Replace it with a *good* habit—one that helps you pay attention to the people and things that matter to you. Talk with your children, organize pictures of your grandchildren in a framed collage, play with your pet, clean your house, organize a closet, or wash and wax your car—do something productive!

If you find it difficult to take such positive action, write on a piece of paper, "Instead of contemplating suicide, I will _____." List at least five different positive actions you can take that will help you release your suicidal thoughts. One entry could be, "I will volunteer in my community." Compose a new positive-action list every time you feel suicidal, then refer to these lists whenever you need ideas.

જી જી જી

I REPLACE "I WANT TO DIE" WITH "I CHOOSE LIFE."

"Happiness is a thing to be practiced, like the violin."
— John Lubbock

CREATING HAPPINESS

How can you create happiness in your life when you're in the midst of overwhelming grief or a deep depression? How can you hold on to happiness when you're troubled by the ups and downs of mood swings? Too often, you may place your happiness outside yourself, which can cause endless distress and disappointment. You may chase illusions that lead you to believe that if you only had more money, a better relationship with your parents, or were able to spend more quality time with your partner prior to his or her death, you'd be much happier today.

But the truth about happiness is that it comes from within you and, because of this, needs to be nurtured so it can grow. There are many ways to nurture happiness in your life and then hold on to it. Create a sense of purpose by doing something you really like to do. Combine this sense of purpose with detachment from others; do for others and care about them, but not to the extent where such efforts impact on your independence. As much as possible, live harmoniously by finding some value in everything and everybody. Add a sense of adventure and enthusiasm to your life. And don't forget to laugh. Chuckle at life's ironies, find joy in humor, and even laugh at yourself if you can. With laughter comes the realization that all things come to pass and that life evolves through cycles of change. Resisting the cycles of life brings pain; flowing with the cycles and enjoying them keeps you healthier and happier.

ᑫᐧ ᑫᐧ ᑫᐧ

I LIVE WITH PURPOSE AND DETACHMENT, AS WELL AS ADVENTURE AND LAUGHTER.

"People who suffer a trauma...must reinvent their lives."
— Dr. Kathryn D. Cramer

REINVENTING YOUR LIFE

If you've lost your job, had an accident, been through a divorce, had to take out a loan to pay your bills, ended a relationship, or are in the midst of some other major life change such as a move, illness, or retirement, then you know how difficult times such as these can bring you down.

Some people approach traumatic life events with the attitude of a passive, helpless victim who moans, "Nothing ever works out for me!" or "This is just the way things seem to go for me—another terrible chapter in the story of my life!" Others become angry and resentful and resort to blame and vengeful feelings. They may say things like, "I'll show my boss he can't lay me off—I'll take him to court!" or "I hope my ex gets dumped really badly!" Still others become even more negative about themselves with comments such as: "I'm a failure!" or "I'm no good." And there are those who let traumatic events make them feel depressed or apathetic about life, as they adopt such attitudes as, "I don't care anymore" or "Nothing I do ever matters."

But there's a much better way to deal with traumatic life events. From now on, look at the ways the experiences can teach you and help you. For instance, an illness can encourage you to take better care of yourself; a divorce can give you the opportunity to focus on your needs; a layoff can help get you out of a rut and pursue another career. Sometimes traumatic life events can be beneficial when you can see them as opportunities to reinvent the way you live.

ॐ ॐ ॐ

I SEE EACH EVENT IN MY LIFE AS AN OPPORTUNITY TO LEARN, GROW, AND CHANGE.

"The term clinical depression *finds its way into too many conversations these days. One has a sense that a catastrophe has occurred in the psychic landscape."*
— singer/poet Leonard Cohen

MOOD-ALTERING MEDICATION

Depression has become increasingly common in recent times. The rates of depression were lower for people born in 1900 than for those born in 1920, and lower for the 1920 group than for those born in 1940. Nowadays, roughly 10 to 12 million Americans become depressed each year, although not for the first time—about two million have manic-depressive episodes each year. Depression in young children and adolescents, once believed to be rare, has also increased, with growing evidence that some forms of depression are inherited.

Peter D. Kramer, in his controversial bestselling book, *Listening to Prozac*, notes that eight million people have taken Prozac—but not simply because of clinical or manic depression. He wrote: "People were taking the drug for weight loss and for binge eating, for premenstrual tension and postpartum blues." Why? Because the drug made them feel 'better than well.' Prozac seemed to give social confidence to the habitually timid, to make the sensitive brash, to lend the introvert the social skills of a salesman. Prozac was transformative for patients in the way an inspirational minister or high-pressure group therapy can be...."

Before taking any mood-altering medication, keep in mind that it's best to discover why you feel the way you do. Just because you're down, depressed, or grieving for a long period of time doesn't necessarily mean you're clinically depressed.

ᔭ ᔭ ᔭ

I EXPLORE THE REASONS FOR MY MOODS BEFORE TRYING MEDICATION.

"You feel worthless because all of a sudden you aren't the way you once were. I cried a lot. I was angry."
— Teddy Pendergrass

COMFORT AND SUPPORT

In the early 1980s, singer Teddy Pendergrass sold more than ten million records in a decade-long stretch, and he often performed at sold-out concerts. But his life and career almost came to end in a tragic car accident that left him partially paralyzed. Recovering from the accident forced Pendergrass to make difficult physical and emotional adjustments. With the help of intensive therapy and the support of his wife and children, Pendergrass resumed his recording career. Although he remains in a wheelchair and has limited use of his arms, he is still an active and powerful force in the music world. "I'm more confident and comfortable in my ability, and I'm less afraid," says Pendergrass about his life today.

When you're physically challenged, suffering from a chronic illness, or healing from surgery, an accident, or an injury, day-to-day life can sometimes seem like it's a trial. The simplest activities that others take for granted—or that you were once able to perform with ease—may now be time-consuming, difficult, and exhausting. Physical movement can be painful. And, like Pendergrass, the modifications you have to make in your life can impact your self-confidence.

During such trying times, it's important that you learn to rely upon the strength and support of professionals who are trained to help you, friends and family members who will stand by you, a partner who loves you unconditionally, and care givers who are there when you need them. Ask for help, then be thankful for, and appreciative of, what you receive.

🌿 🌿 🌿

I LET OTHERS BE THERE FOR PHYSICAL COMFORT AND EMOTIONAL SECURITY.

"It used to be that, if I had a good working day, I thought I was a wonderful person, but otherwise I thought I was a terrible person."

— Byron Janis

FEELING GOOD ABOUT YOURSELF

Feeling "blue" or depressed can have a disastrous effect on your self-esteem. Such mood disorders can throw you into rages and fits that cause self-loathing and create guilt and shame, make you feel "less than" others, lead you to continually find fault with yourself, make it hard for you to attain goals or complete even simple tasks, weaken your belief in yourself, and make it hard for you to take proper care of yourself.

Elevating your self-worth, therefore, is absolutely essential to alleviating your mood swings. How can you do this? Here are some self-esteem boosting suggestions. Try one or two each day for a week, then note how you feel about yourself at the end of the week:

- Live one day at a time.
- Accept compliments.
- Do something that you perceive as difficult or scary.
- Focus on your past successes.
- Give yourself credit for an accomplishment.
- Do something you enjoy or at which you feel you excel.
- Spend time with people who affirm your worth.
- Say this affirmation aloud: "I think and act with self-confidence."

ஃ ஃ ஃ

I RAISE MY SELF-ESTEEM AND SELF-CONFIDENCE THROUGH THE POSITIVE THINGS THAT I DO FOR MYSELF.

"Forgiveness saves the expense of anger, the cost of hatred, the waste of spirits."

— Hannah More

FORGIVENESS

Do you have a propensity for dwelling on old hurts and past mistakes? You probably can't practice forgiveness when grudges stand in your way; you certainly can't look forward to the future with any sort of positive outlook when you get an almost perverse pleasure from hanging on to transgressions made by yourself or others. As Charles E. Jinks observed, "The main difference between optimism and pessimism resides in the notion of memory. The pessimist aptly recalls the hurts and failures of yesterday, but simply cannot remember the plentiful possibilities of a new tomorrow. The optimist has a hopeful future already memorized."

According to American Indian tradition, "enemies" such as failure and hurt are sacred because they can make you strong. The unfortunate things that have happened in your past can teach you how to become stronger in the present and how to succeed in the future. But if you can't forgive what's gone on in the past, then you're going to remain an angry, vengeful, negative, perpetually pessimistic person.

How can you change this propensity? Take a moment to recall a hurt or failure from the past. Ask, "How has it made me stronger or wiser? How has it provided me with lessons that have helped me grow? How has it brought new opportunities into my life?" Focus on the positive aspects of yesterday's hurts and failures, and then say, "I can let this go now. I forgive." With each act of forgiveness, you create a positive foundation on which to build a successful future.

෯෧ ෯෧ ෯෧

I HEAL MYSELF AND IMPROVE MY LIFE THROUGH THE ACT OF FORGIVENESS.

"The whole trouble is that we won't let God help us."
— George MacDonald

SPIRITUAL SUPPORT

There will always be times in your life when you must mourn an especially painful loss, such as the end of a romantic relationship. But if you focus on the enormity of the pain that lies ahead of you, the seemingly endless days of sadness and loneliness, and the myriad holidays and special times you'll no longer share together, you might be so overwhelmed that you will think you can't possibly get through such a difficult time. You may consider suicide. You may rely upon food, sugar, drugs, or alcohol to ease your pain. Or you may use denial, vindictiveness, or even geographical relocation to try to deal with your feelings at this time.

Even though you must—and will—get through this difficulty, you don't have to endure it alone. God's help is always available to you, especially in times of intense sorrow and pain. You can turn to this Higher Power and trust this Guiding Voice so you can have faith that all things change, every wound heals, and all is eased through the passage of time. You may wish to use the following passage from Isaiah (60:20) as a daily or even hourly reminder of the promise that a spiritual resource is there for you:

> *Thy sun shall no more go down;*
> *Neither shall thy moon withdraw itself:*
> *For the Lord shall be thine everlasting light,*
> *And the days of thy mourning shall be ended.*

ॐ ॐ ॐ

I TURN TO MY HIGHER POWER DURING TIMES OF NEED.

"Action may not always bring happiness, but there is no happiness without action."

— Benjamin Disraeli

EXERCISING

E xercise can lift your mood, soothe your restlessness and anxiety, reduce your dependence on alcohol and drugs, ease insomnia, and make you feel confident, secure, and happy. However, when you're depressed, you may find it very difficult to exercise. When your energy level is low and your motivation is minimal, working out may seem less like a prospect and more like an impossibility.

But there are ways to gently push yourself into a routine of exercise. To begin, you need to set aside a specific time of day to exercise. With the approach of warmer weather and longer hours of daylight, both early mornings and evenings are options. If you feel uncomfortable coming into contact with others while you're exercising, choose places to go to where you're not likely to meet many people, such as hiking or walking in the woods, attending a fitness club during nonpeak times, or using aerobic workout videotapes in the privacy of your living room. You might like to vary the kind of exercise you do from day to day to make the regimen more interesting, or you may prefer to engage in the same types of activities each day so that you feel comfortable with your routine.

In the beginning, try to exercise for at least 20 minutes, three times a week. If you miss a day or two, that's okay—just pick up where you left off. And be sure to reward yourself at the end of each exercise session. Take a short rest or nap, or eat a piece of delicious, nourishing fruit.

ぬ ぬ ぬ

I EXERCISE EVERY DAY FOR PHYSICAL AND EMOTIONAL WELL-BEING.

"Weeping and feeling depressed at times is natural, but it drains you. On the other hand, laughing and being happy makes you feel energized. So we—families and friends—appreciate it so much when people allow us to let down our hair, to smile and relax awhile and to enjoy ourselves in spite of it all."

— Vera Kiley, a mother whose daughter
was shot and paralyzed

CELEBRATING LOSS

Sometimes you can't see the importance of laughter in your dark times because you're blinded by tears. Being overly serious while grieving can be physically and emotionally damaging, depleting your immune system so you become more susceptible to illness and more hopeless about life.

That's why being open to seeing the positive, humorous side of situations, even when it comes to "serious" matters such as death and funerals, can help you stay both mentally and physically healthy. In his biography of Harvey Milk, the outspoken, popular gay San Francisco supervisor who was brutally murdered, author Randy Shilts described the unusual funeral service in which Milk's friends, family, and colleagues mixed the sweet with the bitter. Milk's box of ashes was wrapped in his favorite comic strip and the initials R.I.P. were spelled out in rhinestones across the box. His ashes were scattered in the ocean along with purple Kool-Aid and bubble bath. The lavender cascade of bubbles that resulted was a fitting tribute to the gay public official who often equated politics with theater and had a flair for the dramatic.

Today, think of how much more sense it makes to rejoice at the end of a life. Then do so in your own way.

ॐ ॐ ॐ

I CELEBRATE MY LOSS IN WAYS THAT MIX THE SWEET WITH THE BITTER.

"Nothing can bring you peace but yourself."
— Ralph Waldo Emerson

INNER PEACE

How do you begin your search for inner peace when you may often be at war with yourself? Begin by identifying any of the following aspects of your life in which you feel you're not at peace:

- my body,
- my career,
- my relationships,
- my family,
- my finances, and/or
- myself.

After you identify one or more areas, remember that whatever the conflicts presented by these areas are, you may be so busy blaming or punishing yourself for your dissatisfaction that you forget to take steps to resolve that issue. That's when it becomes important to examine one area of your life and ask, "What would create greater harmony in this situation?" If you can't answer that question or feel that a solution is out of the question—for example, a partner who won't admit that he or she has a drinking problem—then you need to ask, "What would I like to do about this?" On a piece of paper, write down this goal and then all the possible options for achieving it—the possible as well as the seemingly impossible. Try to see as many possibilities or creative links between possibilities as you can. Review your answers. Accept some; discard others. Then make an action plan so you can bring peace to this area of your life.

ఞ ఞ ఞ

I RESTORE PEACE IN MY LIFE BY RESOLVING A CONFLICT.

"Time is the only comforter for the loss of a mother."
— Jane Carlyle

THE LOSS OF A MOTHER

Mother's Day may be a particularly hard holiday for you to deal with due to the past or recent loss of your mother (or a female figure whom you regarded as your mother). Even if your early connection to your mother wasn't always the best or, as you grew older, you grew apart from one another, that doesn't mean that you now don't miss her or regret all the things you didn't get to do or share with her. As Lillian Hellman wrote in *An Unfinished Woman*, "My mother was dead for five years before I knew that I had loved her very much."

Your mother doesn't have to be deceased for you to feel her loss today. Perhaps you're no longer speaking to one another or are setting limits on the amount of time you spend with her because of your inability to get along when you're together. Maybe seeing or thinking about your mother brings back childhood memories that you'd rather forget. Or, perhaps she has remarried and started a new family, making you feel excluded or unwanted.

No matter how you experience the loss of your mother right now, remember that time will blunt any pain you may feel. If you were lucky to have warm and happy memories of her, use these today to console you in your loss. If your relationship with her wasn't all you would have hoped for, comfort yourself today in "mothering ways"—nurture and comfort yourself, and be gentle with yourself. Also, keep in mind the words of Renita Weems, who confessed, "I cannot forget my mother. Though not as sturdy as others, she is my bridge. When I needed to get across, she steadied herself long enough for me to run across safely."

ৡ ৡ ৡ

I FOCUS ON THE POSITIVE ASPECTS OF MY RELATIONSHIP WITH MY MOTHER.

"Give us to go blithely on our business this day, bring us to our resting beds weary and content and undishonored, and grant us in the end the gift of sleep."
— Robert Louis Stevenson

ESTABLISHING SLEEP CYCLES

Depression and sleep disorders usually go hand-in-hand. You may want to stay in bed a lot, although you may have difficulty sleeping or staying asleep for long periods of time. Or you may wake up in the early morning darkness feeling frightened, anxious, worried, or weepy.

If you have trouble falling asleep at night or have trouble waking up in the morning, you may notice an increase in depression, mood instability, and irritability. You may try to sleep late on weekend mornings, but usually this behavior disrupts your body's rhythm. What you need to do is set your internal "biological clock" so you go to bed at the same time each night and get up at the same time each morning, although this can seem unrealistic due to your inconsistent job schedule or your pressing family responsibilities.

However, there are ways to adjust your routine so you can gradually create more opportunities for a restful night's sleep. Strive to live by the motto: *"Early to bed and early to rise..."* Really make an effort to go to bed about the same time each night and get up at around the same time each morning—even on weekends and holiday mornings. Exercise daily, which can help keep your biological clock in working order. Make adjustments in your schedule to compensate for Daylight Savings Time the week before the actual change. And take late-afternoon naps if you can work these into your schedule.

🕉 🕉 🕉

I HONOR MY SLEEP CYCLES SO I FEEL ENERGIZED AND REFRESHED.

"Sticks in a bundle are unbreakable."

— Kenyan proverb

SUPPORT GROUPS

A support group that brings people together who have experienced loss or who are dealing with mood disorders can be helpful in many ways. The group can help you feel that you're not alone and encourage communication so you can express feelings you're unable to discuss with others. The group can help you see that things in your life might not be as bleak as they may seem to you, and it can provide you with a sense of hope as you see that those with similar problems are getting better all the time. The group can also provide valuable education and information you might find beneficial to your own healing and recovery. And, you might find that you are forming lasting friendships with fellow group attendees.

To locate a support group for your specific needs, call your local mental health hotline or a nearby hospital, check the community calendar listings of support groups in local newspapers, or ask your therapist or doctor for referrals. If there are several groups available, attend each at least once to discover which one feels most comfortable and can provide you with the greatest degree of healing and support.

The first time you attend a support group might not be easy. But keep in mind that the community of others can be personally nurturing and empowering. While one stick alone can easily be snapped, a bundle of sticks together becomes strong and unbreakable.

❧ ❧ ❧

I JOIN WITH OTHERS FOR COLLECTIVE HEALING AND POSITIVE GROWTH.

"All change is not growth, as all movement is not forward."
— Ellen Glasgow

MAKING PROGRESS

Part of the reason why you may feel "blue" from time to time may be your feeling that things in your life never seem to turn out the way you want them to. You may fall short of your desires and find that you do not meet the goals you set to become the person you'd like to be. When you're feeling this way, you may stubbornly continue to pursue your dreams despite the possibility of failure, or you may just decide to give up in dejection, self-pity, or rage.

Yet what may appear to be failure, a major setback, or even backward movement might really be part of a gradual progression forward. As Michel Egquem de Montaigne observed, "They have only stepped back in order to leap farther." So many of your so-called failures and losses might in fact be the necessary stepping stones you need in order to be guided along the pathway towards different objectives, new opportunities, or ever greater possibilities.

Today it's important to accept that some things are meant for you to have or achieve; some things are meant to be lost; and some things are meant to be gained. That's part of the cycle of life —birth (gain), life (possession and achievement), and death (loss). Instead of bemoaning what you don't have, rejoice at what you've been given or what you've achieved. You don't have to view what has happened to you as good or bad, a victory or a defeat, a success or a failure, a cause for celebration or a time for mourning. But you can view whatever happens to you as *progress*.

ॐ ॐ ॐ

I KNOW THAT EVERYTHING IN MY LIFE HELPS ME PROGRESS ON MY PATH.

"If we could hang all our sorrows on pegs and were allowed to choose those we like best, every one of us would take back his own, for all the rest would seem even more difficult to bear."

— Hasidic saying

COUNTING YOUR BLESSINGS

Have you ever read or heard stories about those who have had to endure incredible pain, surmount unbelievable odds, or struggle three times as hard as the average person to attain something others take for granted? There are well-known people that fit such descriptions. Helen Keller grew up blind, deaf, and unable to speak in a world that commonly treated such individuals as less than human. Franklin Delano Roosevelt suffered with polio throughout his life, yet provided the country with strong leadership in a world that was torn apart. Eddie Rickenbacker floated aimlessly in a life raft for 21 days in the Pacific Ocean, not knowing if he would be rescued or die of thirst. There are others—strangers you come to know, whose stories fill magazines and newspaper columns. And there are those you don't even know who are struggling at this minute for their next breath, to cope with the loss of a child, to end painful abuse, or who are trying to negotiate entering a building as they sit in a wheelchair. At this moment, if you had the opportunity to switch places with any one of these people who has such difficulties to bear, would you?

If you're not satisfied with yourself or your life, it may be tempting to think that things would be so much better if you had what others had or if you were more like someone else. But you can't walk in anyone else's shoes unless you're willing to go the distance. Today, be grateful for what you've been given in your life—count your blessings!

☙ ☙ ☙

I AM CONTENT WITH MY SITUATION; I COUNT MY BLESSINGS.

"What poison is to food, self-pity is to life."

— Oliver G. Wilson

GETTING OFF THE PITY POT

Poison can change food from a source of nourishment to a source of illness. So, too, can self-pity taint life, changing it from an exciting adventure you're free to engage in to a stiff prison sentence that keeps you confined to a dark, barren cell.

Self-pity is an attitude, often learned in childhood, that reinforces how ineffectual you think you are today, how bad you think you look, and how everything in your life is hopeless. You may think you're worthless because you never got the best grades when you were a kid—and that's why your friend got into graduate school and not you. You may think you look awful because your mother always used to poke fun at you about your weight—and that's why no one will ask you out on a date. You may think your life is hopeless because your father always told you that you'd never amount to anything—and that's why you lost your job.

While the messages you received while you were growing up may not have been the most nurturing—or may have even been denigrating—you received them at a time when you were a powerless, dependent child. Today you're no longer powerless, and you're far from being a child—you're independent and free. Approach life as if it's a nourishing banquet table, with a wide array of delectable foods that will make you feel healthy and strong. Release the hold that the negative messages of the past have on your present life. Release your feelings of resentment and blame. Instead, live freely and enthusiastically...TODAY!

ॐ ॐ ॐ

I ESCAPE MY SELF-PITY PRISON AND LIVE HAPPILY AND FREELY.

"Even when a bird is walking, we sense that it has wings."
— Antoine-Marin Lemierre

OVERPOWERING WEAKNESS

When a bird hops around on the ground, it becomes vulnerable and weak; at such a time, it would be easy for a cat to quickly snatch the bird in its mouth. Yet, when the bird is in flight, it becomes powerful and strong.

Do you focus on your individual strengths so you can become stronger? Or are you more conscious of your weaknesses and vulnerabilities? One of the greatest mistakes you may make in your development as an individual is spending too much time and effort trying to correct your weaknesses before you capitalize on your strengths. What's more beneficial to your growth is recalling your moments of success rather than focusing on your times of failure. That's why Delores Caleagno advised, "If you don't focus on strengths, you're playing a losing game."

Everyone is stronger when they keep their successes and strengths—not their failures and deficiencies—utmost in their mind. The legendary coach of the Green Bay Packers, Vince Lombardi, was aware of this concept. Before a game with Green Bay's arch rival, the Detroit Lions, Lombardi showed films of the successful running plays previously used against the Lions. He believed that his team would be more likely to take the field with confidence by showing them what had worked in the past, not what had failed.

Today, can you soar with your strengths in mind, or will you let your weaknesses ground you? Focus on what you do best, and you'll surely feel better about yourself.

இ இ இ

I MAKE A MENTAL LIST OF MY STRENGTHS TO OVERPOWER THOUGHTS OF MY WEAKNESSES.

"When you get into a tight place and everything goes against you, till it seems you could not hold on a minute longer, never give up then, for that is just the place and time that the tide will turn."

— author Harriet Beecher Stowe

GETTING HELP

You have five choices when you recognize that you have symptoms of depression, grief, or chronic mood swings. You can start employing self-help techniques and strategies you read about on your own or learn from others. You can join a support group designed to address your specific needs, or build your own support system, which will include understanding friends or family members. You can begin individual treatment with a psychiatrist or psychotherapist. You can combine self-help with outside support and/or professional help. Or, you can feel so hopeless and apathetic that you can decide not to do anything; in essence, you give up on the possibility of ever getting better.

It's not hard to see that the last choice is really not a choice at all—not if you want to start to feel better today. It is merely a response to the "apathy cycle," whereby those experiencing grief or depression decide not to do anything at all to help. But it's at this critical time, when all you want to do is stop the world so you can get off, that you need to awaken your mental senses and make a choice. While it's often hard to start anything when it's new, unknown, and appears to require a large energy and time commitment, that's precisely when you need to take the first step. When you're depressed or grieving, you deserve all the help you can give yourself.

ॐ ॐ ॐ

I CHOOSE TO GET ALL THE HELP AND SUPPORT I DESERVE.

"Your profession is not who you are, it is only a costume."
— Unknown

GETTING TO KNOW YOU

Sometimes when you retire from your profession, sell your own business, or lose a job that you enjoyed, you may feel depressed or even want to die. That's because you've defined who you are by what you did; once the "costume" of your profession, business, or position is taken away, you feel naked and vulnerable. Without it, you lack direction and purposefulness in your daily life. All you may be able to focus on is what you no longer have, making it hard for you to seek out other interests.

Yet a career "costume" is just one of many you may wear. There's the costume of a full-time parent, a college or graduate school student, a member of a self-help group, or a leader in a community organization. You "wear" a costume when you devote your time and energy to a special cause or group, when you plaster your car with stickers that proclaim your recovery program, or when you don a uniform that identifies your connection to a company or special interest.

But do you always need to wear a costume? Sometimes it's okay to walk around without a uniform, slogan, or insignia. Sometimes it's okay not to have your identity be defined by a job, cause, belief, or organization.

Today, devote time to getting to know and appreciate your naked, costumeless self. Discover new hobbies or interests, and pursue them. Uncover latent talents and abilities, and release them in a variety of ways. Become acquainted with the kind of person you are, and strive to become friends with that person!

❧ ❧ ❧

I SHED MY "COSTUMES" AND DISCOVER THE REAL ME.

*"Depression—that is what we all hate. We the afflicted.
Whereas the relatives and the shrinks, the tribal ring, they
rather welcome it: you are quiet and you suffer."*
— author Kate Millett

FAMILY SUPPORT

Your family can help or hinder your healing and recovery from
depression or grief. If they devalue you because of how you
feel, display patronizing attitudes towards you, express impatience, refuse to understand the basis of your feelings, react to you
with anger, or avoid taking part in any aspect of your treatment,
such things can have a negative influence on your recovery—or
even sabotage your efforts.

But if your family can communicate with you as well as listen to
you, remain patient and tolerant during the slow process of healing
and recovery, accept and encourage positive growth and change,
and even participate in some way in your treatment or healing
process, your desire and commitment to feel better can grow
stronger. Some ways in which one or more family members can
participate in your healing are:

- attending an open meeting of your support group with you;
- meeting with your therapist;
- talking to one other openly and honestly, without judgment or
  criticism;
- expressing their concerns and asking questions; and
- sincerely asking, "What can we, as a family, do to ease your
  pain or help you?"

❧ ❧ ❧

I KNOW THAT MY FAMILY'S SUPPORT WILL ENHANCE MY
HEALING AND RECOVERY EFFORTS.

"We ought to hear at least one little song every day, read a good poem, see a first-rate painting, and if possible speak a few sensible words."

— Johann Wolfgang Von Goethe

CREATING BALANCE

Do you find you get caught up in a succession of mundane activities each day with barely enough time to catch your breath? Too often the schedules you set for yourself or try to live by can make you depressed or "blue" when you find that you never have never enough time for yourself, for the things you want to do, to make thoughtful decisions, and for relaxation.

The best way to modify any stressful schedule is to become aware of it. For a week, monitor how you use your time. That is, determine how much time each day you spend:

- eating;
- grooming/caring for your appearance;
- sleeping;
- exercising;
- working (at a job or in your home);
- socializing;
- engaging in recreational activities (reading, dancing, playing games, etc.);
- meditating or relaxing;
- doing routine household/yard chores; and
- volunteering.

Look at the patterns and time imbalances that emerge. Then set about restructuring your day and week so you can make time for the things you really want to do.

ॐ ॐ ॐ

I BALANCE MY TIME IN WAYS THAT WILL ALLOW ME TO ENJOY MYSELF AND MY LIFE.

"I am in that temper that if I were under water I would scarcely kick to come to the top."

— John Keats

VISUALIZING THE FUTURE

When people who aren't troubled by "blue" moods or depression think about the future, their feelings are often a mixture of pluses and minuses. They imagine more pleasant possibilities than improbabilities and spend some of their time daydreaming—creating ways in which the future may work out that fill them with optimistic anticipation. In effect, they're hopeful and thus take actions in the present that will ensure the positive outcomes they desire in the future.

But when you're troubled by depression or despondent moods, it can become harder to imagine anything hopeful happening in the future. Your tendency is to focus on the minuses rather than the pluses. This negative thinking can prevent you from making constructive plans about the future. It's this loss of hope that keeps you locked in despair and that casts a pall over your ability to look ahead.

Yet, just as you visualize unfortunate things happening in the future, so too can you visualize positive occurrences. Although it may be difficult at first to create a scenario in your mind in which you come out a winner in all the situations in your life, know that you can do it. As Norman Vincent Peale advised: "Visualize yourself as sound, healthy and filled with the vitality and boundless life of your Creator. Look upon yourself as the unique individual that you are....Affirm peace, wholeness, and good health—and they will be yours."

ও ও ও

I VISUALIZE MYSELF IN HAPPY AND JOYFUL SITUATIONS IN THE FUTURE.

"Nothing lasts forever—not even your troubles."
— Arnold H. Glasow

CHANGING YOUR LIFESTYLE

Do you believe your mood swings were initially instigated by specific life circumstances or experiences? Do increased levels of stress trigger or exacerbate your despondent moods?

The way you live your life and feel about yourself can affect your levels of instability and depression. These factors may be the whole problem, or they may simply make matters worse. That's why alleviating stress in your life and making positive changes in your lifestyle can enhance your overall well-being and help stabilize your moods.

First, take stock of things. List at least five sources of tension and pressure in your life—such as chronic health problems, job stress, smoking, divorce, and menopause. Select one that triggers or worsens your mood swings.

Now focus on this situation. What are some strategies you can use that might help you lessen the impact this one area has on your life? Talk to others who have had or who are going through a similar situation, seek advice from your therapist, read a book on the subject, or brainstorm strategies on your own. Implement a technique for a few days, then see if it helps. If it doesn't, try something else or use this same procedure for another situation on your list of five. When you can take positive steps towards effecting change, you're also taking positive steps towards stability and wellness.

ᎩᎯ ᎩᎯ ᎩᎯ

I TAKE AN HONEST LOOK AT MY LIFESTYLE AND CHANGE AREAS THAT NEGATIVELY AFFECT MY WELL-BEING.

"It is possible to get sugar even from a cracked sugar bowl."
— Ernest Holmes

PROBLEMS AS CHALLENGES

A Vietnam veteran who was recovering from the loss of his legs asked one of his physical therapists, "What good is all this rehabilitation doing? I'm still going to leave this hospital a helpless cripple."

The therapist replied, "It's true that you will leave here a helpless cripple as long as you focus on only one thing—what you've lost. But what about those things you still have—a strong body, a fully functioning mind, and the potential of things to come?" Today, this veteran works with paraplegics, challenging *them* in the same way his physical therapist challenged *him*.

Everyone has limitations and imperfections. Having two legs, two arms, and all your senses intact doesn't guarantee that you aren't handicapped in other ways—emotionally, creatively, motivationally, or spiritually—or that you don't create or impose limitations yourself because of your doubts, fears, and insecurities.

But such things don't have to be permanent obstacles to your growth. Focus on what you possess rather than on what you don't have or believe you don't have. What matters most is not the perfection of your "sugar bowl," but the value and worth of its contents. Today, instead of believing something is a predicament you *can't* deal with, view it as a difficult challenge you *can* overcome. As Mother Teresa once remarked to a young woman who was describing her personal problems in painful detail, "Problems! Problems! Everyone always refers to these things as problems. Is there not another word we can use? How about 'gift'?"

🌿 🌿 🌿

I ACCEPT THE CHALLENGES PRESENTED BY ALL THE "GIFTS" IN MY LIFE.

"Every morning you come in yelling 'Rise and Shine! Rise and Shine!' I think, 'How lucky dead people are! But I get up. I go!'"
— from *The Glass Menagerie,* by Tennessee Williams

HANDLING BURNOUT

Think about a light bulb. It has an average life of many thousands of hours, so it can shine brightly for months. But eventually it's going to burn out.

Human burnout is the gradual dimming of what once was bright—the lost excitement and energy you once felt for a job, a cause you once believed in, an athletic endeavor for which you once trained religiously, or a relationship to which you once devoted your life. Burnout is the overwhelming sense of fatigue, frustration, and "funk" you feel when you don't get what you want from your life, when you don't know how to get what you want, or when you feel trapped or pressured to stay in unrewarding situations.

Avoiding burnout is a lot like installing a new light bulb. Examine any dimmed "light bulbs" in your life today by asking, "What in my life is wearing me down?" Perhaps your career isn't as promising as it used to be, going back to school isn't stimulating you or is a lot more difficult than you imagined, or a relationship isn't making you as happy as you once were. You can then ask, "What will it take to make me feel challenged, interested, and excited again?" All it may take is a simple change. Take on a new project at work or volunteer a few hours a week to feel valued and valuable. Join a study group at school or enlist the help of a tutor. Or have a candlelit dinner with a loved one.

❧ ❧ ❧

I RENEW AND RECHARGE THE INTEREST I ONCE HAD IN ALL THE THINGS IN MY LIFE.

"Our true life lies at a great depth within us. Our restlessness and weaknesses are in reality merely strivings on the surface."

— Emanuel Swedenborg

CENTERING MEDITATION

Have you ever seen the ocean in a storm? The water is in constant, frightening motion, capable of sinking boats, eroding shorelines, and sweeping away entire homes. Yet, below the surface is a stillness that enables the tiniest fish to dart gently to and fro.

Within you is a similar "center"—a part of you that's capable of being calm and still in the midst of the most trying circumstances. Being centered in this way is like being a tree in a storm: while wind, rain, lightning, and other elements may affect you on the outside, your roots still hold you fast and firm in the ground.

How long has it been since you've felt the sensation of having your feet planted firmly on the ground? Aikido masters who teach their students to maintain their centers claim that centering can generate incredible personal force that enables one to withstand the power of many. To gain your center, stand with your feet about a foot apart. Keep your spine straight. Bend your knees slightly. Hold your hands in front of you with your elbows bent, slightly above waist level. Now inhale deeply. Imagine the energy rising up through your feet. Then exhale gently and slowly, feeling the energy flow out through your hands. Repeat this process three times, twice a day, centering and strengthening yourself on a daily basis.

ɤɜ ɤɜ ɤɜ

I DO A CENTERING MEDITATION TO KEEP ME FIRMLY PLANTED IN PEACE AND SERENITY.

"I am larger, better than I thought. I did not know I held so much goodness."

— Walt Whitman

IMPROVING SELF-IMAGE

Do you believe your critics—that is, those people whose opinion you value, but who often have done very little to deserve such attention? Perhaps one of your critics is a parent who brought you up to believe that you weren't a very worthwhile person. Another critic may be a sibling who has always tried to better you in senseless competitions. One of your critics could be someone you think of as a friend but who rarely has a kind word to say. Maybe your partner is a constant critic who finds fault with nearly everything you do. Or perhaps you yourself are your most outspoken and vicious critic, filling your own mind with negative self-talk and confirming your inability to take effective action and make meaningful decisions in your life.

Ralph Waldo Emerson said, "Whatever course you decide upon, there is always someone to tell you that you're wrong." When you give your critics the authority to dictate how you should be, you allow them to fulfill the role of an influential movie critic who has the power to denigrate the hard work created by a movie studio, director, screenwriter, or actor. Your critics can destroy your self-image and self-confidence—if you let them.

Today, paste or tape your picture on a large piece of paper. Around this picture write phrases that praise who you are in ways that make you feel good about yourself. You might write, "A great cook!" "A blockbuster parent!" "A four-star lover!" "Funny!" "Talented!" Add to your "good review" phrases once a week; in so doing, you'll be creating a self-image that is enhanced more and more with the passage of time.

ぬ ぬ ぬ

I USE PRAISE RATHER THAN CRITICISM TO IMPROVE MY SELF-IMAGE.

*"Sometimes I go about pitying myself and all the time I am
being carried on great winds across the sky."*

— Indian saying

SPIRITUAL TRUST

Do you remember the story of the man who thought God had deserted him during a most troubling time in his life because he only saw one set of footprints along the difficult path he had just walked? When he asked God why He wasn't with him when he needed Him the most, God told him that he had only seen one set of footprints because He had been carrying him.

Whether you realize it or not, the help of God is always near. All you need to do is open your eyes in faith, belief, and trust, and let yourself be carried through your particular difficulty. Relying upon a spiritual resource through prayer or meditation can help you realize that there isn't a problem that can't be solved, a teardrop that won't be dried, a weary body that won't be energized again, or a lost soul who can't be found.

When you can't see through your dark times because you're blinded by your pain and tears, strengthen the faith you need to get you through the difficult times with the following poem by an unknown author:

> *My life is but a weaving between my Lord and me,*
> *I cannot chose the colors, He weaveth steadily.*
> *Sometimes He weaveth sorrow, and I in foolish pride,*
> *Forget He sees the upper and I the underside.*

ড়৹ ড়৹ ড়৹

I TRUST IN MY HIGHER POWER TO HELP ME THROUGH THESE TOUGH TIMES.

"There was a tiny range within which coffee was effective, short of which it was useless, and beyond which, fatal."
— from *The Writing Life*, by Annie Dillard

CUTTING OUT CAFFEINE

Caffeine can cause mood elevation, as well as "the blues" and depression, nervousness, hyperactivity, jitteriness, irritability, insomnia, anxiety, shakiness, restlessness, a pounding heart, lethargy, and headaches. The more you drink it, the more you crave it, which is why many consider this beverage to be a mood-altering food-drug.

As Joan Frank commented in an article in the *San Francisco Examiner Image*, "I found myself face to face with a long line of people resembling extras off the set of *Night of the Living Dead*: shuffling along, pale and twitching, empty cups in hand—murderous. Miserable...for a writer, it's more essential than food. Great American novel? Coming right up. We're talking second only to cocaine here, and hoarded as covetously."

To discover if caffeine is a negative mood-enhancer, note how you feel after you drink a caffeinated product as well as how you feel a few hours later. If what you discover is a high-level energy surge followed by a blue or even depressed mood, it might be wise to limit your intake of caffeine or give it up entirely.

Remember, caffeine is present in regular as well as some decaffeinated coffees. It's also found in tea, a variety of soft drinks, cocoa, and chocolate products. Although it may be difficult to give up caffeine, initial symptoms such as a general feeling of tiredness, a mental fuzziness, a temptation to have something caffeinated, and a mild but persistent headache decrease over time—and often go away completely after two weeks.

ะจ ะจ ะจ

I ASSESS THE IMPACT CAFFEINE HAS ON MY MOODS AND MAKE AN APPROPRIATE CHANGE.

MAY 30

"Imagine that a soldier has been wounded with a poisoned arrow. The doctor arrives to remove the arrow, but before he can do anything, the soldier says, 'Wait! Before you take out the arrow, I want some information. I want to know who shot the arrow, why he shot it, what he looks like,' and so on. Now if the doctor stops to answer all the questions, what do you think will happen to the soldier?"

— Buddha

TRYING ANOTHER WAY

The correct response to the question Buddha asks of one of his disciples is that the soldier will most likely die. Buddha tells the disciple, "It is the same with your questions. I have no intention of being concerned about your speculation and analyzing. I am interested only in teaching how you put an end to suffering."

If you only analyze your failures, then the temptation is to perpetually re-examine situations, rather than to create a new experience or do something to alter your present perspective. While it's appropriate to discover the root cause behind any type of failure, obsessive analysis only leads to self-deprecation, immersion in the past, and depression.

In his book, *Gentle Roads to Survival*, Dr. Andre Auw recalls a film he saw about a psychiatrist who was training mentally retarded men and women to assemble a bicycle brake. Whenever they would place a part on the bike incorrectly, the doctor would say in a very gentle voice, "Try another way." The trainees then reversed the part and discovered that it fit. Auw observed: "These young people...acquired a motto to help them with apparent failure: Try another way. I think this motto could benefit all of us when we are inclined to analyze our failures rather than trying new, creative alternatives."

❧ ❧ ❧

I FOCUS ON TRYING ANOTHER, MORE PRODUCTIVE WAY TODAY.

"I started getting outside for a few minutes every day, just sitting on the porch because it was so hard for me to move to be seen and, like a miracle, my deep depression started to lift."

— Participant in a depression study

LIGHTENING YOUR MOODS

Exposure to full-spectrum light—light that contains all the wavelengths of sunlight—positively influences mental as well as physical health. Not getting enough of this type of light can have a profoundly negative effect on mental outlook, moods, and overall well-being. Inhabitants of Northern countries who are deprived of sunlight for months at a time have extremely high rates of suicide and alcoholism. In America, people are spending greater amounts of time indoors, are traveling more by vehicle than by foot or bicycle, and often work in office buildings that depend upon unnatural fluorescent lighting.

What are your reactions to light? Do you notice that your mood has improved now that the days are getting longer? Do you find that you feel despondent on cloudy days and worse after a series of gray, rainy days? Do you notice that you have more problems with depression and mood swings in the late fall and early winter, especially if you are forced to get up for work in the dark?

To get the light you need, spend at least a half hour a day outside, even on cloudy days. When indoors, work, read, or watch television near a window. Replace bulbs in fluorescent fixtures with full-spectrum bulbs, which can be purchased at hardware and specialty stores, and many nurseries. But keep in mind the danger of skin cancer from overexposure to sunlight, especially when the sun's rays are the strongest.

ॐ ॐ ॐ

I USE LIGHT AS A NATURAL MOOD ELEVATOR.

"It is one of the secrets of Nature in its mood of mockery that fine weather lays a heavier weight on the minds and hearts of the depressed and the inwardly tormented than does a really bad day with dark rain sniveling continuously and sympathetically from a dirty sky."

— Muriel Spark

PAYING ATTENTION

When you're experiencing a particularly despondent mood, the incipient stages of grief, or a deep, dark depression, you probably aren't cognizant of the beauty of the day—the bright sunshine, lush greenery, and symphony of bird songs that fill the air. Even if you are aware of the soft morning, the warmth of the afternoon, or the comfort of the evening, it may not matter to you; your heartache or oppressive mood may cast a shadow over the positive effects that such things could have upon you. Or the beauty of this day may even make you feel worse, as if someone were mocking your mood or grief by saying, "All around you is joy and beauty, but you can't enjoy or appreciate it because of how you're feeling."

As hard as it is, when you're extremely depressed or feeling very low, you have to take steps to emerge from your darkness and see the light of day. You need to make an effort to stay in touch with friends, to spend some time outdoors, to stick to your daily routine, or to ask for help. Such activities can help you find that tiny ray of hope that can help pull you out of your gloom and doom.

Today, seize every opportunity you can to fight your dark mood. Take advantage of the fair weather, read something uplifting, talk to a good friend, or dress attractively.

ॐ ॐ ॐ

I FEEL BETTER WHEN I NOTICE THE BEAUTY OF THIS DAY.

"I was suicidal, as a matter of fact, and would have killed myself, but I was in analysis with a strict Freudian, and if you kill yourself, they make you pay for the sessions you miss."

— Woody Allen's character, in the film *Annie Hall*

LOSSES AS GAINS

Gerald Coffee is a retired Navy captain who was held as prisoner of war for seven years in a cell that allowed him to take only three steps in any direction. He survived the long, lonely years when he never knew whether he'd be rescued or not by repeating a simple prayer: "God, help me use this time to get better." In spite of the fact that he could only communicate with his fellow POWS by tapping on the cell walls, he managed to learn French, recite Kipling and Shakespeare, compose his own poems, and keep his sense of humor. Today, Captain Coffee addresses major corporations on the subject of keeping their faith and their sense of humor during difficult times, using his hardship to inspire others.

It may seem as if only certain people can turn painful situations into advantageous ones, without a thought to giving up. That's not so. Even if you've suffered losses that might be considered tragic—for example, if your home burns down, you lose your hearing, your parents die within months of each other, or you have a life-threatening disease—you can hasten the healing of your losses if you see them as enriching your life rather than diminishing it. That doesn't mean you have to welcome or embrace difficulties; what it does mean, however, is that you need to accept them. "Losing is the price we pay for living," wrote Judith Viorst in her book, *Necessary Losses*. "It is also the source of much of our growth and gain."

☙ ☙ ☙

I FOCUS ON THE POSITIVE OUTCOMES THAT ARISE FROM THE TRIALS IN LIFE.

"Man must cease attributing his problems to his environment and learn again to exercise his will, his personal responsibility in the realm of faith and morals."
— Albert Schweitzer

RATIONAL THINKING

Assessing blame is easy. After all, don't you, like most people, know what it's like to fail? Sometimes, in your effort to seek easy solutions to your problems or to quickly assess why you feel the way you do, you may point out the shortcomings in others so you don't have to take full responsibility for a particular situation. An example would be if you said: "I'm depressed because my family was completely dysfunctional." This is a very common illustration of distorted thinking—where bad things happen to you, but you immediately assign fault to others. Or, you may feel blameworthy yourself, either as a result of what you were taught in your childhood or due to your low self-esteem. For example, you might say, "It's all my fault. Everything always is."

The distorted perception involved in blaming your family for your misfortune is that almost all dysfunctional families create problems for its members as these individuals grow up; the distorted perception involved in blaming yourself is that your perceptions always translate into reality. It's up to you to alter these distortions in your thinking by taking responsibility for them and then creating rational responses to them. For example, you can say, "While it's true that I grew up in a dysfunctional family, that's not the sole cause of my depression; thus, I'll stop blaming my family for all my difficulties," or "My opinions about myself change all the time, depending on my mood. But I'm not always at fault, so I'll stop indulging in self-blame."

૪૦ ૪૦ ૪૦

I TAKE RESPONSIBILITY FOR MY LIFE AND SEEK RATIONAL SOLUTIONS TO MY PROBLEMS.

"It's funny how dogs and cats know the inside of folks better than folks do, isn't it?"

— from *Pollyanna,* by Eleanor H. Porter

INTERACTING WITH ANIMALS

Studies have revealed what pet lovers already know—animal companions can be very beneficial to human emotional health. Pets give and receive unconditional affection, are true friends that ask no questions and pass no judgments, and teach people about love and responsibility in uniquely enjoyable ways. How can you not respond positively ways to a warm, shaggy dog curled at your feet in the bed; the purr of a cat as you stroke its soft fur; the melodious song and cheery antics of a caged bird; the gentle rhythm of fish as they swim in their tank; or the engaging habits of the multitude of other outdoor and indoor animals you may think of as your pets?

Your physical well-being can also benefit from interactions with a pet. Dogs require walking, so they are a great excuse to get outdoors on a regular basis. Caged animals and indoor pets depend upon you to maintain a cleaning, grooming, and feeding schedule, which inspires you to abide by a daily routine. Finally, animals—like humans—thrive on touch and other forms of physical contact, thereby forcing you to pay attention to your interactions with them.

If you have a pet, enjoy his or her company as much as possible today. If you don't have one, consider getting one. But if allergies or your living situation prevent you from owning a pet, volunteer to take a neighbor's dog for a walk or offer to cat- or bird-sit for a vacationing neighbor. Animals can give their spirit to you in ways that contribute positively to your overall sense of well-being.

🐾 🐾 🐾

I SEEK OUT THE COMPANY OF ONE OF MY ANIMAL FRIENDS TODAY.

*"I do have tremendously difficult times. Whether that's ge-
netic or caused by difficult times that were genetic in my
family, or whether I in fact inherited some of it, it doesn't
matter... But I am given a tremendous amount of joy in the
work that I do and the people whom I work with. And if
something is working, it can definitely release some of the
sadness."*

— Elizabeth Swados

THE ART OF FEELING

Playwright Elizabeth Swados is one of many creative people
who has wondered about a depression connection in families
with artistic success and mental illness. In her play, *The Four of Us,*
she wrote about her alcoholic—and eventually suicidal—mother
and her schizophrenic brother. Swados, among others, has noted a
high correlation between those in the fields of creative writing, visual arts, acting, and dance; and family histories that include frequent moves, alcoholism, and divorce. In effect, artists tend to
apply their own experiences to their craft, and in so doing, use this
"autotherapy" as a way of healing the past.

Why does it seem, too, that your own creativity and depression
go hand in hand? Whether you're trying to write, express yourself
musically, or act, it may seem that your depression inspires your
creativity. You may be far more prolific in your poetry writing when
you're "blue" than when you're feeling rosy; you may sing your best
after the end of a relationship rather than when you're in the midst
of it; you may paint more passionately on nights when you're sleepless with grief. Perhaps it's the intensity of your feelings that enables you to create from the heart, maybe it's your mind's way of
coping with adversity in positive ways, or maybe it's a gift from
your Higher Power that enables you to use your strengths during
those times when you feel the most bereft.

&a &a &a

I REMEMBER THAT IT'S THE ARTIST THAT CREATES THE WORK,
NOT THE DEPRESSION.

"As I practiced telling myself, 'I'm doing the best I can,' I began to think about the things I did right. At first I couldn't come up with anything. One day I caught myself thinking, 'I love my red shoes.' I said it out loud. After that, every time I found something I liked about myself, I wrote it down so that I could refer to it when I was feeling sad and alone."

— author Julia Thorne

LISTING YOUR ACHIEVEMENTS

When you're a child, there are usually adults around who are taking care of you, who let you know when you're "good," who support the things that are important to you, and who point you in the right direction in life. But when you reach adulthood, oftentimes you're the only one who can give such things to yourself. At times this autonomy can be liberating and exciting. But when you're troubled by low self-esteem, it can feel isolating and lonely to be your sole cheerleader. You may have difficulty weathering times when you feel dependent upon the approval and praise of others and don't receive it. When you're able to focus on yourself, you may identify so many things you think need changing or immediate attention that you're unable to see anything praiseworthy. You may find it difficult to recognize the positive things you do or the wonderful qualities you possess. You may seek out a relationship with someone who can parent you rather than with someone who can be your peer.

Today it's time to begin to parent yourself so you can raise your self-esteem and learn how to recognize your own admirable qualities. Create a special "achievements" list that you keep beside your bed. Add to this list each day (for example, one source of pride could be that you're "a loyal friend"), and reread your entries whenever you need a self-esteem boost.

ﺸ ﺸ ﺸ

I WRITE DOWN MY ACHIEVEMENTS AND REVIEW THE LIST REGULARLY.

"Strange feelings....Just a sort of unexplained sadness that comes each afternoon when the new day is gone forever and there's nothing ahead but increasing darkness."
— Robert M. Pirsig

FEARING DARKNESS

Think about what it would be like to walk through the woods at night without a flashlight. You'd be at the mercy of every root, stump, rock, and hole. Although you may be so familiar with the woods that you could take the same path in daylight without a problem, at night it would be like walking the path blindfolded— and for the very first time.

During the day, your "paths" are often well lit, well traveled, and accessible. You do familiar things—drive to work on the same route, perform the same tasks, keep the same hours. You interact with the same people—co-workers, customers, service people. You have access to the members of your support network—a therapist, family, friends.

But at night you may not have such a familiar route to follow when you're having a hard time. Even though some of your past difficulties may have taught you to trust in the slogan, "And this, too, shall pass," you may not know how to get through feelings of fear, sadness, doubt, anxiety, and insecurity. You can choose to stumble in the dark alone or you can walk easily with the light provided by others whom you know and trust. Reach out to a friend or loved one who will listen to how you feel and reassure you that all is well. Let this trusted person illuminate your path tonight.

❧ ❧ ❧

I RELEASE MY FEAR OF THE DARKNESS WITH THE HELP OF ANOTHER.

"Food probably has a very great influence on the condition of men."

— German philosopher G.C. Lichtenberg

FOOD ALLERGIES

Some kinds of food may seem to aggravate your mood swings. This could be because you've developed an intolerance to them or even an allergic response. After eating certain foods, you may experience fatigue, irritability, acne or other skin rashes, anxiety or a racing pulse, sinus congestion, bloating, gas, sweating, difficulty breathing or swallowing, or diarrhea.

For many people, dairy products can be particularly aggravating. Others react to products that contain wheat, yeast, eggs, meat, peanuts, or tomatoes. A visit to an allergist could reveal positive reactions to certain foods, or you can conduct an experiment with any food you feel might be exacerbating your mood swings. For a two-week period, eliminate one particular type of food from your diet. Be sure to read the labels of all foods you're eating, because you may find this food in items you wouldn't think to avoid. For example, if you wish to exclude dairy products, you won't be able to eat ice cream, cream, yogurt, milk, and cheese; you may also need to eliminate baked goods.

After a two-week abstinence from a particular food, ask yourself if you feel any better. If you do not, then reintroduce this food but eliminate another food in your diet for two weeks. Continue to carefully read product labels, and conscientiously monitor your reactions in a food journal. Over time, you can eliminate offending foods from your diet one at a time.

ﾟ ﾟ ﾟ

I ADJUST MY DIET IN ORDER TO STABILIZE MY MOODS.

"I was shipwrecked before I got aboard."

— Seneca

SEEING THE GOOD

It may be hard to break the habit of thinking solely from a negative perspective. You may exaggerate minor events in your life, turning everything into a worst-case scenario. For example, you may say, "I have a cold that's probably going to turn into pneumonia." You may overgeneralize, reaching a broad conclusion based on one piece of evidence—for example, you may say, "My lover left me—I'll never be loved again." Or, you may filter your thoughts by only looking at one aspect of a situation, to the exclusion of everything else; for example, "My mother and I don't get along, so the family picnic is going to be a disaster."

Author and teacher Leo Buscaglia asked, "Why do some people always see beautiful skies and grass and lovely flowers and incredible human beings, while others are hard-pressed to find anything or any place that is beautiful?" Focusing on the negative may be a habit you learned from growing up in an unhealthy childhood home. Or it may have come from coping with numerous disappointments in adulthood. But no matter the origin, you may find it hard to perceive the good in anything or anybody.

Today, think more positively. Instead of focusing on the negative, find just one positive thing in your life. Perhaps it is a beautiful sunny day. Or, you may be blessed with wonderful friends. Maybe you love your job, or you appreciate the close relationship you have with your children. Practice seeing the good for a while, and soon you'll find yourself coming up with two, three, or even more blessings in your life.

ૠ ૠ ૠ

I FOCUS ON THE POSITIVE PEOPLE AND THINGS IN MY LIFE.

> *"The world leans on us. When we sag, the whole world seems to droop."*
>
> — philosopher Eric Hoffer

LIVING WITH LOSS

During your middle years, you may become more conscious of the signs of advancing age in your parents, aunts, uncles, and siblings. These people aren't the elderly relatives of your grandparents' generation, whose deaths you may have experienced at a young age and at a time when you hadn't formed a lifelong connection. Rather, they are the adults who shaped and formed the landscape of your youth. You may wonder how it's possible that they're slowing down and need help from you, refusing to believe that as you advance in age, so do they. At the same time, a common occurrence for many individuals at this time of life is being forced to endure a series of traumatic events that challenge your resilience and ability to cope.

Such a series of losses is also experienced in the gay and lesbian community, where those who have been infected with the HIV virus advance to full-blown AIDS and then die from complications of the disease. Many young gay men and women have had to endure the loss of longtime companions and members of their circle of friends; their parents and family members have had to cope with the loss of children who they thought would outlive them.

An anonymous 66-year-old woman gave her advice to those who must live with such losses: "Now, my beautiful, intelligent, wonderful son has AIDS. ...It's been really difficult to deal with his possible death....How do I cope? I have always been a people person. I have many friends and organizational involvements. I belong to a church. I concentrate on people and keeping up with relationships."

℮ ℮ ℮

I COPE WITH LOSS BY LIVING LIFE TO THE FULLEST.

"Nothing evades our attention so persistently as that which is taken for granted....Obvious facts tend to remain invisible."
— author Gustav Ichheiser

RECORDING ACTIVITIES

Many people, particularly when they feel depressed, tend to overlook or minimize their accomplishments, taking for granted the things they do every day or the people with whom they come in contact. As a result, they often get to the end of their day and conclude, "What a waste of time! I accomplished nothing." This perception transforms into low feelings of self-esteem which, in turn, feed into depression.

Keeping track of your activities can provide you with a realistic and accurate view of the events in your day. There are two ways to accomplish this task. One is to write down every single activity you perform in a day, from the big things, such as driving to work, to the little things, such as picking up a toy or ironing a shirt. While this chore can be time-consuming—you may fill several pages of a small notebook for just a half day—doing it for a day or two can be helpful.

Another approach is to record the major events of each day. Break them into three categories: goals attained or tasks completed (for example, doing the laundry or applying for a job), pleasurable activities (such as taking your dog for a walk or going to a movie), and daily routines (such as making dinner or reading your mail). Keep your entries simple. Then, at the end of the day, review your diary. What you'll discover is that, in fact, you've accomplished quite a lot in your day and have experienced a number of pleasurable moments. Acknowledging your achievements can help you feel better about yourself and your life.

ॐ ॐ ॐ

I CREATE AN ACTIVITY DIARY TO SHOW MYSELF WHAT I ACCOMPLISH EACH DAY.

"I wasn't holding any babies. People came to work with their babies and passed them around. I would go over and say hi, but I would never touch them. Finally, I took someone's baby. I felt fine. Sad and fine. It's always there, as you can see. Life goes on. That's the good news. You find other ways to fulfill life."

— Christine Cornell

LIVING WITHOUT CHILDREN

Christine and Richard Cornell began trying to conceive in 1988, five years after they wed, but Chris's endometriosis made her infertile. In 1991, after six cycles of fertility drugs and intrauterine insemination, they took a break from treatment and explored adoption, but their name was placed on a long list, and they were never called. Being forced to give up her lifelong dream of being a mother was difficult for Christine, and the loss hit Richard hard, too.

Richard said that even though he was angry, "As time goes on, you heal, and the anger subsides. Over the past year or so, we've moved on towards being childfree. What does that mean? You can't be stuck. It will eat you to death."

You may share in the Cornells' frustration, anger, and sadness over being childless. Maybe you want to get married and raise a family, but haven't found the right person. Perhaps you're married and are trying to conceive or adopt. Maybe your partner doesn't want children, and you're trying to reconcile your differences. Or perhaps you have a health problem that will make it difficult or impossible to conceive.

Today, take deliberate steps to refocus your life. Become closer to your nieces and nephews. Think about adopting pets. Start a hobby. Or, join or form a support group for those who share your experience.

ॐ ॐ ॐ

I FACE LIFE WITHOUT CHILDREN IN POSITIVE WAYS.

*"Ladies and gentlemen, I would like at this moment to an-
nounce that I will be retiring from this program in two
weeks time because of poor ratings. Since this show was
the only thing I had going for me in my life, I have decided
to kill myself. I'm going to blow my brains out right on this
program a week from today."*

— from the film *Network*, written by Paddy Chayevsky

REGULATING MEDICATION

Do you keep old prescription medications hidden away in case
you want to commit suicide at some later time? Do you allow
your doctor to write new prescriptions when you still have a gen-
erous supply of the old ones? Do you fill your prescriptions at different pharmacies so you can maintain a large quantity of
medication?

Today, limit your prescription reserves by flushing all the old
drugs down the toilet. Next, telephone your doctor or therapist or,
at your next appointment, talk honestly about any suicidal tendencies you may feel. For your protection, request that prescriptions be filled in small quantities or that you be prescribed
medication with few side effects or interactions. Then discuss
your situation with an understanding and concerned pharmacist.
Drugstores often keep computer records of just what drugs are sold
and when. Your pharmacist can place a special mark by your
name to cue the computer if it appears you have too much medication. Then, you can be asked to return what's left of the old
medication before any new medication is dispensed.

Finally, share how you feel and what steps you've taken with
your suicide support network. Let them know the medications
you're taking and where you keep them in the house. Eliminating
the temptation to commit suicide keeps your focus on facing life's
challenges.

❧ ❧ ❧

I REGULATE MEDICATIONS I HAVE ON HAND FOR MY OWN
PROTECTION.

JUNE 14

*"If you are depressed, ask God what you can do for Him;
not what He can do for you. Then wait for the answer."*

— Unknown

SPIRITUAL MEDITATION

Meditation is the process of clearing your mind of stressful
thoughts or negative feelings so you can experience physical
relaxation and inner peace. It's a way to open yourself up to "communicate" not only with your "inner self," but also with a spiritual
"guide" such as your Higher Power. By making this contact, you gain
knowledge, inspiration, and guidance about the people, places,
and things in your life so you can handle them more calmly and
effectively.

How do you meditate? There are no hard and fast rules. Some
people sit in a quiet, candlelit room, their eyes closed; some listen
to soothing music, recorded nature sounds, or a guided meditation
tape; some chant one word such as *om* or *peace*; some use the
soothing scents of aromatherapy; others combine long-distance
running, camping, or beach walks with meditation. No matter
what form of meditation you choose, what's important is to be still,
in a quiet space. As Hands Margolis says, "Only in quiet waters,
things mirror themselves undistorted. Only in a quiet mind is ad-
equate perception of the world."

To begin meditating, select a place where you won't be interrupted and an appointed time each day; in that way, you become
"conditioned" to calm and still your mind in this space and at that
time. Keep your breathing deep and steady, your body relaxed, and
your thoughts stilled so you can be open to the messages from
your Higher Power.

ℬ ℬ ℬ

I MAKE CONSCIOUS CONTACT WITH MY HIGHER POWER
THROUGH MEDITATION.

"I am bigger than anything that can happen to me. All these things, sorrow, misfortune, and suffering are outside my door. I am in the house and I have the key."
— Charles Fletcher Lummis

TAKING CONTROL

So many things may seem to loom over you each day. There may be your addiction to drugs, alcohol, food, cigarettes, or people that require a great deal of time and attention. There may be your fears to express love, to experience your feelings, and to be comfortable in your solitude. There may be your anxieties over abandonment, rejection, loss, or failure. There may be your sensitivities to the moods of others or your desire to make everyone happy. There may be the miseries of your childhood or regrets over decisions made in the past. There may be an unhappy marriage, a troubled son or daughter, or the death of a loved one. Sometimes there's even the world in general—all the people, places, and things in your life that seem to be part of one gigantic tidal wave that hovers above you, threatening to crash down at any time.

But nothing in this life has absolute power or control over you, unless you let it. The negative conditions you believe are lurking in the shadows, ready to spring upon you at any moment, are of your own creation. Rather than being a self-sabotager—someone who gives up control—be a self-confidence builder—someone who takes control. Do your best at all times, be determined to get more out of life, lower your perfectionistic standards, and live one day at a time. Remember, the only thing in this life bigger than you are is your Higher Power.

ॐ ॐ ॐ

I TAKE CHARGE OF HOW I RESPOND TO MY LIFE.

"And I believe I've changed a lot, by the way, in many areas. I think I'm mature enough to see the patterns; I'm not always strong enough to change them. The big things, like when your father dies, that feeling of loss—I don't think I will ever get over that."

— Barbra Streisand

CELEBRATING YOUR FATHER

Barbra Streisand was only 15 months old when her father died, apparently during an epileptic fit. She says she remembers the loss in her body and psyche. After going through years of therapy to deal with a number of issues, she stopped. "I just said, 'There are things I can't change. There are patterns set up in childhood that are so strong.'"

You may identify not only with Barbra's loss, but also with her comment about childhood patterns. Many of the thoughts, feelings, and behaviors you have today may be a result of your relationship with your father while you were growing up. The child within you may still be crying out for a father with whom you can share your victories as well as your upsets, your pain as well as your growth, your failures as well as your successes. As an adult, you may feel cheated out of a wonderful relationship with your father because of your past history, or saddened because your relationship with him ended when he died.

A loving, healthy father is a great blessing. But instead of thinking about your father with anger, bitterness, sadness, regret, dejection, or depression, today look back and remember three good things about your father.

ﭼﻪ ﭼﻪ ﭼﻪ

I CELEBRATE MY FATHER TODAY.

"I do not enjoy the pain, but I understand it better. I now begin to look for the message behind the pain sooner than I did before."

— author Andre Auw, Ph.D.

TUNING INTO YOUR BODY

Periods of breakdown in the way your body functions can be important indicators in the relative illness or wellness of your body so you can respond accordingly. For example, If you twist your ankle sliding into home plate, the initial pain and tenderness and then the ensuing swelling lets you know that your ankle isn't going to be able to perform at its full capacity for a while. So you elevate your ankle and ice it, and then use crutches or limit your activity until the pain subsides.

Just as the pain from an injury is an indicator of a breakdown in your overall physical health, so too is the discomfort expressed by one or more of your body's "early warning system" weak points. Every body has these areas that send messages to help avert a full-blown illness. For example, a tickle in your throat or a soreness when swallowing may only occur when you're not getting enough rest or not eating the proper foods. Some people have sensitive stomachs that give them the same message; others have irritable bladders or joints that swell.

By paying closer attention to your body, you can learn to identify your weak points. They'll send you important signals to alert you to your susceptibility to physical or mental distress. Recognizing those signs can help you notice the potential of illness or injury in its subtle—and avoidable—stages so you can take the appropriate corrective measures for continued good health.

ॐ ॐ ॐ

I AM ALERT TO MY BODY'S EARLY WARNING SIGNALS.

"I went in one end an emotional basket case and came out the other end my full height, with my shoulders squared away."

— Michael, a person who suffers from depression

USING MINDFULNESS MEDITATION

When Michael and his wife lost the house in which they raised four children, he realized that he had become so depressed that he couldn't even take a part-time job to meet the mortgage payments. He had tried everything to shake the depression from his mother's death, his father's Alzheimer's, his job loss, his abstinence from alcohol, and his negative experiences with drug therapy. Not knowing where to turn, Michael tried a nonpharmacological approach and attended an eight-week program in mindfulness meditation that has provided thousands with measurable improvement in their depression.

The central technique in mindfulness meditation is to sit quietly for a period of time with the eyes closed, paying attention only to one's breathing. Whenever attention wanders away from each breath, the thought or emotion that has provided the distraction needs to be briefly noted, but then attention is once again returned to breathing. When this technique is practiced regularly—for example, for 45 minutes a day over a period of eight weeks—a deeper level of calm and stability can occur, thereby decreasing anxiety and increasing one's well-being.

Michael keeps up with his mindfulness meditation on a daily basis. "My meditation can consist of sitting at the window with a cup of coffee, watching the birds," he explains. "I'll just think, This is my time now. There's nothing but me and those birds and my coffee. I can switch off the world."

ря ря ря

I SUSTAIN A REGULAR PRACTICE IN MINDFULNESS MEDITATION FOR INNER PEACE.

"Were it possible for us to see further than our knowledge reaches, perhaps we would endure our sadnesses with greater confidence than our joys."

— Rainer Maria Rilke

EXPRESSING SADNESS

When Henry David Thoreau was at his retreat on Walden Pond, he wrote of a life lesson he learned after enduring a stretch of rainy days. At first, as he watched the rain, he expressed his dissatisfaction that he was housebound because of the gloomy weather. But then he felt happiness at seeing the bean seeds he had recently planted being watered. As the rain persisted, he observed that even if the seeds rotted in the ground, the rain "...will still be good for the grass on the uplands, and being good for the grass, it would be good for me."

In moments of sadness, the seeds of new growth are often planted. You may cry because you know you're dying. But the person you are now will soon be transformed into someone new—a soul who has moved on to a different plane in the universe. You may cry because someone you love is dying. But the person he or she is now will become someone new to you after they're gone—a beloved companion who has left you with endless memories and reasons to smile. Or you may cry because you feel sad, overwhelmed, frustrated, scared, or alone. But such tears will cleanse your soul and leave you refreshed and with a different perspective.

Today, remember that sadness and joy are both an integral part of the life process; without one, the other can't exist. Think of your tears as that gentle, nurturing rain that Thoreau witnessed years ago. The tears you now shed have to fall so that new stirrings of growth can occur within you.

৯১ ৯১ ৯১

I ALLOW MY TEARS TO WATER MY SOUL.

> *"Aliveness is not necessarily about feeling better, curing ills, or solving problems; it is about feeling more, being in touch with a larger dimension of awareness."*
>
> — Richard Moss

BECOMING MORE AWARE

Imagine that you have the opportunity to take a coast-to-coast trip across the United States. You can stop wherever you'd like, spend however long you want at any location, and have no set timetable. Are you going to focus solely on reaching your destination and simply drive there with tunnel vision? Or are you going to release of the need to arrive at a specific time, and simply enjoy the scenery, the people you meet along the way, and the interesting places you happen upon along the way?

Every day you have the opportunity to go on a "cross-country trip"—a once-in-a-lifetime adventure never to be repeated on any other day. How do you wish to spend your time? By focusing on all the things you don't have, all the negative feelings you have, and on all the setbacks you've experienced? Or do you wish to enjoy every minute and sometimes stop to savor a unique opportunity?

At any given time, you can let go of your focus on upsetting people, things, and events. By removing them from your mind, you open your senses so you can experience everything and everyone around you. From this moment on, resolve to pay attention to what's happening in your world beyond your problems and troubles. Appreciate the journey in each minute.

సౌ సౌ సౌ

I OPEN UP TO A LARGER DIMENSION OF AWARENESS.

"To live with shame is to feel alienated and defeated, never quite good enough to belong. And secretly we feel to blame. Shame is without parallel a sickness of the soul."
— Gershen Kaufman

RAISING YOUR SELF-ESTEEM

Shame comes from the pain of believing you aren't good enough. Many life events can affect this belief by impacting on your self-esteem and self-worth. Personal failures, such as not receiving a job promotion, rejection and criticisms, and making mistakes, are a few of the many situations that can contribute to your feelings of shame.

To conquer shame, you need to build your self-esteem. Rather than let life events and the judgments and criticisms of others influence how you feel about yourself, focus instead on actions you can take that will help you improve your view of yourself. You can start by taking good care of yourself. Pay attention to what you eat. Dress well. Exercise sensibly and get enough rest. Meditate. Use daily affirmations. Participate in spiritual activities. Pursue a hobby or craft. Write in a journal.

Then get your living space in order. Clean out clutter. Tackle a household project you've been putting off. Weed your garden. Put a fresh coat of paint on a favorite piece of furniture. Donate old clothing and other items to a charity.

Finally, continue your education. Take a class. Learn a new skill. Join special interest clubs. Take part in community activities. Work as a volunteer.

Adding one or more of these activities to your life can enhance your self-esteem and minimize your feelings of shame.

ॐ ॐ ॐ

I ENHANCE MY SELF-ESTEEM BY DOING POSITIVE THINGS FOR MYSELF.

"And then he gave a very long sigh and said, 'I wish Pooh were here. It's so much more friendly with two.'"
— Piglet, from *Winnie the Pooh,* by A.A. Milne

STARTING A SUPPORT GROUP

Starting a support group for others affected by depression, "the blues," or the death of a loved one is not as difficult as it might seem. Invite friends whose personal experiences coincide with those of the group, and include members of your own support system. Contact hospitals, professionals associated with mental health organizations, and therapists and psychiatrists in private practice who can spread the word about the support group.

Locate and then reserve a convenient public meeting place for your group, such as a room in a school, church, library, or other building. Confirm a time, then post flyers or place a notice in the community calendar section of your local daily or weekly newspaper that details the place, time, and purpose of the group.

At the first meeting, work with other group members to define the group in ways that will help to meet everyone's needs. Include in this discussion the length and frequency of meetings, finances, how the meeting will be facilitated (either within the group or by a health-care professional), the format of the meeting, topics for meetings, and how group responsibilities will be shared.

Support groups can be wonderful places to meet new, empathetic friends. As one anonymous member of a support group said, "We share our ups and downs at meetings and elsewhere....It has helped me more than any other thing....It has certainly helped me to help others."

ஃ ஃ ஃ

I START A SUPPORT GROUP OR HELP SOMEONE ELSE TO FORM ONE.

"Our dilemma is that we hate change, but we love it at the same time. What we want is for things to remain the same but get better."

— Sydney J. Harris

CHALLENGING FEAR

How often do you complain that you could do something—if only something or someone wasn't preventing you from doing it? Day after day, you may suffer with feelings of depression, but rather than getting help you rationalize, "Well, I can't go to therapy because I don't have time." Week after week, you may grieve the loss of your partner, but rather than going out and socializing, you say, "I can't go out, or people will think I didn't love (him or her)." Month after month, you let your children run you ragged but you explain, "I can't discipline them because I've never been very good with kids." Year after year, you stay in the same unhealthy relationship, but you justify not leaving by saying, "I can't break up with my lover because I'm afraid (he or she) will commit suicide."

What's important to recognize is that saying "I can't" is just another way of saying "I fear." If you could eliminate your fearfulness, just think of all you could do. There would be nothing to prevent you from taking risks, traveling to new places, becoming more intimate, changing careers, going back to school, or setting limits with your children.

If you don't welcome change in your life, it's going to be harder and harder for you to respond to other life challenges. Today, try out a new behavior or attempt to handle things in a unique fashion. Change your response from "I can't" to "I can." In so doing, you can push aside or even remove the obstacles you've placed in your path, and challenge your fears.

ɬa ɬa ɬa

I TAKE STEPS THAT MOVE ME AWAY FROM FEAR AND TOWARDS CHANGE.

"Told that someone's mood disorder has evolved into a storm—a veritable howling tempest in the brain, which is indeed what a clinical depression resembles like nothing else—even the uninformed layman might display sympathy rather than the standard reaction that 'depression' evokes, something akin to 'So what?' or 'You'll pull out of it' or 'We all have bad days.'"

— from *Darkness Visible,* by William Styron

CLINICAL DEPRESSION

Clinical depression differs from the normal sadness associated with "the blues," grieving, and low-grade despondent moods. Clinical depression:

- is more intensely painful: "I sometimes sit and stare at the wall for hours while crying."
- lasts for longer periods of time: "For years I've never been able to label what I was going through."
- interferes with day-to-day functioning, making it nearly impossible to attempt even the most routine activities: "I feel like I'm in a grave and someone is continually throwing dirt in to cover me."
- is a destructive emotion: "I constantly dwell on bad things happening to me or my family....I always think I'm going to die tomorrow."
- is more than just an emotion; it's an illness with a wide array of symptoms: "These episodes feel very much like a horrible physical illness."

If you're clinically depressed, remember that you're not alone and that there's help and hope. Clinical depression is one of the most treatable emotional conditions. Seek help today!

ৡ৯ ৡ৯ ৡ৯

I SEEK HELP FOR MY CLINICAL DEPRESSION; I KNOW THERE'S ALWAYS HOPE.

"Weep with me when I weep. Laugh with me when I laugh. Don't be afraid to share this with me."
— St. Anthony's Hospital brochure

CARE GIVING

You needn't feel completely helpless or alone in your sadness if someone close to you is diagnosed with a serious or life-threatening illness. There's wonderful advice for care givers contained in the St. Anthony's Hospital (Alton, Illinois) brochure titled, *Twenty-five Tips to Help Those Facing a Serious Illness.* The brochure emphasizes that whether you're an AIDS buddy, volunteer in a hospital, provider of home health care, or are the partner, close friend, or family member of someone who's seriously ill, the main function you can provide is to be there emotionally for the person who's sick.

This doesn't mean merely having plenty of superficial contact with the person who's ailing. It means that this individual must feel genuinely cared about. What matters is how you interact—how much you show that you care about what happens to him or her, how often you make visits, and how well you tend to physical as well as emotional needs when they're expressed. Concrete actions not only speak louder than good intentions, but they also help you feel better about the upsetting situation.

Today, communicate directly and openly with one another about that person's illness. You might ask, "Do you want to talk about your feelings with me?" You may find that both of you have a lot of sad emotions that need to be expressed. Share your tears, for it's a very cleansing, healing, and beneficial activity.

ॐ ॐ ॐ

I AM A TRUE CARE GIVER WHO PROVIDES MY FRIEND OR LOVED ONE WITH COMFORT AND SUPPORT.

"We must have courage to bet on our ideas, to take the cal-culated risk, and to act. Everyday living requires courage if life is to be effective and bring happiness."

— Maxwell Maltz

CHANGING IRRATIONAL RULES

Challenge your depression or despondent mood today by changing one of the irrational rules you live by—a rule that keeps you stuck in your "blue" feelings. One rule might be, "I can-not allow myself to make mistakes." Write this statement on a piece of paper, then describe how this rule affects you, impacts your life, and influences how you interact with others.

Then, list all the ways in which this rule is unreasonable or de-structive by finishing this statement: "This rule is irrational, un-reasonable, and destructive to me because _____." One way you might complete this statement is by writing, "...I'm trying to do something that's not within my power, so I always set myself up for failure, which makes me feel bad."

Once you've convinced yourself that the rule is irrational, un-reasonable, and destructive, you can change it. Think up a new rule—one that's realistic, attainable, and that won't harm you or others. An example could be: "Every mistake I make has a positive result that I need to discover." Write the new rule on a piece of paper. Commit it to memory by saying it out loud three times. Then list the actions you can take that will help you put this new rule into effect.

Changing an old, negative, and destructive rule into a new, pos-itive, and instructive one takes courage. But the reward of greater happiness is worth it.

ॐ ॐ ॐ

I COURAGEOUSLY CHALLENGE THE IRRATIONAL RULES THAT GOVERN MY MOODS.

"To me there are three things everyone should do every day. Number one is laugh. You should laugh every day. Number two is think—spend some time in thought. Number three, you should have your emotions move you to tears. If you laugh, think and cry, that's a heck of a day."

— Jim Valvano

LIVING AND DYING

"Jimmy V" started as an assistant basketball coach the year he graduated from Rutgers; by age 23, he was head coach at Johns Hopkins. He went on to Bucknell, and then to Iona, a small Catholic school in New York with a mediocre basketball program. When he coached there, he hugged his players as they came off the court and yelled encouragement. In five years, he led Iona to a 95-46 record and two NCAA tournament appearances. When he was only 34, North Carolina State hired him, and he led his teams to two conference titles and seven NCAA tournament appearances.

But in 1992, a spinal scan for back pain revealed bone cancer. He bore his chemotherapy and pain gracefully, continuing as a broadcaster for ESPN and ABC. When he accepted the Arthur Ashe Award for Courage at the American Sports Awards two months before his death, he arrived in a wheelchair and shuffled to the podium. There he delivered a message that came deep from his heart. He concluded his speech with these memorable lines, "I know I gotta go. But I have one last thing to say. Cancer can take away all my physical abilities. It cannot touch my mind, it cannot touch my heart, and it cannot touch my soul. And those three things are going to carry on forever."

❧ ❧ ❧

I REMEMBER THE MIND, HEART, AND SOUL OF A LOVED ONE.

"An optimist expects his dreams to come true; a pessimist expects his nightmares to."

— Laurence J. Peter

OPTING FOR OPTIMISM

It has been estimated that 10 times as many people suffer from severe depression as was the case 50 years ago. But is that such a surprising statistic? With businesses failing, inflation rising, unemployment lines growing, unrest at home and abroad, and the number of violent crimes soaring, it's increasingly difficult to find positive people and uplifting topics of conversation. Pessimism is all around you, while optimism is suspect.

Think about the conversations you have with people. Do you prefer to talk about the problems and hassles in your life, or do you focus on personal achievements and light-hearted, entertaining anecdotes? Do you find yourself drawn to those who discuss tragic topics and doomsday predictions, or do you prefer to listen to those who make you laugh or who have something interesting and exciting to share?

The other side of nightmares are dreams; the other side of pessimism is optimism. Optimism, although not "in vogue," has been known to fight depression, enhance personal achievement, ease the symptoms of stress, and result in improved physical, emotional, and spiritual health.

Today, you have a choice as to how you're going to act. Can you stop looking for or focusing on the dark side of life? Can you switch to a more positive outlook and seek out pleasurable people and activities? Choose now: Will you be a pessimist or an optimist?

❦ ❦ ❦

I OPT FOR OPTIMISM TO CREATE POSITIVE OUTCOMES IN MY LIFE.

"You go on a diet. Then you eat some chocolate cake, and you punish yourself by feeling guilty. Half an hour of punishment for the chocolate cake. It's absurd."
— author Peter McWilliams

GETTING RID OF GUILT

How do you go about clearing your guilty conscience and the accompanying feelings of low self-esteem and depression? Guilt over anything—cheating on a diet, cheating on your taxes, or cheating on your spouse—is really anger at yourself about something you didn't think you should have done, or something you should have done, but didn't. Either way, you lose because you not only did or didn't do something, but you're also mad at yourself because of it.

Guilt is an absolutely useless emotion. Its sole purpose is to inflict self-punishment. If you enjoy feeling guilty, then you probably enjoy punishing yourself. But if you don't, then there are positive ways for you to make things "right" in your mind so you no longer feel guilty.

First, face the music and admit what you did. This means being honest with *yourself*, not necessarily having a "true confessions" session with someone else. Next, stop the behavior that's causing you the guilt. If you're guilty over hitting your child, then decide that physical punishment will no longer be an option in disciplining. Then, seek professional help or support in working through your guilt. Heed the advice that is given you.

Finally, forgive yourself by identifying what you learned from this experience, and resolve to respond differently next time.

❀ ❀ ❀

I TAKE STEPS TO RELEASE MY GUILT.

"Patience is power; with time and patience the mulberry leaf becomes silk."

— Chinese proverb

PATIENT GROWTH

You're part of a universal pattern of growth that renews itself in cycles. Night to day, spring to summer, youth to middle age—all give birth to something new within you. You're not the same person at this moment that you were yesterday; you're not even the same person you were when you read the quotation above. If you can trust in this process of change and renewal, then you'll find that your moods stay pretty consistent. You trust that your periods of darkness will be followed by the light, that solutions to problems will eventually be found, and that injury and illness will heal. But when you're impatient, your moods bounce up enthusiastically with each cycle of growth and renewal, and they fall down with each cycle of dormancy and sameness.

Working in a garden can teach you how to become familiar with such cycles. The seeds that need to be planted in the spring for summer growth can't be planted now, for they won't germinate and strengthen in time for the full summer sun; the fruit trees you prune today won't bear fruit ready for picking until the fall.

You and the projects you undertake, like the seeds you plant, have different seasons. Some spring up quickly. Others take longer to germinate, even longer to bear fruit. All the impatience in the world won't change this process. As Minon Drouet said, "To make a peach you need a winter, a summer, an autumn and a bee, so many nights and days and sun and rain, petals rosy with pollen—all that your mouth may know a few minutes of pleasure." So, too, it is with you.

ya ya ya

I ALLOW MYSELF TO PATIENTLY HEAL, CHANGE, AND GROW.

"People think responsibility is hard to bear. It's not. I think that sometimes it is the absence of responsibility that is harder to bear. You have a great feeling of impotence."
— Henry Kissinger

HELPING YOURSELF

When is "the right moment" to seek help for how you're feeling? Some people feel "the sooner, the better." Others feel it's best to seek help at the first warning signs of depression. Still others ask for help when all their usual attempts to help themselves aren't working. Right now is a good time to think about the criteria you'd like to use to determine the right moment for you to seek help. For example, you may wish to seek help:

- when you can't prioritize or sort out your feelings,
- when you can't get out of bed,
- when you're having problems sleeping,
- when you can't work,
- when you isolate yourself,
- when you start thinking about ending a relationship or quitting a job, or
- when suicidal thoughts start.

Create a list of your own criteria or add to this suggested list. Then, when you feel you need help, contact a health care professional, attend a support group, or telephone a close friend. Taking responsibility for yourself is one way out of your depression.

ॐ ॐ ॐ

I DETERMINE THE RIGHT MOMENT TO SEEK HELP.

"There are boxes in the mind with labels on them: To study on a favorable occasion; Never to be thought about; Useless to go into further; Contents unexamined; Pointless business; Urgent; Dangerous; Delicate; Impossible; Abandoned; Reserved; For others; My forte; etc."

— Paul Valéry

USING POSITIVE LANGUAGE

Read the following words slowly to yourself: *unhappy, gloomy, sullen, weepy, morose, frowning, hopeless, sorrowful, negative, bitter, miserable, despairing, suicidal.* Take a moment to reflect on how speaking and hearing the words makes you feel.

Now read the following list in the same way: *joyful, happy, joking, silly, delighted, inspired, carefree, sweet, jolly, cheery, pleasant, funny, smiling, rosy, wonderful, upbeat.* How do these words make you feel?

When a situation in your life causes you concern—the stability of your job, your relationship, or yourself—the way you sort and label it in your mind can often determine how you feel about it. The labels you use can also influence how you'll handle the situation—by taking positive action or by viewing it as hopeless.

Author Vernon Howard once described a man who every day wrote down "beautiful words" in a small notebook. Each morning the man read aloud parts of his list. When a situation arose during the day, the man would use the words to label the situation. To explain his habit, the man told a friend, "Because I looked at the world only through rose-colored words, I became rose-colored myself."

From now on, resolve to sort and label the situations in your life with positive, uplifting language. Use this language to influence the actions you'll take.

❧ ❧ ❧

I USE POSITIVE LANGUAGE TO RESOLVE THE SITUATIONS IN MY LIFE.

"Pain with the thousand teeth."
— poet Sir William Watson

SOOTHING PHYSICAL PAIN

If you suffer from chronic pain—backaches, headaches, arthritis, or pain from an illness or its treatment—then you know that coping with the pain can drain you physically as well as emotionally. However, you can use natural healing methods for temporary or even permanent relief so you can soothe your body as well as your mind:

- Breathe into your pain. When you're in pain, your breathing may be shallow or you may even hold your breath. This only contributes more to your pain. Close your eyes and imagine the site of your pain as a tight knot. Focus on this as you take slow, deep abdominal breaths. With each breath, imagine the knot loosening.

- Keep a pain journal. Observe when and where you experience pain so you can determine whether there are patterns that you can break. For example, you may discover that your pain is most severe when you miss a day of stretching or exercising, after eating or drinking dairy products, or when you don't get enough sleep.

- Eat chili peppers. This food contains capsaicin, which stimulates secretion of endorphins and reduces the release of a neurotransmitter called substance P, which short-circuits the perception of pain. Include chili peppers in your favorite recipes.

- Use body therapy. Select a massage therapist who can be sensitive to your sites of pain or who's familiar with acupressure. Work together to discover what's most comfortable for you.

🖗 🖗 🖗

I CHOOSE STRATEGIES THAT HELP SOOTHE MY PAIN.

"You have to leave the city of your comfort and go into the wilderness of your intuition....What you'll discover will be wonderful."

— Alan Alda

SELF-LIMITING THINKING

There are those who see themselves as continually failing or having bad things happen to them. In contrast, there are those who routinely see themselves accomplishing whatever they want to do and who mentally program themselves for success.

The difference between someone who submits to defeat and someone who achieves success has nothing to do with ability. Rather, it's "all in the head"—what their mind believes they're capable of.

How can you activate your mind to be filled with less negative "programming" so you can dispel some of the self-limiting beliefs you have about yourself and your abilities? You can do this by "mental reprogramming." First, think about some of your beliefs about your limits. You might say, "I don't stick to getting things done," "I can't ask for help when I need it," "I'm never going to be good at anything," and so on. Then, for each belief, "reprogram" it with an opposing statement. For example, "I did stick to getting my yard work done last weekend, so I can stick to getting things done," "I can ask for help from my support group, so I can ask for help when I need it," "I am good at working with computers, so I can be good at some things," and so on. Say each new statement aloud. Then, the next time you think a self-limiting thought, use this reprogramming method to think in more positive terms.

❧ ❧ ❧

I REPROGRAM MY THINKING SO I MAKE POSITIVE PROGRESS.

"If a person has experienced the depths of despair and the heights of elation, they have a way of articulating what those contrasts are about."

— Fred Goodwin

MILD MANIC DEPRESSION

A milder form of manic-depressive illness, cyclothymia, is often characterized by continual mood swings. The ups and downs may last from weeks to months, but never develop into a full-fledged manic-depressive illness. Unlike someone who's depressed, if you're mildly manic you may enjoy the ups you experience and not recognize that you have a problem until you experience the symptoms of depression.

What are some of the "manic ups"? They include:

- increased self-esteem or grandiose thinking;
- a decreased need for sleep;
- racing thoughts or the inability to stop talking;
- an increased sex drive;
- an inability to concentrate or to prioritize;
- a desire to take large risks or impulsive actions; and
- overdoing things socially, on the job, at school, or around the house.

While it may be tempting not to view mania as a form of depression—you may feel so good that it's difficult to think you might have a problem—the fact that you eventually experience depression symptoms that are quite the opposite of those on the above list indicates that you may need help. Seek treatment to smooth out your mood swings so you don't feel so high—only to feel so low.

ఇa ఇa ఇa

I SEEK HELP FOR MY HIGH AND LOW MOOD SWINGS.

"Today is not yesterday...How then, can our words and thoughts, if they are always to be the fittest, continue always the same? Change, indeed is painful, yet ever needful...."
— Thomas Carlyle

TREATING DEPRESSION

Early treatment strategies for depression were bizarre, cruel, and, in most cases, useless. In ancient Greece, priests threw depressed patients into the sea from a high cliff. Other priests waited in boats in the water below to rescue the patients from drowning. In ancient Phoenicia, the mentally ill were boarded on a ship and set adrift. During the Middle Ages in Europe, exorcists coaxed "demons" from the bodies of those who acted strangely. As late as 1806 in the United States, a Vermont man was treated for depression by having his head held down in a bucket of water. When the first treatments were unsuccessful, his head was held under for increased lengths of time until he drowned.

Treatment for mood disorders is now based on providing effective and appropriate help. Since many infectious diseases such as mononucleosis and infectious hepatitis can generate psychiatric symptoms, medical treatment is important. Daily stress as well as the stress of traumatic life events can cause depression, so changes in lifestyle as well as meditation and relaxation techniques can help. Hormonal imbalances of the thyroid gland can create a mind-body connection that can respond to treatment. Know that you can seek help and find relief!

ஃ ஃ ஃ

I LIVE WITH DEPRESSION WITHOUT SUFFERING WITH IT.

"I can pardon everybody's mistakes except my own."
— Marcus Cato the Elder

AIMING FOR PERFECTION

Do you believe you must be unfailingly competent and almost perfect in everything you undertake—or you'll lose the respect, love, and approval of others? Do you believe in the existence of perfect love and a perfect relationship—or you won't find the right person so you'll be able to live happily ever after? Do you believe that your worth as a person depends on how perfectly you achieve the things you do—or you're no good?

Such perfectionistic thoughts are unrealistic. A more rational assessment of your worth depends on your capacity to be fully human and alive. Belief in a perfect partner and perfect love often results in unhappiness and resentment in the search for the "perfect fit." And believing you must always be perfect can make you hesitant to try anything for fear of failure.

Promoting realistic thinking, rather than perfectionistic thinking, is one way to get through this. Whenever you find yourself thinking about one of your beliefs about perfectionism—for example, "I should be able to do everything perfectly" or "I ought to have no conflicts with my partner," ask yourself, "Is there any rational support for this idea?" Discovering that your ideas of perfection are of your own irrational creation—rather than the way things really are—can help you let go of your need to always hit the mark right on the bull's eye. As George Fisher said, "When you aim for perfection, you discover it's a moving target."

ॐ ॐ ॐ

I SIMPLY DO MY BEST AND KNOW THAT IT *IS* THE BEST.

Dawn is a shimmering of the horizon.
Dusk is a settling of the sky.

— Tao

SAYING GOODBYE

Sunrise and sunset together represent the measure of a day. When the sun rises, the moon sets; when the moon rises, the sun sets. Without such alteration, a day would neither have a beginning nor an end. It would not be complete.

So, too, are there cycles in your life. There are endings as well as beginnings. It's easy to view the loss of a loved one as an ending; you may also understand that your life after this loss can be a beginning. But until you effectively say goodbye to your loved one, there may be a certain level of emotional incompleteness that may prevent you from moving beyond the loss to a new beginning. One way to say goodbye is to write a letter as if your loved one were still alive and could hear the letter being read. Write about what's emotionally incomplete between you—the things you wanted to say, but weren't able to; the conflicts you wanted to resolve, but were left hanging; the things for which you wanted to make amends, but couldn't; the dreams you wanted to share, but didn't.

Write as long as you feel the need to write. You'll know you're finished when you write: "I love you" and feel there's nothing more to say. Imagine that your loved one is sitting across from you. Read your letter aloud. If your throat gets tight or your tears fall, let them. Then "look" at your partner and tell him or her goodbye. Not goodbye to the love and memories you shared together, but goodbye to the pain and confusion you once had, which has now ended.

૭ૹ ૭ૹ ૭ૹ

I SAY A FINAL, AFFECTIONATE FAREWELL TO A LOVED ONE.

"As I continued my healing, I learned depression was once the traditional path to 'soul fitness,' the way exercise is the path to body fitness today. For hundreds of years, melancholy was treasured as the characteristic of creative genius, the introspective quality that gave birth to great talent, leadership, and invention. I began to ask myself: If depression was once of use, could it not be converted into alliance again?"

— author Julia Thorne

THE BENEFITS OF DEPRESSION

In spite of having to deal with periods of mood instability, many people who are working to overcome their depression can boast of amazing accomplishments, personal achievements, and a more enjoyable life. Through their recovery and healing, they discover that their lives can be the way they want them to be. They learn to dream, and they realize that they can achieve their goals. So, too, can you.

There may be a wide range of areas in which you're interested—from sports and recreational activities to carpentry and wood carving to community service for the elderly. Think of the interests you look forward to pursuing in the future. Consider ways in which you'll pursue those interests.

There may be a number of fields in which you feel you're talented or quite knowledgeable—from consumer advocacy to plumbing to horticulture. Think of all the things you're really good at. What skills would you like to develop further?

There may also be significant achievements you've made—from successfully raising a family to making amazing progress in your growth and development in spite of extreme mood swings. Praise yourself for your most significant achievements. Then think of others you'd like to make.

ฆ ฆ ฆ

I TAKE PRIDE IN MYSELF AND MY RECOVERY.

"Exercise is a common prescription for depression, and that no doubt helps explain why I've averaged more than 85 miles a week since the early '80s."

— Scott Douglas

EXERCISE AND DEPRESSION

Many times when people are depressed, grieving, or stuck in "the blues," they will hear: "Why don't you get outside for some fresh air? Take a walk. Go for a run. Ride a bike. Just get moving, and you'll feel better." More often than not, these suggestions are beneficial. But for those people who are or who were habitual exercisers prior to experiencing depression, a loss, or emotional downswings, such advice can sometimes make them feel worse.

For Scott Douglas, an avid runner since the ninth grade who could run close to a five-minute mile pace in a 10K road race, running was at times an antidote to a depression that began for him in the 1980s. However, on some mornings, just the thought of running was too much. The grip that depression had on him was sometimes so powerful that it immobilized him; it was all he could do to get out of bed. His running went from being an antidote to his depression to a symbol of his mental state. He explained, "On such days, running was one more activity that had previously brought me joy, but was then just another in my seemingly endless list of chores. This was so, even though I knew from such experiences that even a few miles would bring a brief abatement of my condition."

Scott's solution to his dilemma was to first seek medical help. His doctor told him that medication could really be of great benefit to him. With it, he could run consistently and enjoy it much more than he had in the past, for he could view running less as a barometer of his psyche and more as an advantage to his life.

❦ ❦ ❦

I AM OPEN TO RECEIVING HELP FOR MY DEPRESSION.

"Guilt upon the conscience, like rust upon iron, both defiles and consumes it, gnawing and creeping into it, as that does which at least eats out the very heart and substance of the metal."

— Robert South

HONORING YOUR VALUES

Your "blue" moods or depression may be the result of a guilty conscience. You feel guilty whenever you violate the conscious or unconscious rules you live by. Whenever you violate the rules, your inner voice says you deserve to be punished. If you're not punished by outside forces, you punish yourself with feelings of inferiority, illness, anxiety, hopelessness, and depression.

To heal yourself, you need to stop violating your moral values and the standards by which you'd expect others to live with dishonesty, scheming, cheating, or self-criticism. You need to start today to bring your behavior into alignment with a rational vision of the kind of person you'd like to be. That doesn't mean that from now on you'll never feel embarrassed, have to endure the anger and disapproval of others, need to make amends, or forgive yourself for mistakes. But what it does mean is that once you admit your guilt to yourself and make efforts to rectify any wrongdoings, you give your cloud of doom and gloom permission to dissipate. You release the hold guilt has upon you.

Now is the time to conduct a searching moral inventory. Ask yourself if you're living up to your standards of behavior. If the answer is no, are you willing to examine your behavior and make the necessary changes so you no longer feel guilty?

ॐ ॐ ॐ

I DO RIGHT SO I START TO FEEL RIGHT.

"I do not believe that sheer suffering teaches. If suffering alone taught, all the world would be wise, since everyone suffers. To suffering must be added mourning, understanding, patience, love, openness and the willingness to remain vulnerable."

— Anne Morrow Lindbergh

FALSE BELIEFS AND NEGATIVE MESSAGES

During the sensitive, vulnerable years of childhood and adolescence, you may have been barraged with dozens of negative messages which shamed you, embarrassed you, or made you believe you were worthless. But just because your father may have said to you, "You're never going to amount to anything" doesn't make it true. Just because your mother may have said to you, "You're so fat and homely" doesn't make it true. Just because your peers may have said to you, "Your family's crazy" doesn't make it true. Just because your teachers may have said to you, "You're not college material" doesn't make it true.

Just because you've heard and perhaps still hear negative messages doesn't mean they're true or that you have to accept them. Even though such messages have inflicted hurt upon you and caused you to suffer, you can learn something from them—that you can take positive steps to reject such false beliefs and negative messages.

Write one false belief or negative message on the top of a sheet of paper. You might write, "I'm no good." Say the belief or message out loud. Then, fill the paper or repeat the following statement several times: "I reject this belief." Do this a few times a day or for several days, until you feel comfortable tearing the paper into tiny bits and throwing it away.

ॐ ॐ ॐ

I REJECT FALSE BELIEFS AND NEGATIVE MESSAGES.

"If I am not for myself, who will be for me? If I am for myself alone, what am I? If not now, when?"

— Hillel, *The Talmud*

SELF-LOVE

If you were in the midst of the most perfect, wonderful, satisfying love affair, what do you imagine your lover would be doing for you? Asking you how you feel? Attentively listening to you? Comforting you with hugs and gentle caresses? Doing something nice for you, like preparing a delicious meal or putting your favorite music on the CD? Surprising you with a bouquet of flowers or a special gift? Reassuring you that you're doing well?

You deserve to have such time, attention, and energy lavished on you. But it's unhealthy to expect or believe that such things ought to come from someone else. You need to live each day as though you're in a glorious, satisfying, comforting, and never-ending love affair—with yourself! How can you demonstrate such self-love? Give yourself a little gift—a take-out order from your favorite restaurant, tickets to a ball game, or a bunch of freshly picked flowers. Compliment yourself on some of the things you did today, your appearance, or on a risk you're taking. Set aside time each day for play, exercise, rest, and meditation. Say affirming statements to yourself such as, "I deserve to be treated well; such treatment will begin with me." Then, each night before you go to bed, tell yourself, "I love you." Treat yourself as if you were your perfect lover—with gentleness, kindness, and respect—and view yourself in warm, loving ways.

୬ଫ ୬ଫ ୬ଫ

I BEGIN A LIFE-LONG ROMANCE WITH MYSELF.

"Life shrinks or expands in proportion to one's courage."
— Anaïs Nin

INNER COURAGE

When you decide that you want to lift yourself up out of your depression or "blue" moods, then you need to have the courage to do those things that will make you feel good about yourself instead of the things that make you feel terrible. That may mean that you need to take an unflinching and honest look at yourself to see what you may be doing that's not helping to change how you feel. You may need to fearlessly identify and observe the ways you're pulling yourself down. And you may have to call upon your inner strength to make a firm decision that you want to discontinue such negative thinking or self-defeating behaviors.

Today, you can make up your mind to start doing the things that give you pride and pleasure in yourself and in living. If you enjoy playing a musical instrument, going on day trips or long drives, working with wood, canoeing, playing softball, or horseback riding, then do these things. Start to alleviate your low moods by bringing them under control in positive ways—through meditation, by keeping busy, by spending time outdoors, or by maintaining a balance of rest and good times. And develop new attitudes that can help you enjoy yourself and your life more. Be good to yourself, refuse to feel guilty, focus on living one day at a time, laugh, and endorse and affirm all your efforts. The courageous actions you take today have the potential to affect the quality of your life for years to come.

ぷ ぷ ぷ

I CALL UPON MY INNER COURAGE TO LEAD ME BACK TO LIFE.

"'Tis greatly wise to talk with our own hearts, and ask them how we stand toward God and heaven; where we have failed; and how we may avoid failure in the future; how to grow wise and good; how others bless, and be ourselves approved, by God, and conscience, and our fellow-men."
— Edward Young

MEETING YOUR SPIRITUAL NEEDS

Each day you may try to meet your physical needs by eating, sleeping, and exercising. You may attempt to meet your emotional needs by sharing your feelings with others. But how do you meet your spiritual needs? These needs include quiet time for meditation, connecting with the wonder and splendor of nature, developing inner peace through relaxation, and asking for spiritual guidance through prayer.

Perhaps the only times you meditate are when you're bored or stressed out. Perhaps the only times you take a walk in the woods are when someone pulls you out of bed or away from the television. And perhaps the only times you pray for help and guidance are when you're in the middle of a crisis or overwhelmed by your emotions.

It's certainly easy to ignore spiritual needs. They don't cry out for attention like your other needs do. You won't starve if you don't meditate, and you won't pull a muscle by not praying. But you also may not be able to feel better without a spiritual resource. From now on, set aside five minutes a day in which you can close your eyes, breathe deeply, and share who you are and how you feel with your Higher Power.

🐟 🐟 🐟

I MEET MY SPIRITUAL NEEDS.

"All animals except man know that the ultimate purpose of life is to enjoy it."

— Samuel Butler

LIVING IN THE WORLD

American naturalist John Muir wrote that "most people are *on* the world, not in it—have no conscious sympathy or relationship to anything about them—undiffused, separate, and rigidly alone like marbles of polished stone, touching but separate." Muir's own sense of enjoyment and appreciation of life led him to found the Sierra Club, to campaign in Congress to preserve the natural wilderness, and to establish Yosemite National Park.

When you're depressed, you're of the world but in your own world—a world that excludes no sympathy or relationship to anything or anyone around you. But you can re-enter the world by developing inner awareness in four areas:

- In yourself. Ask: "Is there something I can do to create greater health and wholeness in myself?" Take these actions.
- In your work. Ask: "How can I promote greater cooperation and understanding? Can I communicate my ideas more clearly? Can I include a new person on a project?" Take these actions.
- In your relationships. Ask: "What can I do to connect with my friends, my family, my partner, my neighbors? How can I expand my circle to include others?" Take these actions.
- In your environment. "What can I do to clean up my living space? Are there ways I can help the plants and animals in my area?" Take these actions.

ಱ ಱ ಱ

I ENJOY LIFE BY CONNECTING WITH MYSELF AND THE WORLD AROUND ME.

"If life is a bowl of cherries, what am I doing in the pits?"
— humorist Erma Bombeck

MOOD DISORDERS

A mood is an emotion that temporarily discolors all aspects of your life. When you're angry, for example, that anger often extends out to people and things beyond the source of the anger. For many people, such moods aren't a problem because they often dissipate quickly. But for others, moods may persist long after the triggering circumstances have passed. It's when a mood goes beyond its "normal" lifespan that it can become a serious liability to healthy emotional functioning.

When a mood or moods impair your work, relationships, and potential for happiness, then you have a mood disorder. You may have a depressive disorder in which you experience one or more periods of major depression in your life. Or you may have a bipolar disorder—a series of moods that include at least one manic period and one or more periods of major depression.

Knowing all you can about mood disorders empowers you to make good decisions about your treatment, lifestyle changes, living space, parenting style, career, and relationships. Being educated enables you to ask the right questions and empowers you to discover on your own, or with the help of another or others, the most appropriate self-help or professional treatments. Visit the library or your local bookstore to locate books on the subject and treatment of mood disorders. Subscribe to newsletters with valuable wellness information produced by mental health organizations. Attend workshops and seminars, where you can meet others who share what you're going through.

ﻬ ﻬ ﻬ

I EDUCATE MYSELF ABOUT MY PARTICULAR MOOD DISORDER.

"Now what can I tell you? Last year, two or three—goes way back, I suppose—I can remember entertaining suicidal thoughts as a college student. At any rate, I've always found life demanding. I'm an only child of lower middle-class people. I was the glory of my parents. 'My son the doctor,' you know. I was always top in my class. Scholarship to Harvard. Boy genius. The brilliant eccentric..."

— from the film, *The Hospital*, written by Paddy Chayefsky

MAKING A PHONE CALL

Do you believe you can't possibly be depressed because of all the things you have—an enviable college degree, a successful job, an impressive financial portfolio, beautiful children, a comfortable home, gorgeous clothes, or striking physical features?

Take the example of the corporate lawyer who practices on Fifth Avenue in New York City and sometimes stares out his window on the 30th floor. He thinks of all the things he has—a beautiful country house in Connecticut, a perfect wife, more money than he needs, a secure job, and the respect of his family, friends, and colleagues. "How can I say I'm not happy?" he asks. "Look at everything I have. Who would believe me? Who could I talk to? What would people think of me?" So, day after day, he sits at his desk and tries to avoid the window, because all he wants to do is jump out and end his misery.

You're not alone in your feelings of confusion and despair. Nor are you alone in your reluctance to want to reach out for help. But help is just a telephone call away. Today, contact a hotline or make an appointment with a therapist. Ask for help.

৯৯ ৯৯ ৯৯

I ENTRUST MY FEELINGS TO SOMEONE QUALIFIED TO DEAL WITH THEM.

"Look well into thyself; there is a source of strength which will always spring up if thou wilt always look there."
— Marcus Aurelius

BELIEVING IN YOURSELF

A writer knows that a first draft is just the initial step towards creating a manuscript. There's often much polishing and revising that needs to be done before the writer can send the manuscript to a publisher. And even when the writer is willing to share the book with the world, what is then involved is the process of waiting to hear from a publisher, possible rejection letters, or disappointment that stems from having to do additional research or to rewrite further.

Every day in your life is like a first draft. It's just a first step you take in working towards the kind of person you'd like to become and the kind of life you'd like to have. Sometimes this can feel bright and exciting, like finishing your first draft of a novel. So you may end the day on a satisfied, relaxed note. Other times it can feel dark and depressing, like the hard work and dedication that's involved in believing in your book when others don't. Then you may end your day feeling restless and unfulfilled.

The writer uses a belief in his or her talents to get through the "dark times" of self-doubt and waiting for a publisher. So, too, can you make it through your dark times by focusing on the skills you have. Before you begin your day and then again before you go to sleep, identify at least three of your strengths. By seeing what you do best, you'll be sharpening your determination that can lead to achievement and success.

ॐ ॐ ॐ

I BELIEVE IN MYSELF IN TIMES OF DARKNESS AND IN LIGHT.

"Since modern man experiences himself both as the seller and the commodity to be sold on the market, his self-esteem depends on conditions beyond his control. If he is 'successful,' he is valuable; if he is not, he is worthless."

— Erich Fromm

RISING ABOVE FAILURE

When Thomas Edison and his assistants had finished an improved prototype of the first electric light bulb, Edison handed the bulb to a younger helper. As the boy nervously carried the fragile bulb up the stairs, he dropped it. Hours more work had to be put into producing another light bulb. When it was finished, Edison handed it once more to the boy who had dropped the first one, who gingerly carried it to safety in another room.

In that simple gesture, Edison may have changed the boy's feelings of self-worth from failure and incompetence to success and self-confidence. Rather than let his young worker wallow in a mistake, by giving him another chance Edison taught the boy that he could rise above his failure. Being unable to rise above your mistakes and failures can prevent you from getting up when you've been knocked down. But failure can be a learning experience. From now on, look upon the mistakes and failures in your life as valuable teachers. Instead of saying, "I blew it," ask, "What can I learn from this?" And then, "How can I use what I learn so I can try again?" Your capacity to learn from your mistakes and move on will be key to your ultimate success and achievement—as well as to a secure, serene self-image.

ﾃ ﾃ ﾃ

I RISE EACH TIME I FALL AND LEARN SOMETHING IN THE PROCESS.

"I don't know who—or what—put the question. I don't know when it was put. I don't even remember answering. But at some moment I did answer 'Yes' to someone or something. And from that hour I was certain that existence is meaningful and that, therefore, my life, in self-surrender, had a goal."

— Danish philosopher Dag Hammarskjöld

INNER FEARS

Are you troubled by inner fears? You are if you don't like your job or relationship, but you're afraid to change. You are if you're afraid to take chances. You are if there's something you'd really like to do, but you're afraid if you try you'll fail. You are if you'd like to be more successful, but feel you don't deserve it. You are if you're afraid that if you make the changes you'd like, people won't like you. You are if you'd like to experience more success in your life, but you're afraid you can't handle it.

Many people stay in dead-end jobs and unhappy relationships because they're afraid of change. The unknown is full of threat. So no matter how bad their situation and how horrible it makes them feel, they stay in it because they at least they know what to expect. They aren't willing to say yes and surrender their fears.

The next time you face a challenge in your life that causes you fear, visualize yourself doing the thing you fear. Get as clear a picture as possible. What are you doing? What do you look like? How do you feel? Then ask yourself, "What's the worst thing that can happen if I do this?" Think about your answer. Exploring the consequences can help to dispel your fear of the unknown. Your inner fears will be shadows that fall away in the light of greater awareness.

ॐ ॐ ॐ

I DEAL WITH MY FEARS BEFORE I TRY SOMETHING NEW.

"Noble deeds and hot baths are the best cures for depression."
— from *I Capture the Castle*, by Dodie Smith

GAZING MEDITATION

More and more people are using relaxation techniques—also referred to as meditation—to make themselves feel better, to gain more of a sense of control in their lives, to give them a feeling of safety, to enhance the ability to sleep, to restore clear thinking, to refresh their mind, to diminish tension, and to increase the ability to deal with symptoms of depression.

There are many different ways to meditate, but any way you choose leads to the same result. One meditation you can do while taking a hot bath or sitting quietly in your favorite chair is called gazing. Set the object of your choice on a surface that's at eye level and about a foot or two away from you. Choose something simple such as a flower, a burning candle or stick of incense, a crystal, or a favorite stuffed animal. Take three deep abdominal breaths, then gaze at the object while keeping your eyes and body relaxed. Notice everything about the object—its texture, shape, color, size, and how it smells. Trace the edge of the object with your eyes as you take in all the minute details that you might not ordinarily notice. If you become distracted, simply return your gaze to the object.

Practice the gazing meditation twice a day for two weeks. Each day, compare how you felt before trying the meditation and then after. At the end of two weeks, consider whether this meditation has affected your mood or helped you to respond in more positive, effective ways in your life.

ॐ ॐ ॐ

I PRACTICE MEDITATION TWICE A DAY FOR INNER PEACE.

"Depression was a very active state really. Even if you appeared to an observer to be immobilized, your mind was in a frenzy of paralysis. You were unable to function, but were actively despising yourself for it."
— from *Kinflicks*, by Lisa Alther

EARLY WARNING SIGNS

As you become more aware of your low moods or periods of depression and how you feel during them, over time you may discover early warning signs that can alert you to an impending downturn in your emotional state. Such signs may be quite subtle, such as carelessly stepping off a curb out onto a busy street instead of looking both ways first; what this may tell you is that when you start to pay less attention to protecting yourself, you're feeling down. Others may be more recognizable, such as staying in bed on a beautiful summer day, eating junk food, or feeling like giving up.

One way to help you get in touch with early warning signs is to make notations in a Daily Planning Log. On a sheet of paper, create four columns. In the first column, titled TIME, divide the time in which you're usually awake into one-hour blocks, starting from when you get up to when you go to bed. In the next column, titled PLANNED ACTIVITY, write what you expect to do within that one-hour time period. The next column, titled ACTUAL ACTIVITY, is where you enter what you actually did in that one-hour block. The last column, titled HOW YOU FELT, is where you record how you feel about your actual activity compared to your planned activity. When you start to pay attention to such early warning signs, you can then take action that can help you to avoid a long-term "blue" mood or a deep depression.

ॐ ॐ ॐ

I LEARN WHAT MY EARLY WARNING SIGNS ARE.

"There is perhaps no more effective way to relieve psychic pain than to be in contact with another human being who understands what you are going through and can communicate such understandings to you."
— from *Resilience*, by Frederic Flach

FRIENDS AND SUPPORTERS

One of the most common catalysts for recovery from grief, despondent moods, or depression cited by individuals is the support another or others gave them. All people need at least five good friends or supporters they can call on when they need someone to talk to. Some of the things supportive people can give are:

- empathy—they can say, "I understand what you're going through" or "I've been there, too";
- recognition of strengths—they can point out and validate individual achievements;
- attention—they can set aside time to listen as well as to encourage fun activities for a balanced recovery;
- open-mindedness—they can accept the good as well as the bad, the silly as well as the serious, the mundane as well as the shocking;
- acceptance—they can acknowledge the ups and downs in the recovery process without being judgmental; and
- help—they can provide guidance for each step along the way.

Think of five people who can be your support. If you can't identify five friends or family members, consider joining a support group or contacting a health care professional so you make contact with others who could be part of your support list.

ﾟﾟ ﾟﾟ ﾟﾟ

I SELECT FIVE PEOPLE I COUNT ON TO BE THERE FOR ME.

"Man spends his whole life running from feeling with the mistaken belief that you cannot bear the pain. But you have already borne the pain; what you have not done is to feel all that you are beyond that pain."

— Bartholomew

RELEASING YOUR FEELINGS

There's an old story told by Chuang Tzu about a man who was so afraid of the sight of his shadow and the sound of his footsteps that he ran away from them. But the more he ran, the faster the footsteps sounded after him and the more swiftly his shadow followed close behind. Falling into a panic, he ran faster and faster until he finally died of exhaustion. What he didn't realize was that if he had only stopped running, what he feared would stop chasing him. Resting in the shade of a tree would have made his shadow disappear and the sound of the footsteps cease.

You may believe that your feelings are the cause of your pain, so you run from them. But the truth is that it's the very act of running from your feelings that causes you pain. The more you avoid feeling and expressing your feelings, the greater and longer your pain. If you stop running, your pain stops. Then you're left with a whole lot of unexpressed feelings, often accumulated from years of living in fear. What this signals is that you have work to do—work that may be difficult but may also give you a chance to finally live in the present and experience your feelings as they happen.

Today, begin to feel your sadness, grief, anger, and joy. Begin to express all of your feelings by crying, laughing, screaming, and smiling. Feel them, express them, and release them. Then you can begin to walk in a new direction.

ॐ ॐ ॐ

I STOP RUNNING AND START FEELING.

"Be willing to accept the shadows that walk across the sun."
— Emmanuel

ALLEVIATING DEPRESSION

Many people besides you have experienced depression at least once in their lives. The predominant effect of any depression is a loss of energy. Few things, if any, seem interesting; levels of motivation and enthusiasm drop. Although such emotions may feel terrible, people in the grips of depression are often able to do the chores they need to do to get through each day. They go to work, pay bills, cook meals, and maintain relationships. Such "functional depression" may feel rotten, but life can continue on in spite of it.

But what may make this depression most difficult to deal with is the sense of helplessness and powerless you're experiencing. You may feel as if you're trapped by it, unable to overcome it. Although concerned friends may try to cheer you up by saying, "Things will get better—try to look on the bright side," you're not going to be able to see this bright side until you can discover ways to dispel the shadows of your depression.

What can you do when you're getting or feeling depressed? Seek help while you can; the longer you wait, the harder it gets. Plan your day with a balance of some activities you have to do and some activities you enjoy doing. Give yourself credit for even the smallest things you're able to get done. Call upon spiritual resources. Listen to or help someone else. Get some exercise. And remember that depression passes; focus on living one day at a time.

ஓ ஓ ஓ

I DO THINGS TO HELP ALLEVIATE MY DEPRESSION.

"Peace does not dwell in outward things, but within the soul; we may preserve it in the midst of the bitterest pain, if our will remain firm and submissive. Peace in this life springs from acquiescence, not in an exemption from suffering."
— François de S. Fénelon

HONESTY

Picture in your mind a calm lake, its surface like glass reflecting the sky and the full trees along its edge. A short distance from shore a group of geese float smoothly along the surface. With their long necks extended gracefully, they barely create a ripple on the surface of the lake. You may take in this scene and marvel at how serene it is. But is it, really? What you don't see, below the surface of the water, is a flurry of webbed feet furiously churning. What you're unable to feel is the strong pull of a current that courses through the deep part of the lake. This visualization can teach you a lesson: Things are not always as they seem.

So, too, it may be with you. Your smiling face may not reflect your broken heart. Your efficiency as a worker may not reflect the nervous approval-seeker you are inside. Your responsible adult image may not reflect the hurting, angry child within. And your sleeping face may not reflect the terrible nightmares you dream.

Are you like the smoothly floating geese because you try not to let anyone see your struggles? Keeping up appearances isn't helping you out—or letting anyone in. Today, think about letting go of your deceptions and letting someone in. Resolve to be honest and show the emotions that exist under the surface.

 youth youth youth

I RESTORE INNER PEACE THROUGH HONESTY.

"Chances are right now you are standing in the middle of your own acre of diamonds."

— motivational speaker Earl Nightengale

PERCEPTIONS

The Chinese gardener uses things wisely so nothing is over-looked and lives by the philosophy that nothing is wasted. A good example of this has been exhibited by gardener Peter Chan, whose beautiful gardens have won awards and been featured in magazines and on national television. When Chan moved his family to a new home in Oregon, the yard was filled with hard clay soil and large stones, enough to make even the most skilled gardener unhappy at the prospect of ever making a passable garden emerge from such difficult conditions. But Chan saw the yard not as a problem, but as an opportunity. He enriched the clay soil with compost and used the stones to form neat pathways between the raised beds of his vegetable garden.

Your happiness and satisfaction, like Chan's view of his new property, depend upon your perceptions. If you perceive that you're standing in the middle of a hot, airless desert, then that's where you are. If you believe you're in the middle of a stagnant, smelly bog, then that's where you are. But if you believe you're standing in the middle of an acre of diamonds, then *that's* where you are.

When you're flexible, resourceful, and open to new possibilities, you can see the value, beauty, and potential in any situation. As the *Tao* teaches:

> *Wise people seek solutions;*
> *The ignorant only cast blame.*

Are you standing in your own acre of diamonds and don't even know it?

🪷 🪷 🪷

I SEE THE GEMS IN MY LIFE TODAY.

"Enthusiasm is the yeast that makes your hopes rise to the stars. Enthusiasm is the sparkle in your eyes, the swing in your gait, the grip of your hand, the irresistible surge of will and energy to execute your ideas."

— Henry Ford

SETTING GOALS

How would your life be different if, from this moment on, you made up your mind to do things instead of just trying to do them? How would your actions be different if you eliminated the word *try* from your vocabulary and inserted the word *can*? Instead of saying, "I'll try to stick to an exercise program," you could say, "I do stick to an exercise program." Rather than saying, "I'll try to set aside time to be with supportive people," you could say, "I do set aside time to be with supportive people." Instead of saying, "I'll try to change my diet to improve my moods," you could say, "I do change my diet to improve my moods."

Wouldn't your life be filled with potentials rather than possibilities, intentions rather than insecurities, and results rather than repeated attempts? The difference between believing you can *try* and believing you can *do* is the difference between having doubt in your abilities and faith in yourself.

How do you foster faith in yourself—faith that you can do something? Start by tackling little things. Jog three blocks, not three miles. Schedule one evening a week to be with supportive people. Read one self-help book, not all the books in the library. Change your eating habits at one meal. Set a small, easily attainable goal for something you've wanted to do. Rather than focus on the end result, concentrate on simply beginning.

૪૦ ૪૦ ૪૦

I TAKE ONE SMALL STEP TO A LARGE GOAL.

"I have no money, no resources, no hopes. I am the happiest man alive."

— Henry Miller

MATERIAL POSSESSIONS

Society seems to encourage accumulating material possessions in order to be happy. Every day manufacturers announce new and improved products, the latest must-have gadgets, and "in" fashions. As a result, your dresser drawers and closets may be jam-packed, your living room filled with wall-to-wall electronic equipment, your car loaded with the best options, and your garage and attic piled high with excess furnishings. But are you any happier?

Learning to purchase only what you need, to use it completely or frequently, or to know when to give it away to those who are less fortunate provide the true foundation for happiness. By not buying into the belief that you need to own everything you're told you "have to have," you can reduce the compulsive work ethic of having to work hard and be successful so you can earn enough money to support your lifestyle.

It has been said that great trouble comes from not knowing what is enough, that conflict arises from wanting too much, and that once you know when enough is enough, there will always be enough. Try shifting your focus today from accumulating more to enjoying the things you already have. Sweep away the clutter in your life by cleaning out one area in your home, discarding anything you don't need, and recycling or donating it to a worthy cause. Freedom from wanting everything can help you relax and enjoy the things you already possess.

ぞ ぞ ぞ

I SIMPLIFY THE OVERLOAD OF MATERIAL POSSESSIONS.

"There is an Indian belief that everyone is a house of four rooms: a physical, a mental, an emotional and a spiritual room. Most of us tend to live in one room most of the time, but unless we go into every room every day, even if only to keep it aired, we are not complete."

— author Rumer Godden

DAILY PRAYERS

Do you pray to a Higher Power only before meals at holiday gatherings or just in times of crisis? Ralph Waldo Emerson once observed that "God enters by a private door into every individual." At this moment, whether you "need" your Higher Power or not, do you have your spiritual room ready—or even a door that leads into this room?

One way to welcome your Higher Power into your "house" is to begin communicating through daily prayer. You may wish to use a familiar prayer each night before you go to bed, perhaps one learned by rote in childhood: "Our Father, who art in heaven..." "Now I lay me down to sleep..." or "The Lord is my Shepherd, I shall not want..." You may like to rely upon spiritual readings from other religions or cultures. You may prefer to create your own prayer— one that addresses the particular areas of your life in which you feel you need spiritual guidance and wisdom. Or you may like to repeat an affirmation, a short proverb, or a helpful slogan.

What's most important about opening your "house" and making this spiritual room available is that you do it every day. By making such communication part of your routine, you may discover a more profound—and much more rewarding—relationship with God.

ঞ ঞ ঞ

I FIND TIME EACH DAY TO PRAY.

"What the hell are you talking about a tumor? Do you know what your trouble is? You don't have enough to occupy your brain so you put a tumor there to fill the space."
— Martin Balsam's character in
Summer Wishes, Winter Dreams

PHYSICAL SIGNS OF DEPRESSION

Sometimes depressions and "blue" moods can feel very much like physical illness or may even be disguised as such. You may complain of backaches, headaches, muscle tension, flu-like symptoms, nausea, chest pain, stomachaches, constipation, fatigue, weight changes, or sleep problems when, in reality, you're experiencing a physical response to your depression. But because of the physical symptoms, you may use over-the-counter medication for temporary relief or make an appointment with a physician.

When the medication doesn't work or your doctor's physical examination reveals that no disease is present, you may start to exhibit characteristics of hypochondria, excessively worrying about your physical health. You may abuse drugs or alcohol to soothe the physical aches and pains you're experiencing. Or you may become wildly imaginative, speculative, or morbidly negative about your physical ailments, believing your chest pain signals heart disease, or that your poor concentration and headaches signal brain tumors or Alzheimer's Disease.

While depression is a physical disorder, because it's first and foremost associated with changes in brain chemistry, the accompanying psychological symptoms are what need to be treated. Drug therapy and psychotherapy are both viable methods of initiating helpful intervention for depressive disorders.

&a &a &a

I PAY ATTENTION TO THE PHYSICAL SIGNS OF EMOTIONAL STRESS.

"I don't like people who have never fallen or stumbled. Their virtue is lifeless and it isn't of much value. Life hasn't revealed its beauty to them."
— from the film *Doctor Zhivago*

NECESSARY GROWTH

"Hard times" is a label you may often hear during times of great unrest or social and economic change. But even hard times can offer opportunities for growth, times of pleasure, and rays of hope. While the Great Depression was, economically and emotionally, a miserable time, it was also a great time in the entertainment industry. In fact, the 1930s are known as the "Golden Age of Entertainment," for wonderful music, great radio programs, and two outstanding movies—*Gone With the Wind* and *The Wizard of Oz*—were created then.

What if those things you perceive today as hard times—things that make you stumble and fall on your way to growth, self-fulfillment, and happiness—are really times of great opportunity? What you may now view as an obstacle on your road to success or an unbearably heavy load you must carry—a job layoff rather than a promotion, a loss of financial security rather than the ability to pay your debts, an ending of a marriage rather than the celebration of your anniversary, the loss of a loved one rather than another day spent together—could actually be the paving stones you need for building a new road to success. It depends on how you look at your hard times—as obstacles that trip you up, or opportunities that encourage you to climb higher. Believe in the words of an unknown author, who wrote: "I may be in an uncomfortable situation, but it is necessary in order for me to grow."

ॐ ॐ ॐ

I GROW OUT OF ANY HARD TIME.

"Tears may linger at nightfall....Carefree as I was, I had said, 'I can never be shaken.' But Lord, it was Thy will to shake my mountain refuge...."

— Psalm 30

SYMBOLIC CHALLENGES

Hollis Hunnewell had planned someday to take part in the arduous 100-kilometer MacLehose Trail race up and down the nine mountain peaks on China's Kowloon peninsula with his brother Peter, who lived and worked in Hong Kong. But that "someday" came sooner than he expected when his brother was killed in a motorcycle accident. Overcome with grief and exhausted from the 24-hour flight to Hong Kong with his family to claim his brother's body, Hollis came up with the idea to do something in Peter's memory as he "was sitting on a rowing machine at Peter's health club wearing his sneakers."

Climbing all nine peaks in the MacLehose Trail race has been equated with climbing Mt. Everest; it has both trails and severe peaks, and is so grueling that medical stations are set up along the way. Hiking and running through the night without sleep, wearing a miner's headlamp and carrying his brother's flashlight, Hollis finished the 62-mile-plus race in 22 hours and 33 minutes. Even though he already had a bad left knee and hip and threw his right knee out in the race, he has no regrets. He calls his run a gesture of brotherly love—the best tribute he could give his kid brother.

Today, pay tribute to someone you've lost. Seek out a challenge that symbolizes his or her life. Then meet this challenge. In doing so, you'll be paying the highest tribute to your loved one.

❦ ❦ ❦

I EASE GRIEF BY DOING SOMETHING IN MEMORY OF A LOVED ONE.

"Laughter and tears are both responses to frustration and exhaustion....I myself prefer to laugh, since there is less cleaning up to do afterward."

— Kurt Vonnegut

LAUGHTER AND TEARS

Sometimes you may not see the importance of laughter during dark times because you're blinded by your tears, immobilized by your grief, or incapable of feeling anything other than anger. But being able to laugh at life's ongoing daily hassles as well as in the face of incredible tragedies such as illness, death, and loss can provide you with the same much-needed physical and psychological benefits that laughter can give you at other times, including helping keep things in perspective, as well as keeping you in balance when your life seems totally out of balance.

In addition, remaining open to levity in even the most solemn situations can help you stay physically healthy. As Proverbs 17:22 says, "A merry heart doeth good like a medicine." Laboratory studies have shown that laughter affects most, if not all, of the major systems of the human body. Your cardiovascular system is exercised as your heart rate and blood pressure rise and then fall. Your breathing creates a vigorous exchange in your lungs and a healthy workout for your respiratory system. Your muscles release tension as they tighten up and then relax again. In fact, hearty laughter is very much like aerobic exercise.

While crying is important and should not be suppressed, at some point in your distress and pain, continued crying may not be the healthiest thing. But humor is.

ॐ ॐ ॐ

I PUT MY TEARS IN PERSPECTIVE SO I LAUGH.

"Prayer is one of life's most puzzling mysteries. I have sometimes feared it is presumptuous of me to take up God's time with my problems."

— Celestine Sibley

SAYING YOUR PRAYERS

How do you learn to pray? What do you ask for? What do you say? Do you get down on your knees, bow your head, or lift your face to the heavens?

Sometimes, in trying to answer such questions, you may forget the purpose of prayer. You may feel inhibited about praying to an unseen presence. You may feel as self-conscious "talking" to a Higher Power as you do communicating with others. You may let your low self-confidence influence you into thinking that your prayers don't measure up to the eloquence of the sentiments expressed by a moving preacher or inspirational literature. These may be just a few reasons why you may feel unworthy of praying to a Higher Power.

When you begin to think like this, remind yourself why you pray and what it can do for you. Although you may never describe your prayers as articulate or perfect, it's the act of praying that matters. You pray as an expression of your gratitude as well as your suffering, of your helplessness as well as your purposefulness, of your fears and doubts as well as your trust and faith, of your powerlessness and helplessness as well as your strength. As Hannah More points out, "Prayer is not eloquence, but earnestness; not definition of hopelessness, but the feeling of it; not figures of speech, but earnestness of soul." Your Higher Power will hear you, no matter how you choose to pray.

ಜಿ ಜಿ ಜಿ

I MAKE THE EFFORT TO PRAY TODAY.

"When the beginnings of self-destruction enter the heart, it seems no bigger than a grain of sand."

— John Cheever

TIMING MOOD SWINGS

Do you often find that you start your days filled with hope and promise, but end up negative and despairing? Do you sometimes feel like you're a different person in the morning than you are at night?

You may experience an increase in the intensity of your "blues," grief, or depression as the day goes on. If this is the case, take a look at what you're doing in the morning that helps you avoid such intensity. Perhaps you take a few moments before you get out of bed to focus on what you need to get done for the day. Maybe you exercise alone or with a partner. Perhaps you listen to music, write in your journal, or meditate. Or maybe just the simple act of getting out of bed and staying busy helps ease your despondent moods.

To track how the day's progression affects the intensity of your moods, use a scale of one to ten to rate your moods from less intense to more intense to most intense five times a day—morning, noon, mid-afternoon, early evening, and night. After doing this for a week, you'll discover at what time of day your moods are most intense. Then ask yourself, "How am I going to deal with this in the future?" You can replicate activities you perform during your times of less intensity at other times; for example, if you do 15 minutes of stretching and yoga exercises in the morning, you can also do them around the time when you're most susceptible to low mood swings.

ஃ ஃ ஃ

I TAKE NOTE OF HOW THE TIME OF DAY AFFECTS MY MOOD.

"I don't think homosexuality is a choice. Society forces you to think it's a choice, but in fact, it's in one's nature. The choice is whether one expresses one's nature truthfully or spends the rest of one's life lying about it.

— Marlo Thomas

GAY/LESBIAN SUICIDE

You may have had suicidal thoughts at one time or another in the past. In fact, the U.S. Department of Health and Human Services reports that 30 percent of all teen suicides are gay and lesbian youths. When you were initially coming to terms with your sexuality as a teenager, when your first gay relationship ended, when your parents overreacted or rejected you because of your way of life, when you struggled to be happy in a heterosexual relationship or marriage, when you had to deal with the death of a partner or close friend, or when you first learned you were HIV positive—all these difficult situations may have led you to contemplate or even try suicide.

For years, you may have been able to release all thoughts of suicide and lead a relatively happy, stable life. But today, for whatever reason, you may once again be feeling unhappy, hopeless, depressed, and suicidal. That's when you need to call someone. Talk it out with a friend, bring it up at the next meeting of a support group you belong to, or make an appointment with a counselor or spiritual advisor. When you open up, you'll find friends and peers who can be understanding and caring.

Even in your sexuality, you're not alone. Everyone feels like giving up from time to time. But today, don't give in to the feeling.

ॐ ॐ ॐ

I LET SOMEONE HELP ME WHEN I FEEL LIKE GIVING UP.

"Whatever comes, this too shall pass away."
— Ella Wheeler Wilcox

ENDURING THE PAIN

When you're in a distressing situation, it may seem as if all the clocks and calendars in the world have stopped. There you are, trapped forever in your tough time like a fossil in a rock. But time, like everything in nature, moves on. You can trust that the sun and moon will rise and set, the tide will ebb and flow, and the seasons will change. Because you can rely on the fact that such things will happen, you can also rest assured that they're part of the natural rhythm.

Time also takes care of you. One of the best ways to trust that your difficult situation won't last forever is to remember that life, like nature, is forever in motion. Think back to some of the worst times you experienced in the past. Review how they began, how long they actually lasted, and how they eventually ended. What this shows you is that there will, in fact, be a timely resolution to your present difficulty.

You can also take a determined action that symbolizes change, points you in the direction of change, or even moves you towards making that change. For example, you can write how you feel in a journal, update your résumé, or arrange to have a friend help you sort out the things that belonged to a loved one. Remember, it's not really true that what's going on for you right now will last forever. As Charles B. Newcomb observed, "The ebb and flow of will is like the movements of the tides....If you cease your vain struggles and lamentations long enough to look away from the personal self...we realize life is going well with us after all."

☙ ☙ ☙

I TRUST THAT WHAT I'M GOING THROUGH WON'T LAST FOREVER.

"The human body is not a thing or substance, given, but a continuous creation. The human body is an energy system...which is never a complete structure; never static; is in perpetual inner self-construction and self-destruction..."
— philosopher Norman O. Brown

"LISTENING" TO YOUR BODY

Learning to listen to and respect your body can help you uncover and discover more about your emotional state so you can pay attention to the mind-body connection and heal yourself both mentally and physically. Here are some ways you can do this:

- When things in your life that are difficult or painful come up, notice your breathing, your heart rate, and your bodily sensations. Be aware of how things on the outside affect your body on the inside.
- When you experience a sensation such as back pain or a headache, ask: "Are emotions such as anger or fear connected with this pain?"
- Notice how you routinely "talk" to your body by listening to yourself when you look at your body in the mirror. Do you criticize your face, legs, stomach, or hair, or do you give your body positive messages? Do you routinely apologize to others for how you look or gracefully accept compliments that are given? Have you given up on your body, or are you proud of the exercise and diet program you've been able to follow?
- Recognize that every time you eat on the run, skip meals, or fill your stomach with sweets or high-fat, high-sodium foods, you unnecessarily place your overall health at risk.
- Acknowledge that your body, like you, is a miracle.

ॐ ॐ ॐ

I "HEAR" MY BODY'S LANGUAGE.

AUGUST 10

"You need a vacation. You've been cranky since your last birthday. Didn't you know it's in to be over forty now?... They call it middle-age zest."

— writer Linda Morley

AGING ZESTFULLY

Finding yourself with physical limitations due to aging can bring frustration, sadness, and a strong sense of loss. You may miss the things that you're no longer able to do. You may resent health problems when they're painful, make you feel weak and tired, and restrict your movement and your life. You may even get angry at your body because you want to do everything the way you used to—and you can't. As one middle-aged woman commented, "I have reached a stage in my life that I had not given much thought to. Somehow I thought that I would continue as active as I had been in the past. This is not so."

But just because you feel over the hill doesn't mean you can't pedal up it in lots of different ways. Regular physical activity and exercise can help improve energy and increase stamina and endurance—as long as you don't assume you have to continue these activities at the same pace. Try walking, gardening, swimming, and exercising at a slower pace, or for shorter periods of time. You may find you enjoy these activities more when you ignore any feelings of haste or the need for achievement.

Thinking, meditating, watching, and listening are also as worthwhile as more strenuous activities. In your younger years, you may have been too busy and rushed for such reflection. But now that you can't rush, you can turn to these quieter pursuits if you wish.

ঞ ঞ ঞ

I CONSERVE MY ENERGY BUT STILL EXERT EFFORT.

"Laughing at ourselves is possible when we are able to see humanity as it is—a little lower than the angels and at times only slightly higher than the apes."

— Tom Mullen

BECOMING PLAYFUL

If you could learn to laugh at your problems, have fun with your mood swings, see the humor in nearly every situation, or even laugh at yourself, you might be more relaxed and much healthier. And you'd have a much better outlook on yourself and your life.

Play is lighthearted activity that has no express purpose and only one essential ingredient—having fun. But most adults don't usually play; if an activity doesn't have a goal or an end result, such as receiving recognition or some sort of award, then it's often not considered to be a valid way to spend time. And when you're an adult and you're depressed or in the midst of grieving, the last thing in the world you may want to be is lighthearted, playful, spontaneous, or joyful.

How can you add laughter to your life? Let the child in you come out to play. You can do this on your own by playing tug-of-war with your dog, building a sand castle, skipping rocks on a lake, or flying a kite. Or you can spend time with children—at a playground, at a children's museum, or at a weekend carnival. When you're with children, you're guided toward the child within you—your own magical, playful self. The gift you receive when playing with children is that of hope—hope that fresh eyes and fresh energies will repair your sorrows within and the world around you. As Fyodor Dostoyevsky writes, "The soul is healed by being with children."

🙧 🙧 🙧

I LOOK AT THE WORLD THROUGH A CHILD'S EYES.

"Tears are blessings, let them flow."

— Harry Hunter

GRIEVING TOGETHER

When you suppress your feelings of loss, it's the same as putting the lid on a boiling pot of water. The longer you bottle up the feelings, the closer you come to serious and detrimental consequences. You may have difficulty sleeping. You may have difficulty making decisions. You may begin to take prescription medication, abuse alcohol, or eat to dull the pain. You may experience anxiety. You may emotionally withdraw from the world. You may start to feel suicidal. You may direct your anger at others—strangers as well as family members. To keep the pot from boiling over, you need to remove the lid and release the stored-up heat; in other words, you need to express your feelings. As Henry Wadsworth Longfellow said, "There is no grief like the grief that does not speak."

The best way to release your feelings is to first find someone who has suffered intense emotional loss with whom you can establish a grief recovery partnership. You may have a built-in partner for your grief recovery in your own family if you're mourning the same death. If not, there are countless places to look for a partner—at work, your church, in your neighborhood, in your circle of friends, or at a support group.

Once you've found your partner, you both need to commit to being honest with one another so you establish a safe space in which to release your feelings. And you need to agree to absolute confidentiality so the cherished things you share—as well as the things you express with anger and regret—are meant for just the two of you.

ॐ ॐ ॐ

I SHARE MY GRIEF OPENLY AND HONESTLY WITH ANOTHER.

"The more faithfully you listen to the voice within you, the better you will hear what is sounding outside."
— Danish philosopher Dag Hammarskjöld

BUILDING SELF-ACCEPTANCE

The way to overcome despondent moods begins with self-acceptance. Without it, you may see life as a constant struggle. You may make war on yourself and others at home, on the job, and in your relationships. You may suffer tremendous emotional ups and downs and strive to gain approval from the outside to make you feel better within. You actually may attain, succeed, and achieve, but those things are never enough, for deep within you lurks a nagging sense of inadequacy.

Building self-acceptance takes time. At first you may notice that what you think and feel about yourself runs through your mind like a constant monologue—a depressing, degrading, fault-finding, nit-picking monologue in which past mistakes are continually brought up, worries about the future are fearfully piled up, and votes of nonconfidence are added up. In the end, such self-talk undermines your self-esteem, making you feel incompetent, weak, and helpless.

You can turn off your monologue by engaging in more positive self-talk. To do so, every day stand in front of a mirror, look yourself straight in the eyes, and tell yourself some things you like and appreciate about yourself. You might say, "I'm really proud of you for exercising this morning," "You made a difficult decision today—I know that wasn't easy," or "You gave some good advice today to someone who really needed it." The regular approval you hear every day while doing this exercise can help to build and strengthen your self-acceptance.

❦ ❦ ❦

I AFFIRM THE GOOD IN ME.

"Seeing through is rarely seeing into."
— Elizabeth Bibesco

RESPONDING TO EMOTIONAL PAIN

It's inevitable that you'll face the emotional pain that results from the loss of a loved one. You have many choices about how best to respond to such pain; some choices will lead to healing, while others may lead to increased pain. How well you work through your grief will depend on which approach you choose. If you react by gritting your teeth and saying, "I'll just get have to get through this" or "I'm not going to cry because someone has to be strong to provide support for others," then chances are you'll deny or suppress your painful feelings. While such actions as denying or suppressing your grief may get you through your tough times and lead you to believe that you're handling your feelings well, in the end they block emotional healing.

How can you promote emotional healing as you grieve? Accept that it's normal to have painful feelings. Give yourself permission to feel your normal emotions, including your distressed feelings. Rather than saying, "I should be strong," say "Tears are a sign of strength, so I'll let them flow." Express your feelings to at least one other person. Stay in contact with supportive friends and relatives and allow them to help you as much you help them. Maintain a realistic perception of your life and yourself. And engage in problem-solving, which promotes growth. This effort begins when you say to yourself, "I feel so sad, but my life must go on. I want to think about what I can do to start putting my life back together."

🦋 🦋 🦋

I RESPOND TO EMOTIONAL PAIN IN HEALTHY WAYS.

"How often we look upon God as our last and feeblest resource! We go to Him because we have nowhere else to go. And then we learn that the storms of life have driven us, not upon the rocks, but into the desired heaven."

— George MacDonald

TRUSTING CHANGE

All life changes are unsettling, no matter what form they take. The end of a long-term relationship may throw you into an emotional tailspin. Sustaining an injury just at a time when you want to be in top physical condition can make you irritable and angry. Losing a childhood pet can cause you to withdraw from people. But you can also become equally affected or as traumatized by welcome changes, such as getting married, moving into your own home, or going after a coveted promotion.

When you're overwhelmed by change, you can turn to your Higher Power as a source of stability and serenity. By relying upon the faith and trust in a Power Greater Than Yourself, you can face the changes you're going through with clarity and purpose. For, when you turn to a Higher Power, your sense of helplessness, hopelessness, loneliness, confusion, doubt, fear, anxiety, and insecurity can be lifted. Through the act of making a conscious contact with a spiritual resource, you can regain your center and re-establish a sense of inner peace.

In a life filled with change, keep your Higher Power as a constant companion and trusted resource. As Ruth P. Freedman writes: "There is a divine plan of good at work in my life. I will let go and let it unfold."

I TURN TO A HIGHER POWER FOR STABILITY AND SERENITY.

"You never enjoy the world aright, till the sea itself floweth in your veins, till you are clothed with the heavens and crowned with the stars."

— clergyman Thomas Traherne

GIVING OF YOURSELF

When you're recovering from depression or a bout with "the blues," you may find that you feel much better when you're doing something for others. When you give of yourself, your own problems have a way of solving themselves. And you feel better about yourself simply through the act of giving.

You can start learning how to give by being mutually supportive to those who have supported you in times of need. This means being there for others when they need you, as well as allowing them to be there for you when you ask. To do this, resolve to pay more attention to the needs of your friends. Ask them how they feel or if they need your help.

You can then extend this outreach to new friends and acquaintances. When you meet someone you like, extend an invitation for coffee, lunch, or to share an activity. Renew acquaintances with old friends by keeping in touch by letter or telephone.

You might also like to participate in community activities and special interest groups. Your local newspaper often lists what's going on. Or you might like to do volunteer work. Inquire at churches, schools, hospitals, youth service agencies, soup kitchens, food pantries, homeless shelters, the Red Cross, and so on.

৯৯ ৯৯ ৯৯

I GIVE OF MYSELF SO I HEAL MYSELF AND OTHERS.

"Bad times have a scientific value. These are occasions a good learner would not miss."

— Ralph Waldo Emerson

LIFE'S LESSONS

So many things may seem to loom over you from time to time, influencing your emotional state. There may be an addiction to alcohol, drugs, food, or people that seems to require your constant attention. There may be fears that fill your anxious mind—fears about expressing love, being alone, being abandoned or rejected, or of failing. There may be miseries of childhood that don't seem to go away—physical, sexual, or emotional abuse—or present-day stresses—unfulfilling relationships, family illnesses, or general dissatisfaction with your life. Sometimes the world as a whole may seem like a place that's filled with people and events that are tragic or frightening.

At such times, it may be hard to see anything that's good or experience anything that's enjoyable. But as Harry Emerson Fosdick said: "Life is like a library owned by an author. In it are a few books which he wrote himself, but most of them were written for him." Every person you meet, each place you visit, each memory you possess, each change you make, and each circumstance you endure contributes to your library of knowledge and experience. That means you need to be open to what happens around you, to listen, and to learn. Growth comes from learning, but only if you see all the events in life as part of one large classroom.

❧ ❧ ❧

I AM A "STUDENT" OF LIFE AND LEARN FROM MY LESSONS.

"Man cannot remake himself without suffering. For he is both the marble and the sculptor."

— Alexis Carrel

PEACEFUL BREATHING

Sometimes the road to wellness is rocky; you may feel stressed and overwhelmed by the changes you'd like to make, the things you need to do for yourself, and the day-to-day effort it takes to stay on a healing path. At such times of high stress and anxiety, you can practice one or more of the following breathing/relaxation techniques:

- Deep breathing. Take several deep, abdominal breaths while sitting comfortably in a chair or lying on the floor or on your bed. Do this whenever you feel upset or overwhelmed or practice once or twice a day.
- Relaxing sighs. Inhale deeply, then sigh audibly, emitting a sound of pleasurable relief as you gently push the air out of your lungs. Then let the air return to your lungs slowly and naturally. Repeat sighing several times whenever you feel tense.
- Focused breathing. Think of a word or short phrase that makes you feel peaceful and relaxed, such as "peace," "love," or "ocean waves." Sit or lie comfortably and close your eyes. Breathe slowly and naturally, repeating your focus word or phrase in your mind as you exhale. Continue for ten minutes. Practice this technique once or twice a day.

Such simple breathing exercises can relax both the body and the mind.

❧ ❧ ❧

I TAKE DEEP, RELAXING BREATHS TO RESTORE INNER PEACE.

*"It's easy to lose our focus, to get lost in other people, exter-
nal goals, and desires...we lose our connection to the universe inside ourselves. As long as we focus on the outside,
there will always be an empty, hungry, lost place inside
that needs to be filled."*

— Shakti Gawain

SELF-FOCUS

Co-dependency is the act of becoming so absorbed in other people, places, and things that you don't have any time left for
yourself. Caring so deeply about others or focusing so obsessively
on externals can lead you so far away from yourself that you may
forget how to take care of yourself or that you have your own
needs.

Losing yourself in a love affair or relationship, in work or school
obligations, or in caring for an aged or ailing loved one can make
you go days, weeks, months, or even years without conscious contact with yourself. When this happens, you may forget that you
even exist apart from whatever it is you're lost in. That's when you
can ask, "Has staying attached to this person or thing helped
me?" Then you need to learn how to develop self-focus.

From now on, tell yourself, "I'm still here." To bring some of the
focus back to yourself, spend time during the day writing in a journal about how someone or something has impacted your life.
Then consider what it would be like to detach. Ask, "If I didn't have
this person or thing in my life, what would I be doing with myself
and for myself that's different from what I'm doing now?" Make a
list of what you'd be doing. Then choose one thing—and do it!

ॐ ॐ ॐ

I DETACH FROM ANOTHER RATHER THAN ATTACH TO ANOTHER.

"Whatever you may be sure of, be sure of this—that you are dreadfully like other people."

— James Russell Lowell

BIOLOGICAL DEPRESSION

When an imbalance or malfunction occurs in the various neuro-chemicals in the brain, biological depression can result. Biological depression is common; in fact, it's among the most common physical disorders seen in psychiatry. Major triggers for biological depression include some that can be rectified by an individual, such as prescription medication side effects and chronic drug and/or alcohol abuse. Others, such as physical illness or hormonal changes, can be alleviated through some forms of medical treatment as well as holistic healing. But one trigger—endogenous depression—is best alleviated through medication. This trigger represents the most common source of all biological depressions and results in a bipolar disorder, in which depression alternates with mania. Each year, approximately two million men and women have manic-depressive episodes.

During the manic phase of a bipolar condition, you can be positive, excited about life, or even euphoric. You may have unusually high self-esteem. You may be active and brimming with ideas, starting many projects. But once the manic stage wanes, the depression stage often emerges. Each time you cycle through the stages can be confusing and frightening. If you feel you might have a bipolar disorder, you'll benefit best from the diagnosis and treatment of a psychiatrist.

ぬ ぬ ぬ

I SEEK DIAGNOSIS AND TREATMENT FOR MY DEPRESSION.

"Panics, in some cases, have their uses. Their duration is always short; the mind soon grows through them and acquires a firmer habit than before."

— Thomas Paine

DEALING WITH ANXIETY

Anytime you experience an anxious feeling, that's a signal that needs your attention. Perhaps your palms are sweaty, you feel edgy and restless, your breathing is rapid and shallow, your stomach is churning, your knees feel weak, you can't seem to stop shaking, or you feel dizzy and lightheaded. Those are all physical signs that your body's trying to communicate with you, to tell you that there's something going on inside.

If you ask yourself what's going on, you might hear answers like, "I'm really scared to be alone," "I'm having a hard time letting go of this problem," "I'm afraid to say what I feel or ask for what I need," or "I don't know that I'm a good person." You may be feeling frustrated, ashamed, guilty, depressed, or fearful about things that are over and done with or things that have yet to come.

One of the best ways to get through a panic attack is to center yourself in the present. You can do this by remembering such things as the date, the time, and the temperature. Then you can identify objects around you as well as what you're wearing. This simple, two-part exercise can bring you back to the present and ground you in a way that removes you from the space you were in that contributed to your attack. Once you're grounded, it can be easier to work through your anxiety and allay your anxious feelings.

ॐ ॐ ॐ

I CENTER MYSELF IN THE PRESENT TO FEEL LESS ANXIOUS.

"But how do older persons or their families tell the difference between naturally occurring, event-related depression and an illness requiring medical treatment?"
— Dr. Nathan Billig

THE ELDERLY AND DEPRESSION

Dr. Nathan Billig, director of the Geriatric Psychiatry Program at Georgetown University Medical Center and the author of *Growing Older and Wiser*, believes that millions of America's elderly population suffer from clinical depression. But because they don't recognize the difference between mourning the losses of their friends and family members and suffering for too long with the severe, grieflike symptoms of depression, they often don't seek help. Many of the elderly, who often attach a stigma to any sort of mental illness and who may feel little need for "mind doctors," fear that how they're feeling might mean that they will be hospitalized or that they will lose what little sense of independence and freedom they have. Others may associate how they feel with the frightening and generally untreatable condition known as Alzheimer's Disease, rather than with depression, which can readily and effectively be treated. And still others may fear that how they feel connects in some way to dementia, so they never get the help they need.

Loss and illness, which come naturally with old age, do have an impact on an elderly person's physical, emotional, and spiritual well-being. But when the impact goes on for a period of months and states of sadness turn into progressively more morose periods, then it's a good idea to seek a doctor's help. While it may be customary to feel gloomy from time to time while growing older, it's not normal to go through day after day of overwhelming feelings of sadness. Prolonged depression is a treatable illness, and it is never too late for treatment.

ॐ ॐ ॐ

I CAN IMPROVE HOW I FEEL NO MATTER HOW OLD I AM.

"When I first open my eyes upon the morning meadows and look out upon the beautiful world, I thank God I am alive."
— Ralph Waldo Emerson

WONDERFUL YOU

Do you know that native palm trees grow in Arizona—not on the desert, but on the shady side of a mountain? Jutting majestically out from the granite sides of a 2,500-foot canyon in the Kofa Mountains of Arizona are the only native palm trees in the entire state. How do the tropical plants live year after year in the dark, on almost perpendicular sides of the narrow gorge? How can they flourish when the sun reaches them only two hours a day? Botanists who have studied this incredible phenomenon have concluded that the stone walls of the canyon reflect enough light and store enough warmth throughout the day to enable the trees to survive in this seemingly uninhabitable environment.

So, too, can it be with you. You can flourish and grow despite your grief or depression. Even when you don't feel sunny and warm inside, you can take time to notice and marvel at natural wonders. Even when getting out of bed feels like you're scaling a steep cliff, you can issue your mind and body challenges that allow you to do things you never thought you were capable of. Even when the thought of death is appealing, you can choose life—and you can survive against all odds. As St. Augustine remarked, "Men go abroad to wonder at the heights of mountains, at the huge waves of the sea, at the long courses of the rivers, at the vast compass of the ocean, at the circular motions of the stars; and they pass by themselves without wondering."

ᔕ ᔕ ᔕ

I SEE THE WONDERS IN ME.

"Lately it's been a colossal effort to drag yourself out of bed. It's impossible to concentrate on your work. Your head-aches and sleeplessness make it worse. Weekends are no better. Golf used to be fun, but it turned boring. Even sex is a chore."

— journalist Brian O'Reilly

GIVING TREATMENT TIME

You may know you're depressed because you not only feel de-spondent, but you're also experiencing many of the warning signs—a considerable increase or loss in weight, sleeplessness or oversleeping, fatigue, slowed body movements, feelings of worth-lessness or guilt, inability to concentrate or make decisions, and thoughts of death. Now the biggest problem you may face is choosing and then sticking with antidepressant medication or psychotherapy.

The U.S. Department of Health and Human Services says that a typical trial on medication can last four to six weeks, therapy six to eight weeks. There's also a difference in price. Six weeks on the av-erage dose of one of the new antidepressants—Prozac, Paxil, or Zoloft—can cost from $105 to $125, while once a week on a psy-chotherapist's couch for that long could cost $600. Insurance plans generally pay for 80 percent of medications, but only half of therapy.

If the treatment you embark on doesn't begin working within eight weeks, your doctor may start or change medication. If you don't feel therapy is helping after that same time period, you can find a more compatible therapist. What's most important is making a choice and then giving it a chance for several weeks.

❧ ❧ ❧

I WAIT TO SEE THE EFFECTS OF THE TREATMENT I'VE CHOSEN.

"My father told me, 'You gotta keep progressing or you decay.' So rather than atrophy mentally and physically, I just keep forging ahead."

— Clint Eastwood

GROWING OLDER

Even though he's in his sixties, actor/director Clint Eastwood shows no signs of slowing down. "Some people long for retirement," he said. "I don't. I look forward to doing my best work in the present or the future."

In American society, aging is often thought of as an entirely negative experience. Most people are so hooked on youth that they haven't recognized that inexperience and great reserves of physical stamina aren't always virtues; rather, knowing what you're doing, where you're going, and the steps you want to take to get there are the real strengths.

Maturity can give you a chance to do many new things, to develop yourself in new ways, and to set your sights on more distant goals. Just because aging can physically erode your body and slow your pace doesn't mean that your mind is similarly eroded or your determination and faith are fading.

You can find great security in the knowledge that you've still got many more goals you can set and attain—no matter what your age. Think of at least one vital, challenging interest that you'd like to enjoy now or when you retire. Maybe you'd like to learn to fly an airplane, do more creative writing, go back to college, or travel to a foreign country. Visualize yourself enjoying this interest, keep in mind that anything's possible, then take steps to acquire it.

❧ ❧ ❧

I LOOK FORWARD TO MY BEST WORK OR MY GREATEST GOALS.

"We are all serving a life-sentence in the dungeon of self."
— British critic Cyril Connolly

BUILDING SELF-ESTEEM

One of the most self-destructive forms of distorted thinking is called emotional reasoning. This is the mistaken belief that everything you feel about yourself must be true. For example, you may feel you're stupid so you conclude that you must be. You may think that you're not worth anything, so you view yourself as worthless. You may believe that you've never accomplished anything in your life, so you surmise that you'll never accomplish anything. You may label yourself as lazy, so you procrastinate or refrain from taking any action. You tell yourself that you're alone in the world, so you believe that no one wants to be around you.

By imprisoning yourself with such beliefs, you lock yourself into a perpetually low level of self-esteem that ensures that you'll never be released from your depression. The only way around such thinking is by substituting a positive or assertive thought for the negative one—creating a positive comeback for your self-deprecating one-liners. If, for example, "I will never be well" is part of your thought process, then you can write this statement on a piece of paper. Below it, write some thoughts you can use to change that distorted thinking into thoughts that are more positive.

Examples include: "I'm having a hard time right now, but I'm working at getting better," "I'm basically a strong person," "Mood swings aren't anyone's fault, not any more than the flu or cancer. I'm doing the best I can to get well," and "People with the kinds of problems I have do get well, and they stay well for long periods of time."

🍃 🍃 🍃

I PROVIDE POSITIVE RESPONSES TO NEGATIVE THOUGHTS.

"Animals are natural therapists. They offer warmth, unconditional love, the benefits of feeling needed and secure, a sense of family, encouragement to exercise, and sensitivity to your moods."

— educator Janet Ruckert

PETS AS HEALERS

Watching, stroking, playing with, or talking to your pet can have an immediate beneficial effect on your body. The presence of an animal can reduce blood pressure, ease stress, and lower anxiety. Greeting your dog, holding a bird on your finger, or even observing tropical fish in a tank can bring about therapeutic change. Owning a pet is like having an instant relaxation therapist.

Pets can also be self-esteem enhancers. They are always loving, available, and completely uncritical of you. Oftentimes your pets believe that, as their master or mistress, you're the most wonderful person in the world—the center of their universe. So it may not be surprising that, as you talk to your pets and touch them, you say better things about yourself than you would while talking to yourself or other human beings.

Additionally, interacting with your pet can help you adjust to major life changes—job loss, divorce, death, or recovery from an illness or injury. In a study at the Center for Interaction of Animals and Society, the mortality rate among people recovering from severe heart disease who owned pets was one-third that of people without pets.

Finally, the antics of unpredictable, curious, and energetic pets can offer you a daily dose of pleasure and fun. Through pets, you can learn how to laugh and play so you can enjoy life more.

ॐ ॐ ॐ

I LET MY PET HELP ME IN MY RECOVERY.

"Having made a discovery, I shall never see the world again as before. My eyes have become different; I have made myself into a person seeing and thinking differently. I have crossed a gap, the heuristic gap which lies between problem and discovery."

— Michael Polanyi

FUTURE HEALING

There are so many ways in which you can experience healing from grief, depression, or "the blues." Julia Thorne, author of *You Are Not Alone*, wrote about her own recovery: "I didn't use just psychotherapy or medications to get well. Over the years I learned to meditate, get regular exercise, write poetry, eat well, and pay attention to not getting overtired. I learned visualization and relaxation techniques and alternative healing practices. I joined groups and took workshops so that I could be with people. I found it helpful to make a list of things I could do to help myself."

What Thorne discovered was that there's not one "cure" for depression, a "right" or "wrong" way to treat the disorder, or one approach that works better than others. Her recovery options touched upon healing her mind, body, and spirit. This whole-person approach encouraged her to live her life differently, in much healthier and more helpful ways.

Could you benefit from making a list of things you could do to help yourself? In creating such a list, you're not only dealing with how you're feeling and healing in the present, but also on how you'll deal with feelings that need to be healed in the future. Right now, anticipate your need for healing today as well as tomorrow. Think of at least five things you can do whenever you're feeling depressed. Keep this list handy at all times.

ఘ ఘ ఘ

I ANTICIPATE THE NEED FOR FUTURE HEALING TODAY.

"Everything one records contains a grain of hope, no matter how deeply it may come from despair."
— Elias Canetti

KEEPING A JOURNAL

Do you keep a journal or diary? How often do you add to it? On a daily basis? Whenever you're going through a crisis or a particularly difficult time? After you've experienced a life trauma? When something happened to someone else you feel is significant? Or only when you have a few free moments when you're not doing something else—something more urgent?

Getting into the habit of writing regularly in a journal can accelerate your growth, take some of the fear out of making changes or taking risks, make the impact of goal-setting and achieving more significant in your life, track the pattern of your mood swings, reacquaint you with yourself, and help you to pay attention to the small but significant progress you're making. Writing about your feelings, thoughts, and actions can help you get into the habit of taking a personal inventory—looking at yourself to see where work is needed. Through regular journaling, you can also develop a solid and practical awareness of what works and what doesn't work in your life. You can then apply this knowledge in situations and interactions as they occur. If, for example, you feel as if you're about to "fall apart," you can take a few minutes to write about your emotions, the reasons for them, and how you can quiet them. The personal progress you can make by journaling can help you learn and grow.

☙ ☙ ☙

I CREATE AN ONGOING RECORD OF MY PAST, PRESENT, AND FUTURE.

"Life is truly known only to those who suffer, lose, endure adversity and stumble from defeat to defeat."
— Polish journalist Ryszard Kapuscinski

BECOMING VICTORIOUS

When an elephant returns to a former watering hole only to discover that it's rock-hard dry, it doesn't cry out, "Oh, woe is me! Woe is me! This is a disaster! I'm going to die now." Instead, it continues to search until it's able to locate another water source.

Can you find the advantage in your disadvantage? People who can do so not only look for some positive aspect in their setbacks, but actually go one step further. After their initial shock, they gather their resources, overcome their problem, and see opportunities where most fail to see them. Many who have experienced a major loss often go on to achieve remarkable feats in spite of their ordeal because they focus on what they can gain from their circumstance rather than on what they have lost. As Art Linkletter said, "Things turn out best for people who make the best of the way things turn out."

Often it's the most difficult passages in your life that give it meaning and mold you into who you are today. So you can continue to stumble and fall from your misfortunes and losses or you can pick yourself up, dust yourself off, and learn and grow from your experience. One way to do so is to stop labeling your defeats and losses negatively; for example, calling them tragedies, disasters, setbacks, or defeats. Instead, call them gains, gifts, new paths, crossroads, challenges, or victories.

ॐ ॐ ॐ

I MOVE FROM VICTORY TO VICTORY.

"So long as we cannot accept the fact of what we are at any given moment of our existence, so long as we cannot permit ourselves fully to be aware of the nature of our choices and actions, cannot admit the truth into our consciousness, we cannot change."

— author Nathaniel Branden

RESOURCES FOR TREATMENT

Occasional "blue" moods often don't require professional treatment since they're part of the human condition. However, more serious and prolonged periods of depression are cause for concern. Depression, in addition to causing considerable emotional suffering, can also lead to functioning problems that may result in job loss, divorce, estrangement from families of origin, and homelessness.

The feeling of depair experienced in depression may lead you to think that no one can help you or you'll never get out of that state of mind. But there are a number of resources besides private psychiatrists or psychotherapists. Look them up in your telephone directory, or call directory information for a number for your:

- community mental health center,
- county health department or department of social services,
- hotline or crisis line telephone service,
- college or university counseling center, or
- family services center.

ℬ ℬ ℬ

I EXPLORE RESOURCES FOR TREATMENT.

"Pessimist: One who, when he has the choice of two evils, chooses both."

— Oscar Wilde

THINKING YOUR FEELINGS

The way you look at and interpret the events of your life will have a lot to do with how you feel. If you perceive and think about a situation in a very realistic fashion, then the resulting emotions will be normal, and you'll eventually be able to heal from them. For example, the normal emotional response to a loss is sadness or grief, which eventually leads to emotional healing. When experiencing normal sadness, you would not be flooded with extreme pessimism.

But if you perceive a situation in a distorted way, then the results are extreme pessimism, an erosion of your feelings of self-esteem and self-worth, and destructive emotions that increase misery and block healing. Often, when a depression or "blue" feeling begins, most likely it's because you've been thinking in ways that are negative and pessimistic.

Because you may not even be aware of the inner thinking that occurs during times of emotional pain, an effective way to become more aware involves using these feelings as signals or cues. The next time you notice an unpleasant feeling, use this emotion to let you know that something's going on. Ask yourself these questions: "What's going through my mind right now?" "What am I thinking?" "What am I telling myself?" and "What am I perceiving about the situation that triggered this feeling?" While it won't be easy to change your feelings right away, you can become more aware of why you're feeling them.

ஃ ஃ ஃ

I FIND THE THOUGHT BEHIND THE FEELING.

"What is the source of our first suffering?...It was born in the moments when we accumulated silent things within us."
— Gaston Bachelard

FROM VICTIM TO VICTOR

A devastating loss or severe upheaval could be an experience that sends you reeling into helplessness and retreat. Without realizing it, you could begin to behave and feel like a victim. For example, rather than work through the grieving process after the end of a long-term relationship or marriage, you may see your partner as the cause of your pain and the dissolution of your relationship. You may hold firmly to the belief that you did all you could to make the relationship work, while your partner was uncaring and unresponsive. And then you may live for years feeling that life has dealt you an unfair blow from which you can never recover. In so doing, you throw away your chance at happiness by suffering in silence—a victim of a painful life event.

The tendency to feel victimized by life's turmoil is a natural first reaction. But the longer you play out your role as victim, the greater the possibility that you will inflict long-term damage on your health and happiness. When you're a victim, you spend your days waiting for life to begin, but it can't until you release your victim mentality.

In the wake of any traumatic upheaval, you have two mental options. You can view what's happening as a dangerous situation in which you stand to lose something or someone, or you can view it as an opportunistic situation in which you stand to gain something or someone. To empower yourself to grow stronger and healthier, focus on the positive aspects of your trauma rather than on the threat it presents to you.

ఇ ఇ ఇ

I BECOME A VICTOR IN LIFE RATHER THAN A VICTIM.

"If we do not find anything very pleasant, at least we shall find something new."

— from *Candide*, by Voltaire

PARTNERING WITH PAIN

It can be very difficult to be patient and persistent enough to confront the painful times that are part of life. When you encounter a crisis, loss, or another bout with depression, you may often wish you could resolve it immediately. You may desperately want it to be over and done with. You may yearn to get on with living in ordinary, familiar, and safer times. So you may think of the situation as an enemy you've met on your battle with life—a foe that either needs to be annihilated or from which you need to flee.

Treating traumatic or difficult life events as enemies can be harmful. When you view situations in this manner, the underlying assumption is that the world is *doing* that particular thing to you. So the dynamic you set up is one that pits you against the trauma. In your drive to avoid, escape, and conquer the ensuing pain, you may be filled with anger, fear, helplessness, resentment, anxiety, loneliness, and annoyance—feelings that will emotionally and physically drain you.

As painful as some life events are, if you can see them as challenges, then you see yourself joined with the trauma in a partnership in which you work together to seek resolution. In forming this type of relationship with the distressing events in your life, you become involved, hopeful, excited, courageous, competent, empowered, enthusiastic, and energetic. This experience of handling life events as challenges perpetuates growth and helps develop valuable coping skills so you can handle other challenges.

৯৯ ৯৯ ৯৯

I FORM PARTNERSHIPS WITH THE PAIN IN MY LIFE.

"When health is absent, wisdom cannot reveal itself, art cannot manifest, strength cannot fight, wealth becomes useless, and intelligence cannot be applied."

— Herophilus

PERSONAL WELLNESS PROGRAM

Here are ways you can make and keep yourself unwell:

- Don't pay attention to your body.
- See life as meaningless and having little value.
- Do what you don't like and avoid doing what you want.
- Be resentful and hypercritical, especially towards yourself.
- Worry and obsess.
- Avoid deep, long-lasting relationships.
- Blame other people, places, and things for your troubles.
- Keep your feelings inside.

Here are ways you can make and keep yourself well:

- Pay close attention to yourself.
- Express your feelings.
- Do things that bring you joy and fulfillment.
- Love yourself and everyone else.
- Be committed to your healing.
- Develop a sense of humor.
- Make a positive contribution to your community.

❧ ❧ ❧

I DEVELOP AND MAINTAIN A PERSONAL WELLNESS PROGRAM.

"Almost everybody in the neighborhood had 'troubles,' frankly localized and specified; but only the chosen had 'complications.' To have them was in itself a distinction, though it was also, in most cases, a death warrant. People struggled on for years with 'troubles,' but they almost always succumbed to complications."

— from *Ethan Frome*, by Edith Wharton

MANAGING YOUR TROUBLES

There's no doubt that the negative repercussions from a variety of difficult circumstances—the death of a loved one, divorce, being fired or laid off from work, retirement, a major change in your financial situation, or a major illness or injury—can be severe. And yet such changes are an inevitable part of everyone's life. You know people who have suffered from or even been ruined by a difficult circumstance; you also know people who have turned tragedy around and made it work for them. What can you do to cope so you don't make a bad situation worse?

To begin with, don't believe for one minute in counsel or comfort given to you by others—or even yourself—that tells you, "You may feel rotten now, but in a few months you will have forgotten all about this," "Every cloud has a silver lining," "God only gives crosses to those who can bear them," "Lightning never strikes twice in the same place," or "Time is a great healer." While such affirmations may be true, they're really excuses not to take action.

Your greatest power, in the face of any adversity, is your ability to choose how you will react—and then to take action. Focus on gaining internal rather than external control. Then progress from a defensive and helpless posture into a position of inner power.

ॐ ॐ ॐ

I MANAGE MY TROUBLES WITH STRENGTH AND CONFIDENCE.

"Whatever does not spring from a man's free choice, or is only the result of instruction and guidance, does not enter into his very being, but still remains alien to his true nature; he does not perform it with truly human energies, but merely with mechanical numbness."

— Oliver Wendell Holmes, Sr.

CHOOSING A PRACTITIONER

How do you sort through often unfamiliar therapies and credentials so you can choose the best practitioner to assist your healing—and get the most from your choice?

Explore your options while you're feeling good. You'll make a less rushed, more thoughtful decision when you're not distracted by physical and emotional strain.

Set up get-acquainted visits with practitioners you're considering. Although shopping around may cost you money, it can be worth the investment.

Network with friends or members of your support group who have had similar symptoms and have obtained positive results with a particular kind of therapeutic treatment or with a particular practitioner.

Don't be afraid to experiment with different medications or recommended therapies, which could include traditional medical treatments, as well as holistic healing techniques. But be clear about your treatment before you agree to it.

Finally, remember that you're in charge. At any time in the process, don't be afraid to stop treatment if you don't feel it's working for you or if you're not comfortable with your practitioner. Trust your own impressions.

ॐ ॐ ॐ

I FIND CARE THAT'S RIGHT FOR ME.

"Every group has its risk takers, its dancers on thin ice....they are the ones with the finely honed skills, those who dare the most, accomplish the most, fly the highest, have the farthest to fall: the high-wire act in the circus, the pitcher in baseball, novelists among writers, litigators among lawyers..."

— Judith Van Gieson

CONQUERING YOUR FEARS

When you're faced with a choice, have you ever thought, "This is an opportunity I shouldn't refuse," and then walk away from it? You may have been too afraid of the consequences of failing in the opportunity, consequences that may include feelings of disappointment, depression, hopelessness, poor self-image, shame, the desire for perfectionism, and so on. Or you may have been afraid of achieving your goal because of the pressure to continue to succeed in future opportunities or the need to make changes in your life based upon your successes.

Risk-taking can be frightening. The worst risk-takers are the people who say, "What do I have to lose?" They have the attitude that if they don't succeed, such failure will validate the negative feelings they may already have about themselves. The best risk-takers are the people who say, "This is what I have to lose, and this is how I'll try to avoid losing it, yet I'll take the risk anyway."

You may be afraid of trying something new because of unknown consequences; your fears are simply fears of the unknown. So resolve to take charge of your life by facing your fears and learning from them. Instead of asking, "What am I afraid of?," reassure yourself with the thought: "Whatever fears I have, I can conquer them."

❦ ❦ ❦

I CONQUER MY FEARS BY TAKING RISKS.

"All other creatures look down toward the earth, but man was given a face so he might turn his eyes towards the stars and his gaze upon the sky."

— Ovid

CONNECTING WITH A HIGHER POWER

It has been said that in order to feel that you're truly one with your spirituality, you need to study a dozen years under the guidance of a good spiritual teacher. But when you're in the midst of a difficult or painful time, you don't want to take such time. You want immediate results—instant spiritual connection.

The need to feel like you spiritually "belong"—to feel connected with a Higher Power, nature, or the universe—can sometimes become an obsession when you're in a time of great need. Like a starving person who constantly dwells on the thought of food, a spiritually hungry person can only think of the connection to the world of the spirit.

You may run off to spiritual workshops or retreats, carry a religious book with you at all times, restructure your life in order to accommodate a rigorous meditation schedule, or purchase numerous books, tapes, and guidance tools for fostering a relationship with a Higher Power. But, as Emmanuel writes:

> *Is this not life's purpose —*
> *to know that you belong,*
> *that you are safe and eternal,*
> *to know that in your spirit reality*
> *you are already one with God?*

ɣə ɣə ɣə

I OPEN MY EYES AND SEE THAT I'M CONNECTED WITH A HIGHER POWER.

"Please understand that there is no one depressed in this house...."

— Queen Victoria

CHILDHOOD ROOTS

The pain of depression is often amplified by a sense of confusion and perplexity, particularly when you can't find any reason in the present why you're feeling so low. It may be beneficial to reflect on your childhood experiences, which you may or may not be aware of, or which you may have blocked out or denied because they were too painful. Many early life experiences can lead to inevitable depression in adulthood or increase vulnerability to chronic blue moods. These include:

- early losses—from death, divorce, or the emotional absence of one or both parents due to alcoholism, workaholism, or other reasons;
- a harsh atmosphere—from physical abuse, to the emotional abuse inherent in comments such as "You're worthless," "You're not wanted," or "You're stupid and lazy."
- lack of support for growth—from "absentee parenting," over-protectiveness and rigidity, perfectionistic demands, and belittling self-expression and independence;
- childhood abuse and molestation—from physical and/or sexual abuse that profoundly damages a child and leads to long-term effects on self-worth, trust, security, and growth in adulthood.

Most children don't "outgrow" these painful childhood experiences. Thus, it's important that you seek help if you suspect a possible link between how you're feeling now and how you felt when you were growing up.

෯෨ ෯෨ ෯෨

I LOOK BACK TO FIND THE CHILDHOOD ROOTS OF MY FEELINGS.

"My life is a perfect graveyard of buried hopes. That's a sentence I read in a book once, and I say it over to comfort myself whenever I'm disappointed in anything."
— from *Anne of Green Gables*, by L. M. Montgomery

NEVER GIVE UP!

Never giving up, despite the odds or obstacles, is not only a test of your belief in yourself and what you can do, but it's also a symbol of how you approach life. When confronted by impending defeat, failure, disappointment, frustration, or rejection, it may be far easier for you to simply give up. But taking such action can shape the attitude you then bring into every situation in your life. And that attitude can spell the difference between long-term success and satisfaction, or a series of defeats.

Leonard Lyons once recounted a story about a very positive—and enlightening—attitude: "A man sentenced to death obtained a reprieve by assuring the king he would teach his majesty's horse to fly within the year.... 'Within a year,' the man explained, 'the king may die, or I may die, or the horse may die. Furthermore, in a year, who knows? Maybe the horse *will* learn to fly.'" Imagine what your life could be like if you could apply a similar attitude to the challenges and risks you face each day. Even in the midst of an impossible situation, you could see a possibility—a ray of hope, a light of success, a moment of brightness, a time of enlightenment. Such a positive, tough-minded, creative approach could turn certain failure into assured success. From now on, let your attitude reflect a "can-do" philosophy rather than a "can't-do" one. Then who knows? Maybe you can even teach a horse to fly!

୫ଟ ୫ଟ ୫ଟ

I KEEP IN MIND THAT BOTH FAILURE AND SUCCESS RELY UPON MY ATTITUDE.

"What stops you killing yourself when you're intoxicated out of your mind is the thought that once you're dead you won't be able to drink any more."
— from *Practicalities*, by Marguerite Duras

TRYING ABSTINENCE

For years, psychiatrists and other therapists sometimes treated depressed people without recognizing that the depression was frequently tied to chemical dependency. Depression has traditionally been a more acceptable diagnosis than alcoholism, and many alcoholics have been admitted to hospitals for "exhaustion" or "depression" when, in fact, they were suffering from chemical dependency.

Alcoholism is now widely considered to be a primary disorder, rather than a symptom of some underlying depression. But some chemically dependent people are still reluctant to admit they have problems with alcohol or other drugs. This is especially true if you're also depressed. You don't want your depressed moods to be ignored, yet you certainly don't want to be told you're only making your depression worse by continuing to use drugs or alcohol. For, if you admit that alcohol and/or drugs play an important role in keeping you depressed, then that would mean that your continued use of such chemicals would imply that you *want* to remain in this state.

If you suffer from depression, you won't be able to feel significantly better over the long term if you continue to use drugs—recreational as opposed to antidepressants—or drink alcohol. Lasting relief relies upon a sober and chemically unimpaired state of mind. That means that abstinence needs to be part of your treatment of recovery from depression.

❧ ❧ ❧

I INCLUDE ABSTINENCE AS PART OF MY RECOVERY.

"If you have made mistakes, even serious ones, there is always another chance for you. What we call failure is not the falling down, but the staying down."

— Mary Pickford

THE PRIDE IN FAILURE

When you take action to make your life and yourself better, sometimes you may fall short of your desires. Just because you opt to take a risk, make a change, or try something new doesn't always mean it will feel great or work out just the way you want it to. That's why it's important to become comfortable with mistakes, errors, and all forms of failure that may occur in your process of healing and recovery.

Consider the following positive statements about failure. Remind yourself of them whenever you become disenchanted or depressed because a desired outcome hasn't happened, you fall short of a goal, or a change isn't right for you:

- Failure tells you what doesn't work and when to change direction.
- Failure leads to new ideas.
- Failure provides you with an opportunity to try something new.

Without the existence of mistakes, failure, or error, there's no risk-taking and no opportunity for growth. As Kathryn D. Cramer, Ph.D., wrote in her book, *Staying on Top When Your World Turns Upside Down*, "I am sure you remember the old adage: 'To Err is Human/To Forgive Is Divine.'... I would like you to take the adage one step further. Modify the first line to read: 'To Err Is Divine.' Repeat the phrase 'To Err Is Divine' as your first reaction whenever you discover that one of your success strategies has failed. Saying this phrase to yourself can make you proud that you have tried to restore your vitality."

ça ça ça

I TAKE PRIDE IN MY FAILURES.

"Happiness is beneficial for the body but it is grief that develops the powers of the mind."

— Marcel Proust

MOVING ON IN LIFE

Sometimes it may feel like you're spending a lot of your time watching too many people you love die from AIDS, cancer, or other illnesses. It can be devastating not only to lose someone close to you, but also to process at the same time the inevitability that others you know will meet the same fate.

How do you get on with your life despite the constant reminder of death? You have a choice. You can choose to sit back and watch your friends or members in your "family of friends" die, putting your life on hold as you immerse yourself in their imminent passing. Or you can decide, "To hell with it! I'm not going to waste my life being depressed and standing hopelessly by waiting and watching. I'm going to make the most of my life and do what I want to do."

It's not selfish to want to live when others you know are dying. It's part of nature. The cycle of seasons tells you that death is never the end; it always marks the beginning in the process of rebirth. While you need time to mourn, you also need time to move on with your life.

Today, think of the losses in your life as reminders that you need to appreciate the time you've been given. As Peter D'Amato said, "There's a lot of rebirth going on. There's only so long you can stay depressed before you realize that the best memorial to your friend is living a happy life."

🌸 🌸 🌸

I MAKE THE MOST OF THE TIME I'VE BEEN GIVEN.

"Sometimes I have insights, although I couldn't tell you what they are at the moment. I will go into a terrible depression and I'll come out of it with the problem resolved."
— author Susanna Kaysen

PROBLEM SOLVING

One day during her lunch hour, a receptionist in a busy medical office building smelled smoke. She searched for the source and eventually discovered that carpenters who were remodeling an examining room had left a soldering iron on. The unattended iron had burned into the flooring.

She unplugged the equipment, then returned to her desk. But when the office reopened after lunch, a commotion ensued. Doctors smelled smoke and began screaming at the nurses, who in turn began shouting at the office assistants. It took the receptionist several minutes to restore calm, having to explain and re-explain what the problem was and how she had already solved it.

In far too many conflicts, people often become either so agitated or depressed that they forget what the problem is and how simple it can be to solve. They'd rather assess blame, become defensive, ponder the root of the conflict, or overanalyze what's really going on.

When fear, confusion, insecurity, or defensiveness are the tools you use for resolution, you rarely have an easy time reaching a solution to any of the problems you face in your life. So from now on, take time to examine a conflict. Be willing to relax so you can find a number of simple solutions. Ask, "What can I do to create greater harmony to resolve this conflict?" Then take this action.

ɤə ɤə ɤə

I ACT INSTEAD OF REACT TO SOLVE A PROBLEM.

"People don't usually complain to their doctors about their mood or tell them they're nervous and anxious. Instead, depressed people often become excessively vigilant about any physical symptoms and commonly ask for medication to address them."

— Dr. Joseph Gerstein, HMO Medical Director

THE DILEMMA OF DEPRESSION

A common response to depression is to suddenly notice things that are physically wrong with you. You may have more frequent or severe headaches. Your joints may ache. You may have tenderness or pain in your muscles. You may have difficulty sleeping or eating. You may have a bowel irritation or irregularity. You may have an upset stomach or a burning sensation in your chest. You may feel lethargic and achy, as if you're coming down with the flu. You may feel anxious and edgy. Or you may have trouble breathing. At best, you may feel that such physical symptoms are temporary and you just have to get through them. At worst, you may think that you have some horrible disease that's slowly killing you.

If you schedule an appointment with a physician, both you and your doctor may only focus on your physical symptoms. You may be prescribed medication to help alleviate those symptoms. But unless you also discuss with your doctor how you feel emotionally, or what current stresses may be present in your life, you may end up making matters worse. For example, taking certain medications such as Valium, oral contraceptives, or medicines used in steroidal treatment, as well as combinations of medicines, can cause or even exacerbate an existing condition of depression. So, your best bet is to focus less on your physical symptoms with your physician, and to be more willing to explore emotional causes and therapeutic cures.

❧ ❧ ❧

I TREAT MY DEPRESSION, RATHER THAN THE SYMPTOMS OF MY DEPRESSION.

"We also discover that depression has its own angel, a guiding spirit whose job it is to carry the soul away to its remote places where it finds unique insight and enjoys a special vision."

— from *Care of the Soul*, by Thomas Moore

THE VALUE OF DEPRESSION

Do you value the darkness within yourself? As you bear your physical, emotional, and spiritual pain, do you feel that it strengthens you and helps you grow? Do you feel that your emotional struggles are valuable? Are you able to trust that, with time, you will feel better?

When you suffer through any emotional crisis, it's easy to panic or be terrified of your feelings. You might even believe that you're going crazy or that things will never get better. You may admit that how you feel is unbearable so you don't have to try to bear what you're going through. You may accept that since you're part of a society in which there's a stigma against emotional struggle and depression, it's far better to deny your difficulty or numb your feelings with alcohol or drugs than it is to deal with what you must.

But emotional pain is a natural part of life; if you deny it, then you're in effect refuting a part of yourself. There's a value in the darkness within you—a guiding spirit that can help you to acknowledge your feelings and to always keep in mind that pain is necessary for your growth. If you listen to your guiding spirit and allow yourself to appreciate the full value of your emotional experience, then you'll soon heal, grow, and live a full, rewarding life.

ʓa ʓa ʓa

I SEE THE VALUE IN MY EMOTIONAL STRUGGLES.

"There is no point in treating a depressed person as though she were just feeling sad, saying, 'There now, hang on, you'll get over it.' Sadness is more or less like a head cold—with patience, it passes. Depression is like cancer."
— from *The Bean Trees*, by Barbara Kingsolver

IDENTIFYING SYMPTOMS OF DEPRESSION

When you say, "I feel depressed," it can mean many different things. Just as it's common to be aware of aspects of a physical illness or injury that hurt the most or cause the most problems so you can treat them, so too can you become aware of the wide array of depression symptoms and which ones are familiar to you. Common symptoms include:

- sadness, despair, sense of loss, emptiness, feeling blue;
- apathy, indifference, low or no motivation, fatigue;
- an inability to experience excitement or pleasure, a loss of enthusiasm for life;
- increased sensitivity to criticism or rejection, anxiety;
- low self-esteem, lack of confidence, feelings of inadequacy;
- irritability, anger, intolerance, impatience;
- feelings of guilt, self-blame, self-hatred; and
- feelings of hopelessness or helplessness.

Depression is a complex condition; as a result, you may experience a combination of symptoms rather than simply an unpleasant feeling. However, taking stock of your symptoms can make it easier for you to know or select what kinds of self-help techniques or professional treatments can be useful.

ℬ ℬ ℬ

I IDENTIFY MY SYMPTOMS SO I TREAT THEM.

"I think I shall always remember this black period with a kind of joy, with a pride and faith and deep affection that I could not at the time have believed possible, for it was during this time that I somehow survived defeat and lived my life through to a first completion, and through the struggle, suffering, and labor of my own life came to share those qualities in the lives of people all around me."

— Thomas Wolfe

SUPPORTING OTHERS

Are there people in your life who are enduring what you've had to go through who could benefit from your experience, strength, hope, and reassurance? Maybe a family member needs a daily telephone call to feel safe and secure. Perhaps a neighbor who recently lost a loved one could use your comforting shoulder to cry on. Maybe a friend who's bedridden or going through a difficult time could use some of your concern and attention. Or perhaps new members of your 12-step support group would benefit from your message of strength and hope in order to guide them through a difficult time.

If you've ever seen a candlelight ceremony, you know how powerful one candle can be. Countless tapers can be lit from that one small flame until a room, a large meeting hall—even a darkened avenue—is brilliant with light.

Others may see you as a flame from which they can light their candles of hope, health, and happiness. Offer encouragement to those who can use it, give support to those in need, provide strength to those who are weak, relate hope to those who are losing faith, and share your experience and knowledge with those who will listen. Let others light their candles from yours.

❦ ❦ ❦

I SHARE THE LIGHT OF MY EXPERIENCE WITH OTHERS.

"Man's main task in life is to give birth to himself, to become...what he potentially is."

— Erich Fromm

BEING AN INDIVIDUAL

At times, are you like a chameleon, changing colors to please others? Chameleons survive because they're adept at hiding from predators. So you may suppress your sad feelings and pretend to be happy and content. You may avoid sharing your truthful thoughts so you don't challenge the image someone already has of you. You may go along with the decision and choices others make for you about your treatment or recovery even though what they choose aren't your preferences. By doing such things, you may feel that you're displaying yourself in the best light, are handling your feelings well, or are showing that you're someone who's easy to get along with. But who's getting to see your real colors? Aren't you ignoring your own healing and growth while making someone else's needs and opinions more important?

Today, keep in mind that when you hide from others, you also hide from yourself. You don't have to be a chameleon anymore. Show your own wonderful colors today. Be yourself—someone who's different from everyone else. Please yourself first, and make your own needs your number-one priority. As Ralph Waldo Emerson wrote, "What must I do is all that concerns me—not what people think. It is easy in the world to live after the world's opinion; it is easy in solitude to live after our own—but the great man is he who in the midst of the crowd keeps with perfect sweetness the independence of solitude."

ॐ ॐ ॐ

I LET MY INDIVIDUALITY SHOW.

"A lifetime of happiness: no man alive could bear it: it would be hell on earth."
— from *Man and Superman*, by George Bernard Shaw

LIGHTENING UP

Do you feel that you're a happiness-impaired person? Have you thought about trying to make happiness a daily habit, like brushing your teeth? Do you ever wonder if happiness is actually a state of long-term euphoria? Do you find it difficult to imagine yourself transformed into the sort of person who greets each day smiling, brimming with energy, always looking on the bright side of things?

The concept of happiness can be extremely disheartening to a depressed person. One brief, happy moment can make you feel as if something is wrong. As *Boston Globe* columnist Diane White described: "It's difficult to convey how stunning the revelation of happiness can be to a depressed person. It takes you by surprise. The clouds part and suddenly you have a glimpse of what life must be like for people who don't walk around carrying the burden of depression. They must feel good a lot of the time. The thought is very depressing."

When you're troubled by the everyday, walking-around type of depression, you learn to live with it and then oftentimes can't imagine life without it. To be in a good mood, to walk with a spring in your step, or to make a decision based upon positive thinking can be foreign.

But making fun of your depression is one way of dealing with it. When you can do so, you may not pave the way to a lifetime of happiness, but you can certainly create a path that leads towards brief, happy moments each day.

🐟 🐟 🐟

I LIGHTEN UP SO I BRIGHTEN UP MY "BLUE" MOODS.

"I could look like I was together, but inside I was crumbling."
— Cathy Gidley, person suffering from depression

CURING DEPRESSION

Part of the stigma of depression is the feeling that if you let others see how you respond to events in your life or make them aware of your emotional problems, they'll think you're crazy. So you try to hide your feelings or, when they do come out in "crying jags" or angry outbursts, you explain away your tears by attributing them to premenstrual syndrome or a business setback or justify your angry outbursts by citing lack of sleep, the pressure you're under at work, or a difficult decision you need to make. But, as much as possible, you let others see a person with a strong foundation who can handle life rather than one who can barely make it through each day, whose foundation is slowly crumbling.

When 34-year-old Cathy Gidley finally told her husband that she had been depressed for at least half of her life, it was "the scariest thing I've ever done." He urged her to make an appointment with her doctor, who recommended psychotherapy and an antidepressant medication.

Today, Cathy describes her life as the difference between night and day, and says, "I have my life back." So, too, can you get your life back from the grips of depression. Conquer your fears of letting others know exactly how you feel inside. Talk your emotions out with a loved one, detail your symptoms to a health care professional, and follow recommended treatment. You don't have to hide your feelings anymore!

ℬ ℬ ℬ

I AM PART OF THE CURE FOR MY DEPRESSION.

"When I think how it was then, I can't believe it. It was like being in a dark valley, and bit by bit I've climbed out into the sunshine."
— from *All Creatures Great and Small*, by James Herriot

RESTORING YOUR VISION

Famed veterinarian and author James Herriot told the story of a dog named Digger who lost his eyesight. His owner brought him to Dr. Herriot, convinced that the dog needed to be put down. "There's nothing anybody can do for him now," the owner sighed with resignation.

But Dr. Herriot told him he was wrong. "This is where you start doing things for him. He's going to be lost without your help." Dr. Herriot advised the dog's owner to take him on the same paths he and the dog used to walk, but to help the dog steer clear of holes and ditches. He said that the dog could still run on the big lawn in back of the owner's house, but that the owner would have to be on the lookout for things left lying around in the grass that the dog might trip over.

The owner listened, then shook his head. "But I'm having agony...it seems so cruel and unjust for this to strike a helpless animal—a little creature who's never done anybody harm."

Dr. Herriot patted Digger and told his owner. "You're just torturing yourself," he pointed out. "That's part of your trouble. You're using Digger to punish yourself instead of doing something useful." Weeks later, Digger was joyously exploring gorse bushes on his daily walk while his owner exclaimed that both he and his dog were better off than they were before.

How often do you feel as if you're blindly groping around, stumbling over unseen obstacles, and banging into walls? You can resign yourself to having to do such things for the rest of your life, or you can learn how to get around more efficiently.

❧ ❧ ❧

I TACKLE THE WORK I NEED TO DO TO RESTORE MY VISION.

"If you feel depressed, get specific: What are you feeling? Bring the dragon out into the light before it comes out in self-destructive depression, or in an uncontrolled volcanic explosion."

— author Sue Patton Thoele

CONSTRUCTIVE ANGER

It has been said that depression is often anger turned inward, with a resulting suppressed sadness. In effect, it's like weeping without tears. But how can you identify the feelings of anger that trigger your depression when the depression is like a fog that settles over you, limiting your ability to see what you're feeling?

A key indicator is the realization that you're really only depressed when you're not aware of or dealing with your feelings. After all, if you were aware of them and working out what was bugging you, then you would be expressing your feelings rather than suppressing them. Talking about your anger or expressing it in appropriate ways is not depression; rather, it's part of the very healthy process of healing. So if you're feeling depressed, chances are you're angry about something and afraid or reluctant to let those feelings out.

A lot of people carry around unresolved emotional junk—some of which includes suppressed anger. But you can only grow emotionally stronger and become more happy and fulfilled by getting in touch with, talking about, and then releasing your anger in healthy ways. Hitting your partner or kicking a pet isn't a constructive expression of your rage and will most likely lead to anger at yourself as well as guilt and resentment. But you can punch a punching bag, play an aggressive game, or write down your feelings in a journal.

ॐ ॐ ॐ

I EXPRESS MY ANGER IN CONSTRUCTIVE WAYS.

"If money could make us happy, millionaires would rest complete. If sex could fulfill us, those who enter relationships of marriages based upon sex would roam no farther. If power were the source of peace, heads of state would be the happiest people in the world. But persons with much money, sex or power are not always the happiest; in fact they are often the most unhappy."

— author Alan Cohen

RE-EXPERIENCING HAPPINESS

Comedian Dom DeLuise once recounted a time when nothing made him laugh: "Everything was wrong—life was hopeless and I was feeling useless."

When his young son asked what he wanted for his birthday, DeLuise replied with a snap in his voice, "Happiness—and you can't give it to me." But on his birthday his son handed him a piece of paper with the word HAPPINESS printed on it in bright colors. The boy declared, "See, Dad, I can give you happiness!"

Many people believe happiness is measured in material terms—a house, money, lots of clothes. Others insist it's found in enjoyable moments—a sunset, dinner with friends, a walk in the woods. Still others equate happiness with personal victory—achieving something they've worked hard to attain, such as a promotion, a degree, or a home.

Take a moment to reflect on the things in your life that have brought you great pleasure. Have your yesterdays been positive? Do you have a wonderful relationship with a parent? Are you blessed with kind, loving friends? Does your partner respect you and your needs? Have you achieved a personal victory? Such joys and pleasures are the keys to your happiness right now.

🍃 🍃 🍃

I REDISCOVER THE HAPPY EXPERIENCES IN MY LIFE.

"It can strike while one is driving on the highway, shopping at the mall, even ruminating at night in bed: a rush of fear and doom. Soon, one is dizzy, trembling, sweating, gasping for breath. Am I going crazy? Am I dying?"

— journalist Madeline Drexler

HANDLING PANIC ATTACKS

Panic attacks are the ultimate mind/body problem. As many as one in ten people suffers a panic attack at least once in a lifetime; for one to two percent of the population, they're a fact of life. Panic disorders can be caused by a number of factors that often converge at the same time, creating fears of losing control, being suffocated in an actual sense as well as in a symbolic sense—such as being overpowered by other people—and being left alone or abandoned.

People who have had just one panic attack are more apt to have a family history of anxiety disorders. Those who suffer from panic attacks show themselves to be biologically vulnerable, having a lower threshold for fear in their brain's limbic system. Many of those who have panic attacks do so when they've been deprived of sleep, use cocaine, or drink too much caffeine. And while panic attacks seem to come out of the blue, they usually happen during a time of stress or change—after the end of a long-term relationship, dealing with the loss of a loved one, beginning college, having a baby, receiving a job promotion, relocating—or when feelings are being suppressed.

To combat anxiety and panic, treat the causes rather than the symptoms. Frightening feelings of a panic attack can be lessened through anti-anxiety medication, working with a therapist, expressing your emotions, and taking good care of yourself.

ॐ ॐ ॐ

I SEEK LONG-TERM SOLUTIONS TO PANIC ATTACKS.

"If you wait to feel motivated, you may be waiting a long time."

— Dr. David Burns

GETTING IN MOTION

You may intellectually know that to get out and about, to accomplish tasks, or to engage in an enjoyable activity will help improve your mood or ease your grief. But there are times when, faced with a decision to either take action or withdraw into nonaction, you take stock of your reserve of physical energy and decide, "I'm just too exhausted or drained to do anything."

But are you, really? Perhaps too many sleepless nights or poor eating habits have depleted your strength and stamina. Maybe your schedule has been far more active than it has been in the recent past. Or perhaps the activities others are suggesting that you participate in aren't right for you at this time.

Chances are that you're just waiting for the time when you wake up motivated—when you can expend energy with little effort. Think of all those Saturday and Sunday mornings when you'd get up with the idea of accomplishing a lot, and then let the entire day go by without doing anything—not cleaning the house, not reading, not going out to a movie. Those were ideal times in which you could've taken action, but chose not to.

Don't wait until you feel motivated to do something. Get started taking some action, even if it's washing the breakfast dishes, folding a pile of clothes, or walking around the block. Such simple movements can be all you need to pump up your energy level so you get the needed boost to get you out of bed, get off the couch, and get out of your rut.

を を を

I PUT MY BODY IN MOTION SO MY MIND BENEFITS.

"My goal is to live a full, productive life even with all that ambiguity. No matter what happens, whether the cancer never flares up again or whether you die, the important thing is that the days that you have had you will have lived."

— Gilda Radner

ILLNESS AS WELLNESS

Actress, "Saturday Night Live" regular, and one-woman show performer Gilda Radner, who lost a long battle with cancer, kept her spirits up as her health failed by trying to live her life as best as she could. She did this by learning and growing in positive ways from her experience. She valued the people, places, and things in her life. And she kept things lighthearted by using one of her famous punchlines—"If it's not one thing, it's another"—throughout her treatment and recovery.

In your own illness, there may inevitably be some crossroads that are harder to negotiate than others. Flannery O'Connor says about such times, "In a sense, sickness is a place, more instructive than a long trip to Europe, and it's always a place where there's no company, where nobody can follow." How you handle such rough spots will determine whether you can progress down the path of healing, make decisions that are in your best interests, foster the wisdom to accept the things you can't change, and develop the courage to change the things you can.

In her book, *Illness as a Metaphor*, Susan Sontag wrote: "Everyone who is born holds dual citizenship, in the kingdom of the well and in the kingdom of the sick. Although we prefer to use only the good passport, sooner or later each of us is obliged, at least for a spell, to identify ourselves as citizens of the other place." How you live in this other place is what matters.

ఱ ఱ ఱ

I VIEW MY ILLNESS AS PART OF MY WELLNESS.

"Night, the beloved. Night, when words fade and things come alive. When the destructive analysis of the day is done, and all that is truly important becomes whole and sound again."

— Antoine de Saint-Exupéry

NIGHTTIME AS A NEW BEGINNING

Just as each day is a new beginning, so too can each evening be a new start. The falling darkness and rising chill of a fall night needn't frighten you or make you feel sad or "blue"; rather, it can present you with a multitude of fresh, enjoyable, and energizing opportunities. Nighttime can be a time to start on a project you've been putting off or to concentrate your energy on a hobby. Nighttime can be the first night of an adult education class, a bowling league, a support group meeting, or a volunteering opportunity. Nighttime can be the time you take a courageous first step in getting to know someone new. Nighttime can be the time to try a new recipe, start reading a good book, meditate, or take in a first-run movie.

Each night gives you the chance to recharge yourself physically, emotionally, and spiritually after your day's batteries have run down. Each night presents you with endless opportunities to start anew on your goals, your growth, and your interests. Instead of using time you've been given tonight negatively reflecting on the past events of the day, you can enjoy each moment. Each night is a new beginning. You can make light shine in the darkness tonight by enjoying yourself in your solitude, with a close friend or companion, in the company of many others, or with family members.

ॐ ॐ ॐ

I SEE TONIGHT AS AN OPENING RATHER THAN A CLOSING.

*"Problems, unfortunately, can be addicting. Like it or not,
we take a certain amount of pride in the very problems
that distress us."*
— from *A Soprano on Her Head*, by Eloise Ristad

ACCEPTING OTHERS

Do you judge other people's actions by rules you've concocted
about what is and isn't fair? For example, you may say, "If my
family really cared about me, they would realize the difficulties I'm
having and help me out," "If my partner truly loved me, he/she
would take me out to dinner or buy me flowers," "If my friends
were really concerned about me, they would be calling me more,"
or "If the support group really accepted me, they would invite me
to chair the next meeting."

Such judgments are based on a false presumption of fairness—
your own. The trouble is that in personal interactions, everyone
has different ideas about fairness. Your family may feel they're helping you out as much as they can, your partner may show love in
different ways, your friends may call as much as possible, and your
support group may accept you in ways far more significant than
chairing a meeting for a few hours.

By falling into this distorted thinking trap, you're bound to
wind up feeling hurt, slighted, or wronged whenever your ideas of
fairness aren't honored—which can be most of the time.
Consciously or unconsciously, you perpetuate problems in your interactions with others and continue to feel miserable.

The way to end your problems and your distorted perceptions is
to throw out all rules, work together with others so you can
reach compromise on yours as well as their expectations, and appreciate what others are willing to give to you.

꽃 꽃 꽃

I ACCEPT WHAT'S POSSIBLE FROM OTHERS RATHER THAN
EXPECT THE IMPOSSIBLE.

"Be glad you can suffer, be glad you can feel...How can you tell if you're feeling good unless you've felt bad, so you have something to compare it with?"

— author Thomas Tryon

EMOTIONAL ACCEPTANCE

When you were growing up, did you try hard not to complain or whine when you were sick, hurt, frustrated, anxious, fearful, or alone? Did you feel that suppressing tears was a sign of strength—that you were a "big girl" or a "big boy" when you let your feelings roll off your back, rather than down your face? Did you try hard not to show you were scared when the lights were turned out, and there was no reassuring night light to calm your fears and anxieties?

Assuming dominance over your emotions may seem admirable when you're younger, but repression and suppression of your true feelings for years can have damaging effects as you get older. In not being able to feel the draining emotions, it also becomes harder to feel the exhilarating ones. So, while in times of profound sadness and great loss you may act nonchalant and uncaring; in times of humor and lightheartedness you may not be able to smile, laugh, and play; and in times of tenderness and intimacy you may not be giving, open, and vulnerable. Blocking the good also blocks the bad.

When you stop tears, you're also stopping laughter. When you take your anger hostage, you're also holding down forgiveness. When you're suppressing anxiety and fear, you're also suppressing serenity and trust. Today, remember that both feeling and expressing all emotions has value.

ళ ళ ళ

I ACCEPT AND EXPRESS ALL OF MY EMOTIONS.

OCTOBER 1

"Here is a mental treatment guaranteed to cure every ill that flesh is heir to: sit for half an hour every night and mentally forgive everyone against whom you have any ill will or antipathy."

— Charles Fillmore

FORGIVING THE PAST

When the sister of a young man who was brutally murdered finally faced the killer in court nearly a decade after the crime, she told him in a trembling voice, "Wherever my brother is today, he may be able to forgive you for what you've done to him. But I can't. *I can't forgive you!*"

During his weekly ride into a therapist's office, a 20-year-old man always ranted to his dead father: "Why did you have to be so abusive when I was growing up? Why were you so awful? *I can't forgive you!*"

Forgiveness is the ability to let go of anger toward yourself or others. But how can you learn to let go of deep-rooted anger from the past so you can get on with living in the present? Such anger is often a response to feelings you didn't express at the time you experienced them in your childhood, in a former intimate relationship, or during an incident that happened years ago.

Because you didn't express them, these feelings remained "alive" and grew into the anger you feel today. To release the anger, identify when you felt angry in the past and acknowledge that you're still angry today. By recognizing past feelings, you can begin to put your anger behind you. Then think about who you need to forgive. Let go of the anger, and let forgiveness heal your soul.

ஓ ஓ ஓ

I FORGIVE THOSE FROM MY PAST SO I CAN LIVE IN THE PRESENT.

"I have come to the conclusion that the inner beauty of heart and soul in each person is most often hidden from view, like Mount Fuji. Clouds of self-doubt, guilt and fear keep this beauty hidden—not only from outsiders, but even from ourselves."

— author Andre Auw, Ph.D.

SUPPORTIVE COUNSELORS

How can working with a therapist or counselor help when you're depressed, grieving, or experiencing "the blues"? First and foremost, you're able to develop a close and supportive relationship. This sense of support, connection, and caring in a one-to-one relationship can help sustain you through very difficult times and help you to feel less alone and alienated.

Support is only one aspect of treatment that can be helpful. During psychotherapy you're often able to learn more about yourself and to discover patterns in your life that might provide a basis for recurring feelings of depression. You may be guided in ways that put you in touch with feelings you've buried or grief you've blocked. Getting in touch with such emotions makes you aware of them, but with the guidance of a therapist you're also able to open up and express them in appropriate ways.

Finally, the work of a counselor or therapist is designed to help you dispel the clouds that obscure your view of your unique inner beauty and strength. Hopelessness can often be replaced by realistic hopefulness—a sense that you're capable of evaluating choices and options in your life in order to create the most personally beneficial outcomes and the greatest amount of healing.

ꗜ ꗜ ꗜ

I AM GUIDED TOWARDS MY INNER STRENGTH AND BEAUTY.

OCTOBER 3

"Why hoard your troubles? They have no market value, so just throw them away."

— Ann Schade

COLLECTING TROUBLES

Occasional troubles are a natural part of living—everyone has them. But it's not natural to suffer continual troubles. If you're someone who never seems to be able to get off the "trouble train"—always speeding from one troubling station to another—then it might surprise you to know that your problems may not always be the result of outside influences, mean-spirited people, being down on your luck, or an unhappy childhood. The cause of your troubles may be you.

You may think of small infractions by loved ones as major crimes against you; for example, you may believe that a partner who has to work over the weekend doesn't love you anymore. You may imagine emotional injuries that you really haven't suffered; for example, you may believe that a friend who's running a few minutes late isn't going to show up. You may behave in ways that arouse the anger of the people around you, thereby creating interpersonal conflicts. Or, you may place yourself in destructive or life-threatening situations—for example, choosing to walk through a notoriously dangerous section of the city late at night—and then lack the fortitude to get out of these situations.

Such troubles are like strings of worthless bangles and beads you display proudly, proving to the world that yes, indeed, you have them in spades. But these concerns do not add anything positive to your life. Take time to assess one of the problems in your life realistically. What you may find is not a major dilemma, but a minor inconvenience that is not worth your time or attention.

I STOP BEING A TROUBLE COLLECTOR.

OCTOBER 4

"There are parts of a ship which, taken by themselves, would sink... But when the parts of a ship are built together, they float. So with the events in my life. Some have been tragic. Some have been happy. But when they are built together, they form a craft that floats and is going someplace. And I am comforted."

— Ralph W. Sockman

STAYING AFLOAT

If you only remembered the unhappy times you've had, you'd never be able to get out of your depression. You'd be like a ship made of granite—strong because you've weathered your tough times, but incapable of floating away from them. Likewise, if you remembered only the happy times you've had, you'd have a limited vision of your lives. You'd be like a ship made of paper—able to float, but only for a short time.

When you're able to remember the unhappy as well as the happy times—the negative and the positive, the bad and the good, the times of stagnation and growth—then you see reality. When you're able to strive in the present for a balance of opposites, then you move closer to maturity. When you're able to accept that for every difficult day there'll be a good or better one, then you're able to accept life as it is. You're able to float with the currents of life.

There's an old adage, "A ship in harbor is safe, but ships weren't built to stay in harbors." So, too, is it with you. You're the captain of a ship that needs to put to sea and meet its challenges—days of smooth sailing and sparkling blue waters, as well as times of rough seas and enormous swells. But with a realistic outlook, balance, and acceptance, you can weather anything!

ॐ ॐ ॐ

I AM THE COURAGEOUS CAPTAIN OF MY SHIP.

"One of the dreariest spots on life's road is the point of conviction that nothing will ever again happen to you."
— from *The West Wind*, by Faith Baldwin

SELF-MOTIVATION

When you're dejected and pessimistic, you may say, "Oh, what's the use? There's nothing I can do. Nothing." So you may stare off into space, mindlessly watching images on a flickering television screen, or shift into automatic pilot and plod through each day, only vaguely aware of life around you. Overwhelmed by a pervasive sense of futility, you may feel that you're powerless to do anything to relieve your depression. Like a swimmer who fights a strong current, you won't surrender to the current and let it gently carry you safely to shore; like the person who can't swim who thrashes wildly about in shallow waters, you don't have the sense to prevent yourself from drowning by simply standing up.

You may think that you've done or you're doing everything possible to overcome your depression or to alleviate your current situation. But is that really the case? You can't solve all your problems or ease all your feelings at once. You can't put all your worries and cares to rest and find instant happiness.

But what you can do is ask yourself, "Am I doing everything I can to mobilize my resources to fight off this depression, or have I yielded, given up, abandoned the struggle?" Answer the question honestly. Chances are you haven't done everything you could. But you can take small steps that can help you fight against the concept of a dreary lifetime.

ஃ ஃ ஃ

I ASK, "WHAT I DO?" INSTEAD OF "WHAT'S THE USE?"

"Often the test of courage is not to die but to live."
— Vittorio Alfieri

SURVIVING

Suicide has been glorified by many writers as a romantic concept. In the wake of Goethe's 18th-century novel, *The Sufferings of Young Werther*, Europe was swept with a wave of suicides by passionately melancholy young men who were thwarted in love. Suicide victim and poet Sylvia Plath glamorized this final act in *The Bell Jar*. She wrote of the Japanese, who would disembowel themselves when anything went wrong. She imagined that they would sit down, cross-legged and naked, a sharp knife in either hand, pointed at either side of the stomach. "Then," she wrote, "in one quick flash, before they had time to think twice, they would jab the knives in, and zip them around, one on the upper crescent and one on the lower crescent, making a full circle. Then their stomach skin would come loose, like a plate, and their insides would fall out, and they would die." She then added, "It must take a lot of courage to die like that."

What do you think is more courageous: killing yourself, or working through your difficulties, as hard as that may be, and staying alive in spite of the outcome? It may seem as if it would be easier to give up. But just as pain is part of life, so too is pain part of death. In fact, there are no painless suicides. Many suicides end up as botched attempts that can permanently scar and internally damage or physically disable. And, more often than not, what's desired is not to end life but to go on living—without the pain.

Courage is survival—against and despite all odds.

❦ ❦ ❦

I HAVE THE COURAGE TO SURVIVE.

"...mental health policy makers want doctors to appreciate depression as a treatable illness, a psychic pain just as 'real' as an ulcer or a broken arm."

— journalist Richard A. Knox

NATIONAL DEPRESSION SCREENING DAY

Are you feeling persistently down or "blue"? Are you suffering from some of the symptoms cited as hallmarks of depression? If so, then you're eligible for a free screening test on the annual National Depression Screen Day. On this day, you can take the test at one of about 2,100 hospitals, clinics, shopping malls, churches, corporations, senior citizen centers, colleges, and military bases around the country.

The screening is anonymous, although organizers may ask participants if they'd be willing to take part in a follow-up study to see how many people end up in treatment as a result of the screening. The screening takes about one-and-a-half hours. It involves a self-administered written questionnaire, which is immediately scored by a professional, as well as a psychiatrist's lecture on signs of depression and its treatment. A personal recommendation on whether the participant should seek further evaluation and care is also provided.

Organizers say that one of the benefits of the screening is that early detection of depression can lead to early treatment. One participant remarked, "I lost years of my life before my depression was diagnosed. Now I can deal with it."

To find the screening site nearest you, call 1-800-262-4444 and give your zip code.

🐑 🐑 🐑

I TAKE THE SCREENING TEST OR MAKE AN APPOINTMENT WITH A HEALTH CARE PROFESSIONAL.

"It has never been, and never will be, easy work! But the road that is built in hope is more pleasant to the traveler than the road built in despair, even though they both lead to the same destination."

— Marion Zimmer Bradley

TRAVELING NEW ROADS

Think for a moment about a nearby city. Now picture the many roads that lead to that city. One may be a winding, tree-lined country road. Another may be an efficient eight-lane expressway. And still another may be rutted and pot-holed. No matter which road is taken, it will reach the same destination as the others. But what will be different is the experience of the journey, depending on which road you take.

Consider that this city is your life. Every day you wake and need to choose a road that will take you into the city. You can take the quick, efficient expressway or the scenic country road. But you may rarely choose either; instead, you may find yourself day after day on the rutted dirt road. Each day you endure the jarring ride as you're tossed about, concentrating intently on guiding your car around treacherously deep holes, jutting rocks, and soft shoulders. Each day you become exhausted after making such a journey, and you may ask yourself why the road doesn't get easier each time you drive it.

Today, become aware of the existence of other roads you can take on your journey—roads not built on despair and disrepair, but roads that are far more pleasant and provide you with a much easier ride.

ℬ ℬ ℬ

I EXIT FROM THE PATH OF DESPAIR AND ENTER THE ROAD OF HOPE.

"You come into the world alone and you go out of the world alone and yet it seems to me you are more alone while living than even going and coming."
— from *Hundreds and Thousands*, by Emily Carr

SELF-SUPPORT

The journey away from depression can be even more lonely than the journey through it. For as you journey through depression, you often meet others who understand what you're going through, those who share in your experiences, and those who are trained to provide help.

But setting out on the actual emotional, physical, intellectual, and spiritual journey of healing is a solo trip. Step-by-step, you need to make a slow rediscovery of yourself. It takes time to undertake this slow, frightening process that oftentimes requires descending repeatedly to the bottom of your emotional well, where you had banished your unwanted emotions. When you're at the bottom of that well, you may find your strength depleted and your motivation to climb out impaired. You may want to give up. But to retrieve the potential of who you can be and to envision the hope of a better life, you need to hold on—you need to become intimate with all of your emotions, make peace with them, and then nurture yourself in ways that enable you to regain your strength.

It's okay to heal and recover alone. Even though you can enlist the help of others along the way—and greatly benefit from their strength, hope, and experience—ultimately you need to do the work, to make the choices that are right for you, and to know when what you've accomplished is an incredible achievement.

❧ ❧ ❧

I DEPEND UPON MYSELF AND GIVE MYSELF THE SUPPORT I NEED.

"It was as if I had worked for years on the wrong side of tapestry, learning accurately all its lines and figures, yet always missing its color and sheen."
— from *I Change Worlds*, by Anna Louise Strong

KEEPING UP APPEARANCES

Do you often feel "blue" when you look in the mirror and don't like what you see? You may find a lot of reasons to dislike who you are on the outside. Perhaps you think you're unattractive. Maybe you don't like the style of your hair. Perhaps you feel you're too fat or too thin. Maybe you wish you were taller or shorter, more muscular or more lean.

Because you may dislike who you are on the outside, you may lose interest in changing your appearance or taking better care of yourself. You might not bother to wash or brush your hair. You may start eating everything you can get your hands on and avoid monitoring your weight. You may stop exercising. You may wear the same sweatshirt and sweatpants for days without laundering them. You may not shower or brush your teeth. You may do all these things because you figure if you don't like how you look, then others won't either—so it doesn't matter whether or not you're presentable or groomed.

The worse you think you look, the worse you may feel about your appearance; the worse you feel about your appearance, the less you may care about it. The only way out of this vicious cycle is to take the time and devote the energy to caring about your appearance. Today, do something simple. Trim your nails. Wash your face. Wear a clean shirt. Polish your shoes. You'll be amazed at how psychologically beneficial such activities can be.

ॐ ॐ ॐ

I DO THE UPKEEP ON MY APPEARANCE.

"It's not true that life is one damn thing after another—it's one damn thing over and over."

— Edna St. Vincent Millay

MISERY MINDSET

Do you possess a mindset for misery? You may stubbornly cling to personal unhappiness and suffering as if it's part of your personality, blaming outside events and the actions of others on how you're feeling. You're the victim; everything and everyone else are the perpetrators. You have a mindset for misery if you feel that:

- your life has been full of disappointments,
- your life is a struggle,
- the people closest to you often don't care enough about your feelings,
- you have little or no control over the direction your life takes,
- you're incapable of improving your situation because of outside factors,
- people have betrayed your trust,
- your life would be better if people just started acting "right,"
- no one else has to struggle as hard as you do to get what they want, and/or
- you're a victim of bad circumstances.

The only way to get out of the misery mindset is to reset your mind. Reframe each of the above statements and change them into a positive statement—an affirmation of what you really could believe if you changed your negative outlook on life. Then strive to make one affirmative statement happen today.

ॐ ॐ ॐ

I REFRAME A MISERY MINDSET TO CREATE A BETTER PICTURE.

"All our actions take their hue from the complexion of the heart, as landscapes their variety from light."
— Francis Bacon

PAINTING YOUR MOOD

Scientific research has proven that color and light play a significant role in influencing your mood. But even if you don't totally believe in the effects color and light can have on your emotional, physical, and spiritual state, you can think about how you feel when you see brilliant autumn foliage or a breathtaking October moon. You can remember how you feel after three or four days of gray, overcast skies. The bright and vibrant colors may evoke a positive stimulus to your senses, while the gray, dark colors can negatively impact on or depress your senses.

Similarly, the colors you wear and the way you decorate your living space can also be seen as pretty accurate reflections of the positive or negative feelings you have about yourself and your life. Sometimes dressing in a more brilliant or soft color can subtly change your mood from sadness to happiness. Sometimes imagining that you're surrounded by a healing color or a brilliant white light can help lift your spirits.

Today, imagine you have a palette of beautiful colors with which to "paint" yourself and your world. Close your eyes and visualize colors that glow within and around you. Select the color of the energy that your living space emits. Picture the color that surrounds your bed at night. Then take these colors with you throughout the day so you can be a joyous walking rainbow.

❧ ❧ ❧

I "PAINT" MYSELF WITH VIBRANT COLORS AND BRIGHT LIGHT.

"I like living. I have sometimes been wildly, despairingly, acutely miserable, racked with sorrow, but through it all I still know quite certainly that just to be alive is a grand thing."

— Agatha Christie

STRIVING FOR SIMPLICITY

How can you possibly imagine that life "is a grand thing" when life can be so difficult, trying, complex, and painful at times? Perhaps the best way to answer that question is to first ask yourself, "What do I want out of my life?" As you ponder your answer, reflect on what you really want—not just on what you don't have, what you haven't attained, or what you're not getting.

What is it that would matter a great deal to you? In the 1950s, a woman who called herself Peace Pilgrim began to walk across America on a pilgrimage for peace. Paring down her possessions to the clothes on her back and a few items in her pockets, she chose to live at what she called "need-level." Living simply was both liberating and empowering, as Peace Pilgrim explained, "A persistent simplification will create an inner and outer well-being that places harmony in one's life."

Seeking simplicity can clear your vision, free you from creating and chasing unrealistic dreams, and bring greater beauty to your life. So perhaps your answer to "What do I want out of my life?" could be based on something simple, yet meaningful.

As Diane Ackerman explains, "I don't want to get to the end of my life and find that I lived just the length of it. I want to have lived the width of it as well." What do you want out of your life?

❧ ❧ ❧

I KEEP MY GOALS, DREAMS, AND DESIRES SIMPLE.

"Many people say they feel 'sad all the time.' Of course, they're not actually sad all the time, but it feels that way to them."

— author/physician Dr. Patch Adams

COMPONENTS OF HAPPINESS

The concept of living happily all the time may seem impossible, even unnatural, yet it takes no greater effort to be happy every day than it does to be miserable. With all the potential for happiness that could be experienced, it's surprising that so many people are so unhappy so much of the time. One of the reasons is that happiness is treated as an elusive enigma—something everyone searches for but, like a legendary creature, something no one has ever seen.

Yet happiness is made up of many simple components. One component is to help others and be with them. As author Thomas Tryon said, "I think real happiness only comes when we are joined to another human being." This can be experienced by spending time with friends or family, an intimate partner, or new acquaintances. It can also be experienced by giving to others in your community or by volunteering.

Another component of happiness is to have fun; fun is what people have when they're happy. Take, for example, the common occurrence of having to wait in line for anything—to make a purchase, to get seated in a restaurant, to board an airplane. If you're a sad person, then this activity is surely going to propel you into a blue mood. But if you're a happy person, then you'll probably see this as a great opportunity to people-watch, daydream, or engage strangers in conversation.

Today, seek happiness through the company of others and by having fun.

❧ ❧ ❧

I DO THINGS TO MAKE ME HAPPY.

"How you regard depression depends on how you experience it. Because by its very nature, it is associated with endings, and because each ending involves starting over, depression is itself a new beginning."

— author Frederic Flach

CREATING NEW BEGINNINGS

Whenever you experience a loss of someone significant in your life, you need to adjust to a new environment and way of life. This can signify a time of many new beginnings, one of which starts with the often painful task of changing the patterns in your life.

In most relationships, social patterns develop. You and your partner may have seen the same type of movie at the same time each week. You may have gone to the same theater. You may have watched the same television programs, sharing the same pizza. You may have gone to the same restaurants, seen the same people, shopped at the same stores, and eaten the same food. And now you're doing all the things you did before, except now you're alone.

You need to create your own social patterns. That doesn't mean you should stop going to movies, socializing, or dining out. Try a different type of movie, something you'd like to see but might not have because you knew your loved one wouldn't have cared for it. Try a new restaurant specializing in interesting foods. Maintain your former relationships, but include new people you've met or change the surroundings in which you get together.

See this time of painful endings as the time for exciting beginnings.

❧ ❧ ❧

I MOVE BEYOND MY LOSS BY CREATING NEW BEGINNINGS.

"Only accumulated emotional pain and misinformation stand in the way of our loving ourselves and each other fully and without shame, pretense or reluctance. We must therefore encourage each other in the natural process of crying, raging, trembling, laughing, yawning and talking, through which our hurts are healed."

— Christopher Spence

HEALTHY EMOTIONAL BALANCE

When difficulties arise in your intimate relationship, are you able to communicate caring, compromise, and concern? Are you able to listen to, as well as express, the wide range of emotions that are part of the intimate human experience? Are you willing to see a conflict through to its resolution, knowing that you both may have to be in an uncomfortable space until things get better?

True harmony in intimate relationships doesn't just happen. Like two people who sit opposite one another on a seesaw, the feelings of one person can't help but affect the other. In order to bring the seesaw into balance, you each need to adjust to one another, hear all that needs to be said, and validate one another's emotional experience until you can still the board.

Each person in a relationship needs to be committed to discussing and resolving conflict. Positive emotional health in a relationship can only be attained when neither partner allows the other to go on the offensive, retreat to the defensive, overreact, or take what's said too personally. Each person needs to be willing to listen to what the other person wants or needs and to communicate with similar openness and honesty.

ℬℬℬ

I ENJOY A HEALTHY EMOTIONAL BALANCE WITH MY PARTNER.

"I suppose everyone continues to be interested in the quest for the self, but what you feel when you're older, I think, is that...you really must make the self. It is absolutely useless to look for it, you won't find it, but it's possible in some sense to make it."

— author Mary McCarthy

WORTHWHILE RETIREMENT

All human beings need a sense of achievement and accomplishment that comes from satisfying and socially valued work. But when you're forced into retirement or choose it, then you need to continue to develop your self-worth in other ways.

Retirement can give you the opportunity to pursue higher education through enrollment in college, in short-term adult education, or in Elderhostel programs. Volunteer opportunities are available in hospitals, schools, libraries, art museums, and numerous nonprofit organizations. Federally funded volunteer programs for older Americans are available in most communities, such as Foster Grandparents, Service Corps of Retired Executives, and Vista. These programs enable participants to use skills, participate in job training, or explore new interests while serving their community.

You can begin to live your life in liberating and challenging ways. A 91-year-old woman tells how fulfilling her days are: "I do as I please with more freedom than when I was younger; I can decide how to occupy my time and what people I want to know."

Another senior citizen, forced out of his company through reorganization, says, "I find myself almost busier than I was when I worked."

And still another individual explains, "All I could do when I worked was work....Now that I am retired, I belong to a senior advocacy group, I also get paid for role-playing with students at a college of optometry to help them learn to relate better to patients."

ﾔﾖ ﾔﾖ ﾔﾖ

I BUILD UPON MY SELF-WORTH AFTER RETIREMENT.

"We of the craft are all crazy. Some are affected by gaiety, others by melancholy, but all are more or less touched."
— Lord Byron

ART AND DEPRESSION

Is art a sign of mental illness? Are creativity and depression inextricably linked? Do artists share a skewed perspective of life, an alternate take on reality? Are the most artistically gifted also the most emotionally challenged?

Kay Redfield Jamison, professor of psychiatry at Johns Hopkins and the author of *Touched with Fire: Manic-Depressive Illness and the Artistic Temperament*, conducted an exhaustive study of over 150 years' worth of acknowledged creative geniuses, fine and performing artists, poets, and writers, from Percy Shelley to Charles Mingus. In addition to studying their lives, she collected evidence of mental illness—specifically, manic depression—in the families of these great creators. Creativity and manic depression, she inferred, runs in families. But there's a note of caution to add to her research: Not all manic-depressives exhibit high creativity, just as not all mental disorders aid those who are creative.

What's important to learn from Jamison's study is that all forms of creative art can be excellent outlets for troubling mood swings and "blue" moods. Rather than lament your emotional downswings and wallow in despair, choose to create. Write a poem. Outline a novel. Paint a picture. Play a musical instrument. Compose a song. Dance. Sing. Express yourself creatively. When you do, you're helping to smooth out your emotions.

ℒ ℒ ℒ

I CAN BE DEPRESSED AND CREATIVE AT THE SAME TIME.

*"We should stop kidding ourselves. We should let go of
things that aren't true. It's always better with the truth."*
— Buckminster Fuller

TRUTHFUL THINKING

You're probably quite familiar with how powerful and punishing
untruthful negative thoughts about yourself can be. Although
you may work hard to free your mind from thinking such thoughts
or believing in them, sometimes they creep back in. Each time you
allow this to happen, you often experience a loss of self-esteem and
an emotional setback.

Today you need to re-enter in your mind positive truths about
yourself. Whenever a distorted, negative thought slips through your
consciousness, say, "I don't believe this negative thought. But
here's what I do believe." Substitute a positive, affirmative, or assertive—and believable—thought. Here are some examples:

- NEGATIVE THOUGHT: I'm all alone in the world.
  POSITIVE THOUGHT: I have many people who support me.
- NEGATIVE THOUGHT: Nobody loves me.
  POSITIVE THOUGHT: Many people love me.
- NEGATIVE THOUGHT: I'm a burden.
  POSITIVE THOUGHT: I have lots to give.
- NEGATIVE THOUGHT: I've wasted many years of my life.
  POSITIVE THOUGHT: I've done many good things in my life.

Remember: Thinking positively requires practice.

ॐ ॐ ॐ

I PUT THE TRUTH ABOUT MYSELF INTO PRACTICE.

"The bravest sight in the world is to see a great man struggling against adversity."

— Roman philosopher Seneca

PEACE OF MIND

Famed musician and record producer Quincy Jones survived a brain aneurysm and two brain operations in 1974. Since that time, the highly successful and driven record producer, composer, and musician has renewed his belief in the important of having balance in his life. He says, "God has given each one of us approximately 25,000 to 26,000 days on this earth. I truly believe He (or She) has something very specific in mind: 8,300 days to sleep, 8,300 days to work, and 8,300 to give, live, play, pray, and love one another." Now, no matter how busy his schedule, Jones sets aside time for enjoying life to the fullest and for listening to the voice that comes from "divine guidance."

True peace of mind comes not from what you can get from your efforts but from what you can give to others, from how well you can live each day, from how often you allow yourself to play, from your ability to reach out to a Higher Power in prayer, and from your desire to love others.

To find this true peace of mind yourself, resolve to give, live, play, pray, and love another person every day. Do something kind for your partner or a stranger. Enjoy the beauty of the chill autumn mornings and the sound of the crisp leaves underfoot. Play a game with your children or friends. Pray for riches in your life that money can't buy. Set a goal to be the best person you can possibly be and to do your best at all times. And express your love openly and honestly.

ॐ ॐ ॐ

I FIND TRUE PEACE OF MIND.

"I have often been downcast, but never in despair; I regard our hiding as a dangerous adventure, romantic and interesting at the same time. In my diary I treat all the privations as amusing. I have made up my mind now to lead a different life from other girls and, later on, different from ordinary housewives. My start has been so very full of interest, and that is the sole reason why I have to laugh at the humorous side of the most dangerous moments."

— Anne Frank

DYING LAUGHING

Jewish traditions see pain, suffering, and death as part of life and therefore embrace these with a lightheartedness—even laughter—that reduces the pain and teaches not to take anything in life too seriously. Every situation, every experience—even not knowing, as with Anne Frank, whether each day she would live or die—has some humor in it. Humor can't stop you from dying, but it certainly can't hurt; in fact, it helps you to live with and deal with death.

Jewish traditions also teach us that laughter offers new perspectives on fears. Any loss—even complete annihilation, can be turned around with a laugh. Allen Klein, author of *The Healing Power of Humor*, recounts this story: A flood is predicted and nothing can be done to prevent it. In three days, water will wipe out the world. A Buddhist leader goes on television and urges everyone to become a Buddhist in order to find salvation in heaven. The Pope goes on television with a similar message, urging everyone to accept Jesus. But the chief rabbi of Israel takes a slightly different approach: "We have three days to learn how to live under water." While humor can't stop you from dying, as the Jewish tradition says, "It certainly couldn't hurt."

ฦา ฦา ฦา

I TURN AROUND MY LOSS WITH LAUGHTER.

"There is no doubt that life is given us, not to be enjoyed, but to be overcome—to be got over."
— German philosopher Arthur Schopenhauer

GETTING OVER DIFFICULTIES

You may often think how wonderful life would be if things were easier. But reflect back on a particularly rough time you went through in the past. Maybe it was a difficult childhood, a hurtful relationship, an injury or illness, or the loss of a job. Would you be as strong today if it hadn't been for that experience? Hasn't that event "marked" you in some way today—left a little piece of itself on your way of thinking, feeling, acting, or believing?

National Book Award winner Dorothy Allison, whose book *Bastard Out of Carolina* was based on her incestuous and painful childhood, talked about how the past influenced her. "I'm past 40 now," she said, "and it's taken me my entire life to figure out what happened to me as a kid. Because the things you do to survive with some kind of sense of yourself, the emotional maneuverings, really obstruct accurate memory."

Each hard lesson you've had to face in your life has helped you learn and grow in some way. It's as if, as author Katherine Mansfield said, in going through places "...you leave little bits of yourself fluttering on the fences—little rags and shreds of your very life."

Today, remember that you've had to climb a lot of fences. Some were hard to get over; others not so hard. Whenever you face difficulties in the present, ask, "What will getting through this experience teach me? How will this make me a stronger person now and in the future?"

❧ ❧ ❧

I CLIMB THE FENCES IN MY LIFE TO LEARN AND GROW.

"Faith is the root of all blessings. Believe, and you shall be saved; believe, and you will be satisfied; believe, and you cannot but be comforted and happy."

— Jeremy Taylor

HEALING WITH FAITH

Loss of anything in your life—a job, a home, a means of transportation, financial independence, a goal or direction, your health—or of any person dear to you—through separation or divorce, because of relocation, or due to an illness or death—can be devastating. Expressing your sorrow may be about the only way you have of getting through your grief over the loss.

But then, when your sadness has eased, you may become fraught with worry. "What am I going to do now?" you may nervously question. "Where will I go? What shall I do? How am I going to get through this time? Is it always going to be this way?"

Some people, when faced with a loss, can only feel sorrow and worry. Back and forth their emotions go as they alternate between crying and trembling. But what they forget is that while their emotions can go down, they can also go up. John Steinbeck has said that "Somewhere in the world there is defeat for everyone. Some are destroyed by defeat, and some made small and mean by victory. Greatness lives in one who triumphs equally over defeat and victory."

Trust that you can get through your loss, no matter how hard that may seem right now. To do so, remember the adage: "Sorrow looks back, worry looks around, faith looks up." Triumphs over your defeats by looking up from time to time. Then tell yourself, "I will get through this tough time," rather than ask, "How will I get through this tough time?"

ဖြစ် ဖြစ် ဖြစ်

I RELY ON THE HEALING POWER OF FAITH.

"To live is not merely to breathe, it is to act; it is to make use of our organs, senses, faculties, of all those parts of ourselves which give us the feeling of existence."
— Jean Jacques Rousseau

DEPRESSION-BUSTERS

Here are some simple ways to alleviate symptoms of depression while you're waiting for help or trying to keep your moods stabilized. They may not make what you're feeling go away, but they can provide some relief:

- Get out in the sunlight and fresh air as much as possible. If you're stuck indoors, sit or work near a window or in a well-lighted area.
- Ask for emotional support from a family member, friend, or mental health professional. Attend a support group meeting. Get together with someone from your support group to discuss how you're feeling.
- Spend time with friends doing things you enjoy. Establish "getting close time" with your partner, talking freely and cuddling together. Take your dog for a walk. Play with your cat. Spend time with your children.
- Exercise. Work out at the gym, outside, or with a partner or pet. Walk, run, bike, swim, hike—do whatever you feel comfortable doing for at least 20 minutes.
- Focus on your appearance. Take a long, hot bath or shower. Put on clean, attractive, comfortable clothes. Wear jewelry. Style your hair.
- Eat three healthy meals a day. Pack nutritious lunches. Anticipate the desire to snack by setting aside fresh fruits and cutting up fresh vegetables. Avoid caffeine, sugar, and junk food.

ॐ ॐ ॐ

I TAKE POSITIVE ACTION WHEN I'M GETTING DEPRESSED.

"We must learn to accept....To accept life and to accept ourselves, not blindly and not with conceit, but with a shrug and a smile."

— psychologist Harvey Mindess

LETTING GO

When you can't let go of your upsets, difficulties, and disappointments, they become burdens that have a negative impact on how you see yourself and life. There's a story that Dr. Bernie Siegel, author of *Love, Medicine and Miracles*, tells that gives good advice on how to stop struggling with your circumstances, let go, and accept what you've been given:

> A farmer who depends on his horse to plow his field is working the field one day when the horse drops dead. The people of the town say, "That's very unfortunate," but the man says, "We'll see." A few days later somebody feels sorry for the man and gives him a horse as a gift. The people of the town say, "How fortunate," but the man says, "We'll see." A couple of days later, the horse runs away. "How unfortunate," say the townspeople, but the man says, "We'll see." A few days later, the horse returns with a second horse. "How fortunate," say the townspeople, but the man says, "We'll see." One day, while out riding with his son, the boy falls and breaks a leg. "How unfortunate," say the townspeople, but the man says, "We'll see." A few days later, the army comes to the man's farm to draft young men for war, but they can't take the boy because he has a broken leg.

So wait a little today—don't jump to conclusions or act impulsively. Your upsetting moments may decrease or even disappear completely!

❧ ❧ ❧

I ACCEPT WHAT I'VE BEEN GIVEN WITH A "WE'LL SEE" ATTITUDE.

"Sorrow is a kind of rust of the soul, which every new idea contributes in its passage to scour away. It is the putrefaction of stagnant life, and is remedied by exercise and motion."
— author Samuel Johnson

BALANCING YIN AND YANG

Eastern philosophy teaches that life is comprised of yin and yang, polarities that are found throughout nature. You may think of them as day and night, hot and cold, male and female, action and inaction. One extreme complements the other, but only when the dynamic balance of the two forces is brought into harmony. For example, you need moments of silent reflection or your actions would have no direction; conversely, without action, your thoughts can't take form.

But when you're depressed, you often get stuck in one extreme or the other, becoming too yin or too yang. In times of sorrow you may withdraw from others, eat to console yourself, and then feel worse about how you look. You may become apathetic and complain that you feel exhausted all the time, even though you're doing nothing. Or, rather than deal with your sorrow, you may fill your life with so many obligations and keep yourself so busy that you don't have time to rest, relax, or get in touch with how you're feeling.

To get out of one or the other extreme, ask, "Where in my life is a point of excess? What do I find myself doing too much of?" and "Where in my life is the point of deficiency? What in my life do I never have enough of?" Write your insights in a journal, then work out solutions to this question: "What can I do to bring greater balance into my life?"

ॐ ॐ ॐ

I CREATE A NEW, MORE BALANCED PATTERN IN MY LIFE.

"If a snake can't grow, it will strangle. The tightness of a skin that doesn't fit is a signal that it's time to slough it off in order to grow."

— Eknath Easwaran

WHOLE-PERSON GROWTH

Have you ever marveled at the balance of a tripod or a three-legged stool? Like a four-legged animal that loses a leg and must adapt to being slightly off-balance, the three legs can only work together to support a camera or a person when they're carefully positioned.

You're like that three-legged stool when you overcome depression, "blue" moods, or grief, for you need to balance your mental, physical, and spiritual healing in order to create appropriate recovery. If you spend too much time and energy focusing on your emotional needs—seeking support and talking to others, charting your mood swings or writing in a journal, or substituting positive thinking for distorted thinking, then your physical and spiritual needs will be neglected. If you spend too much time and energy focusing on your diet, body image, exercise program, and relaxation, then your emotional and spiritual needs will be neglected. If you spend too much time connecting with nature or in prayer and meditation, then your physical and emotional needs will be neglected.

Today, don't shortchange the importance of your mental, physical, and spiritual growth. To be at your healthiest, change and growth needs to happen in all three areas simultaneously. Just as the snake sheds its skin all at once—not just parts from time to time—so, too, do you need to attend to your whole-person growth.

ॐ ॐ ॐ

I GROW MENTALLY, PHYSICALLY, AND SPIRITUALLY.

"There is more to life than increasing its speed."
— Mahatma Ghandi

SLOWING DOWN

Fall impels bears to hibernate, frogs to burrow into the mud at the bottom of ponds, birds to fly south. Fall induces most creatures to either shut down or leave in preparation for the cold, dark end of the year.

But most people consider autumn a new beginning. Summer vacations are over, and kids are back in school. The end of Daylight Savings Time makes less daylight available for each day's duties, necessitating that the pace be increased. Pressure builds. Holidays loom. The weather takes occasional turns for the worse, causing massive traffic slowdowns and creating even more pressure. Not surprisingly, airlines, trains, automobiles, and stock markets show a tendency to crash during this time.

You may find this time of a year not only a little depressing, but also quite stressful. Keep in mind that when you pick up the pace of the way you live your life, set one too many goals or create too many lists, allow yourself to get caught up in the preholiday panic that sets in the minute the Halloween candy goes on sale, and try to make up for lost daylight time, your physical stamina is going to be sorely strained. And when you can't do all that you set out to do, then you're setting yourself up for emotional dejection.

Today, keep in mind that changes in time don't necessarily mean you need to switch your life to the fast lane. Life isn't a race won by the fastest. So slow down and take time to notice and appreciate the beauty of fall.

ॐ ॐ ॐ

I DECELERATE MY PACE OF LIVING.

"We had always expected depressed people to report mostly body symptoms like fatigue, weight loss, sleep troubles and restlessness."

— psychiatrist Dr. Douglas G. Jacobs

PSYCHOLOGICAL SYMPTOMS

When Dr. Douglas G. Jacobs, a Harvard psychiatrist, created the National Depression Screening Day (part of Mental Illness Awareness Week in early October), his goal was to help combat one of the most common and deadly diseases in America; left untreated, one in seven who are depressed will kill themselves. But what he discovered from the results of his screening were that the most prevalent symptoms of depression were those least visible to health care professionals as well as sufferers themselves: they were psychological, such as a sense of hopelessness or joylessness, rather than physical.

Dr. Jacobs devised a simple test for depression that consists of six statements, which require a true or false response:

1. I find it easy to do the things I used to do.
2. I feel hopeful about the future.
3. I enjoy the things I used to enjoy.
4. I find it easy to make decisions.
5. I feel useful and needed.
6. I have felt so low that I've thought of suicide.

If you answer false to most of the questions, there's a high probability that you're depressed and need help. If you agree with number 6, you should seek professional help immediately.

ʃа ʃа ʃа

I GET HELP FOR THE PSYCHOLOGICAL SYMPTOMS OF DEPRESSION.

"As our own little piece of the world tilts away from the sun, the seasonally saddened would be wise to avoid crowds, kids, cutlery, and Christmas music. Feeling blue? Hug a light bulb."

— journalist John Jerome

SEASONAL AFFECTIVE DISORDER

In the fall of the year, the wobble of the earth tilts the Northern Hemisphere away from the sun, reducing the length of the days. Some people find that this wobble induces a state that medical science calls Seasonal Affective Disorder, or SAD. SAD was officially recognized in 1987, with a listing in the American Psychiatric Association's diagnostic and statistical manual of mental disorders. It's a syndrome characterized by severe seasonal mood swings, most commonly in the form of depression at the onset of winter. In effect, autumn makes you sad.

If you suffer from "classic SAD," you crave carbohydrates, have trouble getting up in the morning, feel befuddled most of the day, and have difficulty processing information. You become anxious and irritable, withdraw socially, and may lose interest in sex. The next change of season will remove all symptoms, but while you're going through your tough time, it may be beneficial to know that SAD sufferers in the United States number as high as six percent of the population.

The "cure" for SAD is light. Obtain relief by spending time in natural sunlight and by supplementing this with healthy "doses" of bright light provided by incandescent or full-spectrum light bulbs before dawn and after dark. This helps you to "restore" the length of your day as well as bring your moods back into balance.

ଔ ଔ ଔ

I TREAT "SAD" BY RECEIVING DAILY DOSES OF HEALTHY LIGHT.

"I've struggled with suicidal feelings my whole life because of this abuse. When you're going through that kind of pain, you think that death could not possibly be more painful."
— Kevyn Aucoin

CREATIVE OUTLOOKS

Today Kevyn Aucoin is known as the Renoir of the fashion industry's makeup artists, including among his clients such people as Whitney Houston, Diana Ross, Demi Moore, Barbra Streisand, and Tina Turner. Aucoin is one of the most influential people working in the fashion business today.

But Aucoin's life wasn't always so glamorous and wonderful. From a young age, he knew he was gay; as he grew older, he began to experience prejudice and abuse. At school he was frequently pushed around and hit. Cars would veer off the road as if they were going to run him over. And he was shot at several times. "Sometimes I knew these people," Aucoin remembers, "but to them I wasn't Kevyn Aucoin, the human being; I was Kevyn Aucoin, the gay target."

When Aucoin was 15, he "came out" to his parents. They began to have more of an understanding about gay people by starting a local chapter of the Parents, Families, and Friends of Lesbians and Gays support group. Aucoin himself escaped the oppression and pain of his past through his creativity. He quit high school, went to beauty school, and moved to New York City. Eight months after arriving in the city, he got his big break working on a shoot for *Vogue*.

You, too, can funnel your despair into a worthwhile outlet. Use your talent and creativity to help pull you out of feelings of despair.

❀ ❀ ❀

I CHANNEL MY ENERGY INTO CREATIVE OUTLETS.

"Life, in my estimation, is a biological misadventure that we terminate on the shoulders of six strange men whose only objective is to make a hole in one with you."

— radio comic Fred Allen

QUALITY LIVING

When you must deal with the imminence of your own death due to AIDS, breast cancer, aging, or a chronic medical condition, the last thing in the world you may want to be reminded of by others is your mortality. Well-meaning friends who now visit you in order to take care of your physical needs rather than spend quality time with you, a caretaking partner who now makes decisions without consulting you rather than "bother" you, or family members who never came to visit before but who do now, clearly show you that more energy is being exerted in support of your dying than of your living. You know you're going to die, everyone else knows you're going to die—but what good is that doing for your physical, emotional, and spiritual states?

You need to surround yourself with people who want to support your living. Choose to be with friends who can still be friends—who want to laugh, share a meal, watch a video, play a game, or take a walk on the beach. Let your partner know that you still have a voice and a choice in things that affect your relationship. Limit interactions with family members who are acting out of guilt rather than love when they come to visit.

Today, be honest with your friends, partner, and family members about what you need to make this day one that is full of reminders about life—and not about death.

ஜ ஜ ஜ

I SURROUND MYSELF WITH PEOPLE WHO SUPPORT MY LIVING.

"Every man has a rainy corner of his life, from which bad weather besets him."

— Jean Paul Richter

THE VICTIM STANCE

Because you don't want something to be "wrong" with you, because you want to be "normal," because you don't want other people to judge you harshly, and because you want to feel "together," you may have a tendency to blame your emotional downs on outside forces, other people, or bad luck. You may begin to see yourself as a victim, duped and deceived by forces beyond your control. You may suspect that you've somehow been singled out and targeted for your particular woes. You may believe yourself to be in no way accountable for all your troubles—all those rainy corners in your life that drench you in grief and misery. In short, you may feel that you're a victim of your circumstances, someone who's totally powerless to do or change anything about one or more difficult events in your life. Gayle Rosellini and Mark Worden describe "The Victim Stance in a Nutshell: I didn't do anything wrong. Somebody else did. Therefore, I have a right to feel bad."

As long as you consider yourself to be a victim, you remain incapable of doing anything to ease your plight. In order to conquer depression, you need to admit that your despair is more than just a passing mood and more than just a normal reaction to disappointments, failures, and tragedies. Abandon the victim stance, take responsibility for where your life is, and then make changes or take actions that can open new possibilities for you. While it may be hard to do anything positive when you're in a depressive daze, it's the first and most important step for overcoming your despair.

ॐ ॐ ॐ

I TAKE POSITIVE ACTION TO GET BEYOND MY VICTIM STANCE.

"Tears are sometimes an inappropriate response to death. When a life has been lived completely honestly, completely successfully, or just completely, the correct response to death's perfect punctuation mark is a smile."
— journalist/author Julie Burchill

LAUGHTER AND TEARS

If you believe that death must be a solemn and sad event, then that's the way you'll treat it. If you believe that humor has no place in your suffering and loss, then that's the way you'll react. But if, on the other hand, you believe that it's possible to maintain a lightness toward everything in life—including the more difficult events like death and dying—then that's what you'll create for yourself.

Perhaps you can add the sweetness of a smile or laughter to memorial ceremonies for loved ones to add a feeling of celebration to the situation. In ancient Rome, the court jester used to follow the funeral procession of his dead emperor in an effort to lighten up the public ceremony. Today, a number of cultures include laughter and joyous celebration as integral pats of their death and grieving ceremonies. The Balinese, for example, believe that the body is just a house for the spirit; therefore, when someone dies, the spirit is finally set free—a time for great celebration. In Mexico, the annual Day of the Dead pokes fun at death. Grinning skulls, dancing skeletons, and sugar-coated coffins help mock, scorn, and laugh at death.

Rather than only grieve for the dead, you can also be happy for the ending. As an ancient proverb states: "To weep too much for the dead is to affront the living."

🦢 🦢 🦢

I CELEBRATE MY LOSS AND SMILE THROUGH MY TEARS.

NOVEMBER 4

"Choose your rut carefully. You'll be in it for a long time."

— Unknown

GETTING UNSTUCK

In his book, *The Healing Power of Humor*, Allen Klein relates a story about two monks who were walking down the road when they noticed a young woman waiting to cross a stream. To the horror of one of the monks, the other picked the woman up in his arms and carried her across the water. The monks resumed their walking. About a mile down the road, the monk who was aghast at his fellow monk's action remarked, "We are celibate, we are not supposed to even look at a woman, let alone pick one up and carry her across a stream. How could you possibly do that?" The other monk replied, "I put that woman down a mile back. Are you still carrying her around with you?"

When you can't let go of things that upset you, perplex you, or disappoint you, you remain mired in a rut. Like the monk who couldn't let go of what the other monk had done, you are—in reality—stuck back at the bank of the stream, unable to move on from that point in time. The only way out of your rut is to do as the monk who had carried the woman did—when he released the woman, he also released his attachment to that point in time. To move out of your rut, you need to accept and let go. In effect, you need to give yourself a kick from behind in order to move forward.

Today, move out of any rut in which you're stuck, think about one thing you'd like to forget. Write this thought on a piece of paper, then rip it into tiny pieces and throw it away.

I ACCEPT, LET GO, AND THEN MOVE ON.

"Life, as it is called, is for most of us one long postponement."
— Henry Miller

PROFESSIONAL TREATMENT

Every day that goes by in which you're depressed, grieving, or in another "blue" mood and you don't seek help to alleviate how you feel is a day lost to you forever. You can never get this day back, nor can you re-experience it in the way you would've liked—by feeling more centered, more stable, and more secure with yourself. Add up the days that you've let go by thus far, and you may be astounded at how much of your life you've let slip by.

So if you're experiencing any of the following symptoms, consult a mental health therapist—a psychiatrist, psychologist, family counselor, or clinical social worker—as soon as possible:

- a pervasive sense of despair or sadness, with very few times in which you experience pleasure;
- severe disruption in your personal relationships or an ultimatum from your partner to get help;
- suicidal ideas or planning;
- physical symptoms of depression (weight loss, sleep problems, loss of sex drive, panic attacks, family history of depression, fatigue, decreased energy); and/or
- a profound hopelessness or apathy.

If you're depressed, in the midst of prolonged grieving, or prone to blue moods, don't let another day disappear. You need and deserve all the help you can get.

ôa ôa ôa

I CONSULT WITH A PROFESSIONAL FOR INDIVIDUAL TREATMENT.

"If we didn't live venturously, plucking the wild goat by the beard, and trembling over precipices, we should never be depressed, I've no doubt; but already should be faded, fatalistic and aged."

— Virginia Woolf

LIVING ADVENTUROUSLY

Imagine the fear and anxiety Christopher Columbus and his crew must have felt as they set sail from the safe shores of their homeland, knowing that they might fall off the edge of the world and never return home. But that didn't stop them from beginning their risky voyage.

Risk-taking means attempting something new, different, or unknown, without the comfort of knowing what the outcome will be. Sometimes you take a risk and achieve positive results—for instance, you talk openly and honestly to a supportive person about how you feel, and you end up feeling better. Or you can take a risk and feel you don't succeed—you talk openly and honestly to a person you thought was supportive but instead is critical of you, and you end up feeling worse.

But whatever the outcome, it's important to take the risk. Being ready to take a risk doesn't mean you won't feel afraid. Fear is a natural reaction to the unknown. But fearing and still taking the risk is what risk-taking is all about. That's why the best risk-takers are the people who ask, "What do I have to lose?" They have the attitude that even if they don't succeed, they—like Columbus—are at least willing to try. As André Gide said, "One doesn't discover new lands without consenting to lose sight of the shore for a very long time."

❧ ❧ ❧

I FOCUS ON THE GAINS IN RISK-TAKING.

"Never let your head hang down. Never give up and sit down and grieve. Find another way."
— baseball player Satchel Paige

FINDING A BETTER WAY

When children are tired, they make their feelings very clear. They just sit down and start to cry. As an adult, you may sometimes feel like a child, ready to sit down and give up doing anything. But you're not a tired child; you can't just sit down and give up doing anything. You're a grown-up living with responsibilities and duties, doing certain activities that you may sometimes find difficult, or going through times that may be long, hard, and trying.

Instead of giving up, you need to find other ways of handling the day-to-day flow of life so it doesn't become personally overwhelming. To begin with, you can ask for help. Not only are there supportive friends and family members who can listen to you, but there are also others who can take on some of your burden of responsibility. You can also rearrange your schedule so you're not doing too much at one time and not enough at others. And you can stay active, arranging to do something fun or productive each Saturday or at least one weekday night per week. Asking for help, dividing up and sharing your duties, and staying active are all potent forces that can reduce your feelings of hopelessness, apathy, and dejection. The energy and motivation gained from adding such things to your life can help you to feel better so you can handle your responsibilities and life's difficulties in more positive and productive ways in the future.

ॐ ॐ ॐ

I MAKE CHANGES THAT HELP ME GET UP, NOT GIVE UP.

"Don't get involved in partial problems, but always take flight to where there is a free view over the whole single great problem, even if this view is still not a clear one."
— Austrian philosopher Ludwig Wittgenstein

PROBLEM-SOLVING

If, while walking through the woods, you tripped over a dead log on the path, fell, and skinned your knee, you could hobble home, clean the wound, and tape a bandage over it. But if, on the next day, you tripped over the same dead log on the path, what would you do? You can treat your injury again and again, but it's never going to get better until you solve the whole problem—the cause of the injury as well as the injury itself.

Such injury and re-injury can also occur on an emotional level. While you might not consciously or willingly allow yourself to be re-exposed to re-injuring yourself, doing so on an unconscious level is quite common. One way is to re-expose yourself to the same painful situation. You could be married to an abusive partner who beats you or is emotionally abusive, but you keep returning to the same abuse. Another way is to think in excessively negative and self-critical ways. If, for example, your partner leaves you, you re-injure yourself each time you berate yourself with comments such as, "What's wrong with me? I screw up all my relationships. I can't do anything right. I'm worthless and no good."

Whenever you face emotional pains, you can make choices that lead to increased pain or to healing. Healing choices promote growth and restoration of health by solving the whole problem, not just part of it.

🦋 🦋 🦋

I PROMOTE HEALING THROUGH POSITIVE PROBLEM SOLVING.

"Feeling is a breath orgasm."
— Joseph Kramer

FEELING YOUR BREATHING

Feelings are intimately connected to your breathing. When your moods change, your breathing changes. When you're nervous or anxious about a first visit or evaluation by a mental health professional, your breathing may be quick and shallow. When you're calm and peaceful—being comforted by a friend or lying next to your partner, your breathing may be slow and regular. When you're emotionally spent or drained from several minutes of crying or venting your anger, your breathing may consist of irregular gasps of air.

While most of the time you may be able to get in touch with how you're feeling from the way you're breathing, sometimes when you're emotionally shut down, you may not know how you feel. To get in touch with such feelings involves becoming more familiar with how your body's responding, almost in the same way you'd become more conscious of your physical responses to a lover's touch.

Pay attention right now to your breathing. Ask yourself the following questions: "Is my jaw tense? Is my stomach in knots? Is it hard for me to talk? Is it hard to keep quiet? Are my teeth clenched? Are my eyes stinging? Are my palms sweaty?" After you've assessed your physical responses, ask yourself, "What am I thinking?" Once you know what you're thinking and how your body is responding to these thoughts, you can clarify and then express your feelings. Today, pay attention to your breathing, your physical responses, and your thoughts so you can learn how you feel.

ॐ ॐ ॐ

I FOCUS ON MY BREATHING TO DISCOVER MY EMOTIONS.

"Difficulty, my brethren, is the nurse of greatness—a harsh nurse, who roughly rocks her foster-children into strength and athletic proportion."

— poet William Cullen Bryant

GOING ALL OUT

Kansas City Royals star George Brett, one of the most dedicated players in professional baseball, was once asked by reporter what he wanted to do at his last at-bat. He replied, "I want to hit a routine grounder to second and run all out to first base, then get thrown out by half a step. I want to leave an example to the young guys that that's how you play the game: all out."

Are you willing to work as hard for something you want, or do you often wish things came to you much easier? A team of researchers at the University of Chicago analyzed the careers of concert pianists, sculptors, research mathematicians, neurologists, Olympic swimmers, and tennis champions to determine what led them to high levels of achievement. What they discovered is that talent alone didn't make them great at what they did; rather, their ultimate excellence was a product of total commitment and hard work over the long term.

Today, begin to live by the words of Bertrand Russell: "To teach men to live without certainty and yet without being paralyzed by hesitation is perhaps the chief thing philosophy can do." Set aside time in which to practice a skill you want to restore or strengthen. Create goals. Strive for improvement. Doing something "all out" will help you to get the most out of the effort you put in.

🎀 🎀 🎀

I GO "ALL OUT" IN THE GAME OF LIFE.

"Depression moods lead, almost invariably, to accidents. But, when they occur, our mood changes again, since the accident shows we can draw the world in our wake, and that we still retain some degree of power even when our spirits are low. A series of accidents creates a positively light-hearted state, out of consideration for this strange power."

— Jean Baudrillard

BEING ACCIDENT-PRONE

When you're feeling down, you may not pay attention to much more than how badly you're feeling. As a result, you may find that through carelessness or lack of concentration, you become more susceptible to accidents—tripping over objects you hadn't noticed were in your way, missing the bottom step on a stairway, bumping into furniture, or nearly rear-ending cars in front of you. Such things may only add to your level of frustration and dejection; you may wind up saying, "I'm so bad off I can't even get out of my own way."

You may not feel particularly good about yourself when you're so down and accident-prone. So it's important to train yourself to focus on simple, positive things you can do to help restore your sense of emotional as well as physical balance. Ask for help when you need it. Change your attitude by appreciating what you can do and forgiving yourself for the things you can't do. Exercise, eat right, get plenty of rest, and expose yourself to light; in other words, take good care of yourself. Set up activities that cause you as little stress as possible; for example, seek out tasks that require little concentration. And keep your faith—things *will* improve!

ৰ্জ ৰ্জ ৰ্জ

I AM CAREFUL AND CARING WITH MYSELF.

"We cannot tear out a single page from our life, but we can throw the whole book into the fire."

— from *Mauprat*, by George Sand

MAKING LIFESTYLE CHANGES

One of the most important ways of overcoming mood swings is to take an honest look at yourself and your life so you can identify all of the sources of tension, stress, and pressure that are part of your day-to-day living. Each of these sources are based on choices you've made—choices which, unfortunately, can create a negative impact in your life that serves to fuel your stress, adding to your despondent moods.

Consider your answers to the following questions: Do you smoke? Do you lack a support network? Are you unhappy in the career you've chosen? Do you have a workaholic attitude? Are you abusing drugs or alcohol? Are you eating all the "wrong" foods? Are you overweight? Has it been years since you've had a complete medical evaluation? Do you live a sedentary lifestyle? Do you try to take on too much yourself or endure too much alone? Do you have chronic health problems that you ignore? Are you living in a stressful environment, such as with an abusive partner? Is your diet poor? Do you isolate yourself from others? Are you unable to handle your financial obligations?

Remember, each of these choices can be eliminated from your life or changed into a positive choice that can make you feel healthier and more relaxed. One at a time, like pages in a book, you can rewrite the book of your life into one with a happy ending.

❧ ❧ ❧

I MAKE BENEFICIAL LIFESTYLE CHANGES.

"It is characteristic of all deep human problems that they are not to be approached without some humor and some bewilderment."

— author/physicist Freeman Dawson

CREATING A POSITIVE FOCUS

In a world that continually emphasizes unpleasant occurrences, there are things you can do on a daily basis to remind yourself that there are also joyous events that are part of the world:

- Keep a "joy journal" in which you list all the gifts that come into your life each day—from a coin you find on the sidewalk to a letter from a friend.
- List several people, places, or things that bring you joy and pleasure—from walking in the woods to being with your children.
- Create a "joyous itinerary" in which you list activities you engage in yourself or with others that are fun and amusing—from playing backgammon with a friend to renting a favorite movie.
- In your work area or preferred areas in your living space, surround yourself with pictures that make you feel happy when you gaze at them.
- Affirm and believe that joy and humor can be a part of every day. As Napoleon Hill wrote, "Whatever the mind of man can conceive and believe, he can achieve." Say out loud or repeat several times to yourself: "I can find some humor in every situation. I can smile at the new opportunities that come my way each day. I can laugh and enjoy the sound of my own laughter."
- Finally, visualize wonderful things happening to you and to those you love.

Խ Խ Խ

I TEACH MYSELF TO FOCUS ON THE POSITIVE.

"In the Olympics, perfection is the goal. And we all cheer heartily for the gymnast, the diver or the ice skater who scores the perfect 10. In our own lives, though, the drive for perfection is not always beneficial. High goals and standards may be admirable, but an excessive desire for perfection can cause trouble."

— The Menniger Letter

PERFECTIONISM

While wanting to achieve a perfect score on a test, striving to attain a perfect "10" in an Olympic competition, struggling to maintain a perfect home, exhibiting the characteristics of a perfect employee, and longing to raise perfect children may be admirable goals, the drive for perfection is not always beneficial. In fact, perfectionism has been linked to depression. In a study of 50 male and female college students, those who believed that they must perform well in most of their activities were often more prone to depression. In a study of two groups of older adults who were undergoing psychiatric treatment, a large percentage of depression symptoms were attributed to those with perfectionistic tendencies. And in a study of children ages 9 through 12, the struggle to be perfect resulted in headaches and eating disorders.

What this means is that for all people, no matter what the age or gender, standards of achievement and goals that are set need to be realistic. As well, they need to have, built into them, more than one level of an acceptable standard of achievement that promotes doing one's best, rather than doing or being *the* best. While it's wonderful to be able to achieve high standards and admirable goals that have been set from time to time, it's also important to be practical and to recognize that failure to always attain such high standards is not the fault of the person, but of the standards that have been set.

გა გა გა

I AM SENSITIVE TO THE TYPES OF GOALS AND STANDARDS THAT I SET FOR MYSELF.

"Remember that death is not to be postponed. The hour of your appointment with the grave is undisclosed. Before you die, do good to your friend; reach out as far as you can to help him. Do not miss a day's enjoyment or forge your share of innocent pleasure....Give and receive..."

— Ecclesiastes 14:12-19

ENJOYING A LOVED ONE

Often death goes hand in hand with the phrase "If only..." It's so common to hear someone declare, after losing a loved one, "If only we had been able to spend more time together," "If only I had treated each one of our moments together as precious," or "If only I had said all the things I wanted to."

Yet relating a litany of "if onlys" does no good once someone is gone. What should matter is not thinking about all the things you would have liked to have done together, but taking action in the present—doing all the things you want to do now, before your loved one is gone. Today is a day you can fill with giving, sharing, nurturing, loving, laughing, and conversing with someone who's dying. Read a favorite book aloud; share your memories as you flip through a photo album; play a game together; sit outside in the fresh air and sunshine; provide a nourishing soup or make a soothing cup of tea; cuddle together; tell not only what's on your mind, but also what's in your heart.

Do all these things while your family member, partner, or special friend is alive so when he or she leaves, you mind won't be filled with "if onlys" or your heart bursting with regrets. You'll be able to mourn the death but know you were there in life.

❧ ❧ ❧

I TREAT EACH MOMENT WITH A LOVED ONE AS A PRECIOUS GIFT.

"A deep distress hath humanized my soul."
— William Wordsworth

PEER COUNSELING

One form of counseling that can be a valuable experience not only for you but also for another is peer counseling, also known as co-counseling or re-evaluation counseling. It's an affordable, helpful healing tool in which both people get time and attention devoted to their issues. It also has the added benefit of helping you to focus for a short time on the issues of your peer counseling partner, thereby becoming a humanizing process that helps to soften the spirit and the soul.

Peer counseling involves two people who know and trust each other, who then set up a peer counseling arrangement. Decide how often you want to meet—such as once a week—and for how long—such as for one hour. It's also a good idea to set aside the same time each week so you both become accustomed to peer counseling on a structured basis.

Divide the time you're spending together in half so each partner receives an equal amount of time. During your time, you can talk about anything you want and express your emotions openly and honestly—but without becoming hostile or abusive. Your partner listens to you, focuses on your issues, and then gives positive support and advice. For the second half of the session, the focus is placed on the partner.

Awareness, acceptance, and letting go are part of the healing process integral to peer counseling. A deep well of compassion for one another can be created as a result of the work you do together and the healing you facilitate.

ॐ ॐ ॐ

I GIVE AND RECEIVE HEALING HELP.

*"Facing it—always facing it—that's the way to get through!
Face it!"*

— Joseph Conrad

HANDLING ADDICTIONS

The morning after the first time you got drunk, do you remember telling yourself that you'd never drink again? But over the next several years, you may have repeated the same routine countless times—getting drunk and then swearing off alcohol the next morning. You may be familiar with other "morning-after" routines—mornings after parties where you had to be high to talk to others or to have a good time, mornings after you woke up next to a stranger because you were using sex to numb your feelings of grief and loss, mornings after nights in which you binged with food to soothe your loneliness or self-hatred. And each morning you vowed to yourself, "It will never happen again"—yet it always did, time and time again.

Today, it's time to take a long, hard look at the role alcohol, drugs, sex, and food have on your life. Is it difficult for you to imagine going without any of those crutches? Is it too frightening to think about trying to find healthier ways of dealing with the empty, lonely, scared person inside you? Now, or at some time in the near future, you may finally reach "the point of no return" when you finally concede that using such things is neither a helpful nor a positive alternative to dealing with your feelings. When you do, be sure to have on hand resources to help you overcome the wide array of feelings that will attempt to push you back to drinking, drugging, food binging, or using sex as an escape: supportive self-help groups, the names of those who have endured what you're going through, and the listings of therapists who can help you.

ya ya ya

I SEEK RECOVERY FROM AN UNHEALTHY ADDICTION.

"...the journey begins by quieting one's insides, making room, leaving time to hear and to notice...the practice of spiritual growth has as its core the practice of silence."
— John Fortunato

RESTORING INNER ENERGY

The ancient Chinese taught that it was wise to emulate the tortoise, a creature that knew when to withdraw into itself to restore its inner energy. Are you like the tortoise? Do you know when it's right to withdraw from conflicts, pressures, and energy drains? Are you able to step back from difficult or painful situations so you can become less confused and more centered?

Whenever you're confused and uncentered, you project your own inner conflicts into the world around you. So rather than resolve situations that already exist, your unsettled feelings serve to escalate them. But when you're at peace with yourself—when you're able to "go within" so you can restore your energy—then you become more capable of seeing disruptive situations clearly so you can act more definitively. You restore peace to the world around you because you have restored peace in yourself.

Cultivating inner peace can involved deep breathing to slow the mind, calm restless energy, and restore the body to a relaxed state; periods of relaxed silence in which to quietly reflect without interruption and to gently relax tense muscles; or listening to a guided meditation tape to expel tension, noise, and discomfort.

But no matter what form of spiritual exercise you choose, practice it each day. It's a simple, two-step process: calm the mind, and listen.

🐢 🐢 🐢

I CALMLY RESTORE MY INNER ENERGY.

"I never think about my limitations, and they never made me sad. Perhaps there is just a touch of yearning at times; but it is vague, like a breeze among flowers."

— Helen Keller

RISING ABOVE LIMITATIONS

Do you sometimes resent the limitations in your life because of how you feel? Maybe you're hesitant to make plans too far ahead of time for fear you'll be in a "bad way" at that time and need to cancel your plans. Perhaps you refuse invitations to social events because you feel you just don't have the energy to be "upbeat" and make sparkling conversation with people. Maybe you feel so low about yourself that you isolate yourself from others. Perhaps you're so afraid of making mistakes or failing that you don't set any goals, take any risks, or strive for any changes.

Helen Keller, who became one of the outstanding women of her time, was both deaf and blind. The story of her journey through life is an enthralling mixture of struggle, strength, and the transforming power of having faith in oneself. Her life invites you to think differently about your own disadvantages and limitations. Especially at times that are particularly hard for you, you too may feel a touch of yearning—a vague breeze of longing for a different way of being, thinking, feeling, and acting. This yearning can feel deep and bitter to you; if it is, then chances are you'll remain limited and disadvantaged. Or the yearning can make you feel grateful and challenged; if it is, then chances are you can rise above your limitations and focus on positive paths that can lead to greater advantages.

🦋 🦋 🦋

I RISE ABOVE MY LIMITATIONS.

*"There are trees that seem to die at the end of autumn.
There are also the evergreens."*

— Gilbert Maxwell

LIFE AND DEATH

Often, when someone dies, you may strive to cloak death in meaning, to imagine what happens after death, speculate about reincarnation, or talk about eternal life. When Maya Angelou, poet and author of *I Know Why the Caged Bird Sings*, was asked, "What's the meaning of life?" she realized that in trying to arrive at a definitive answer, her view changed from week to week. "When I know the answer, I know it absolutely," she said. "As soon as I know that I know it, I know that I know nothing." The meaning of death is equally opaque to everyone; it remains an unsolved mystery.

What really dies when someone dies? Is anything actually destroyed? Because the stilled body will eventually return to its original components of water and chemicals, it's not really destroyed but merely transformed. What about the person's mind? Does it cease to function, or does it make a transition to another existence of a higher plane? No one knows for sure. You are powerless not only over the death of others, but also over understanding the meaning of their death.

When a person dies, the only thing that disappears is the identity—the collection of parts you once called by a name, someone with a unique personality who had a meaningful role in your life. What dies is the physical matter of that person. There's still someone underneath that identity who doesn't die. Where that person goes or how he or she gets there is, like life, beyond your capability to control, change, or comprehend.

ﬁ ﬁ ﬁ

I ACCEPT DEATH AS PART OF LIFE AND LIFE AS PART OF DEATH.

"The best way to cheer yourself up is to try to cheer someone else up."

— Mark Twain

BEING NECESSARY

When you feel swamped by your own problems, paralyzed by your emotions, or struck down by profound loss or misfortune, you can be helped by helping others. You can involve yourself in many different ways in the world around you. Within the context of your home, your job, your partner, your family, your friends, and others with whom you have contact, there are hundreds of experiences that create opportunities for you to reach out to others. You can, as Ralph Waldo Emerson has said, "make yourself necessary" to them.

How can you be necessary? By contributing your best efforts and talents to the situations that involve you. By creating a balance of giving and receiving. By providing comfort and support to others who share in a similar journey to yours. By valuing yourself and others. By offering what you've learned from the lessons of life, and by paying attention to the lessons you're being given in return.

Because every person is necessary to the completion of the whole portrait of your existence, the gift of lift obligates you to extend yourself to others. From now on, don't doubt your value or the value of others in your life. Make yourself necessary to others. Be there for them and be grateful for their existence in your life. By nourishing and nurturing the spirit of other individuals, you'll be allowing your own to flourish and grow.

ℬℬ ℬℬ ℬℬ

I NOURISH MY SPIRIT AND THAT OF OTHERS AS WELL.

"When you finally go back to your old hometown, you find it wasn't the old home you missed but your childhood."
— Sam Ewing

PARENTAL RELATIONSHIPS

Holidays focus on families. As a result, it may be difficult to escape from the emotional downswings caused by memories of old hurts or an unhappy childhood. And it may be even more emotionally trying to interact with your parents. Even though it may be draining to be with them, it may be hard not to want to try once more to get from them the love, attention, support, validation, or apologies you may not have gotten when you were growing up.

It may be futile to get from your parents this holiday season what you didn't get when you were growing up. But that doesn't mean you can't strive as an adult to reconnect with them in the present so you can have a good relationship now—and in the future.

To do so, keep in mind that your relationship today isn't parent to child—it's adult to adult. Instead of making demands on aging and perhaps still dysfunctional parents, expect less from them. Rather than carry old grudges and hurts with you when you go home for the holidays or your parents visit you, take a moment to think about all the things you do appreciate about your parents. Even though it may be hard to find things that are wonderful and warm, at least there may be little things they've done for you that you may discover mean a lot to you right now.

ﱞﱞ ﱞ ﱞ

I FOCUS ON BUILDING A DIFFERENT RELATIONSHIP WITH MY PARENTS.

"There are two ways of meeting difficulties: you alter the difficulties, or you alter yourself meeting them."

— Phyllis Bottome

MEETING DIFFICULTIES

Consider the following list of difficulties that you may encounter in your life: You've lost your job. You've been in a car accident. Your marriage has ended. You've just retired. You're having financial troubles. Do you consider such events tragedies or opportunities?

Now consider this list: You've been offered a job in a new business. Your insurance company and parents have provided you with enough money to buy your first luxury car. Your best friend has introduced you to someone with whom you have a lot in common. You and your partner have decided to sell the house, buy a mobile home, and drive around the country for a few years. Do you consider such things merely strokes of good luck or opportunities?

Frederick Phillips said, "It is often hard to distinguish between the hard knocks in life and those of opportunity." Yet, if you think about it, some of the most beneficial changes you've made in yourself and your life may have been the result of painful circumstances you've had to endure, as well as golden opportunities.

What things have been handed to you recently that you can count as blessings? Whether they were enjoyable or not, each can be perceived as "nudges" that can encourage you to use them as positive tools for self-transformation. Each event can point to change—and out of change can come opportunity.

❧ ❧ ❧

I SEE MY OPPORTUNITIES AS NEW BEGINNINGS.

*"Best of all is to preserve everything in a pure, still heart,
and let there be for every pulse a Thanksgiving, and for
every breath a song."*
— from *The Heart of the Matter*, by Graham Greene

THE GIVING OF THANKSGIVING

Don Butcher was harvesting wheat on his farm in Washington
state when his wife Helen fell ill. Preoccupied with looking after
her, he asked neighboring farmers to store his wheat. After Helen
died on Thanksgiving Day, Butcher came across a passage from
Isaiah: "*And if thou draw out thy soul to the hungry...then shall thy
light rise in obscurity, and thy darkness be as the noonday.*" Butcher
interpreted that passage in a way that become a fitting tribute to
his wife and the life they had led together: he decided that each
year he would ship food he and others had raised to the Soviet
Union. The first year, he shipped the wheat his neighbors had
stored for him.

Since that time, each year around Thanksgiving, Butcher helps to
organize large shipments of foods such as dried beans and wheat,
contributed by other farmers, to be shipped to Russian charities for
distribution. A federally funded program helps offset the cost of the
transportation overseas, but Butcher pays the rest. He includes an
address of an American family with each sack of food so the re-
cipients will have someone to write to and thank. "I want this grain
to go to a family, from a family," Butcher explains. "I want to say it's
not bread alone, but sharing God's love that can make a world of
difference."

This Thanksgiving, do something within your family or outside
your family as a tribute to a loved one who can no longer celebrate
the holiday with you.

ॐ ॐ ॐ

I GIVE OF MYSELF IN HONOR OF ANOTHER THIS THANKSGIVING.

"When a man says he has exhausted life, you may be sure life has exhausted him."

— Oscar Wilde

BEING INTERESTED IN LIFE

"Dear World...I am leaving because I am bored," wrote George Sanders on April 25, 1972. The actor, who had to his credit more than 90 film appearances (including the character who spoke the above line in the movie, *The Picture of Dorian Gray*), an Oscar for his performance as a cynical drama critic in *All About Eve*, and the finances and time to travel the world, somehow found his life too dull. So he swallowed five bottles of Nembutal and penned his infamous suicide note as a farewell to a world that bored him to death.

How often are you bored with your life? What do you do about it? Too often, people complain that they're bored, but they don't do anything more than that.That's why it's up to you to change your feelings of boredom into feelings of interest. If you're bored sitting in front of the television for hours, then turn it off and pick up a book or go for a walk. If you're bored with your work, then scan the classified ads for a more interesting job, or enlist the help of a career counselor. If you're bored in your intimate relationship, then do something out of the ordinary—make reservations at a bed-and-breakfast inn or prepare a special dinner. If you're bored in general, renew an interest in the arts—rent a classic film, enroll in a painting class, or listen to some old records or tapes. It's your responsibility to overcome the boredom in your life. From this moment on, resolve to take the initiative and explore what's available to capture your interest.

※ ※ ※

I TAKE A CONSCIOUS AND ACTIVE INTEREST IN MY LIFE.

"Never think about any one thing for too long."
— Walter Bowers Pillsbury

FORGIVENESS CARDS

The fall and winter season are perfect times to reconnect with old friends and family members. Holidays provide the perfect excuses to send cheery cards and "catch-up" letters, to make telephone calls, and to extend invitations to others as well as to accept them.

But do you sometimes find yourself each year wishing you could reconnect with someone with whom you may have had a falling-out, whom you may have hurt, or who may have hurt you? Since this is the season of endings and beginnings, why not seize the opportunity to try to make peace with some old hostilities or amend some past transgressions.

On your list of people to whom you usually send seasonal cards or letters, add the name of someone with whom you'd like to make a clean beginning or atone for the past—someone with whom you're not necessarily on good terms, with whom you may have quarreled, or with whom there's unfinished business. A simple greeting might be: "Sorry that we've lost touch. I'd like to forget whatever water has gone under the bridge between us and begin anew. If this isn't what you'd like, then please accept my blessings for good wishes, health, and happiness this season. If this *is* what you'd like, then I want you to know how much I look forward to hearing from you."

Sometimes when you share forgiveness and extend a hand, someone else will forgive you and offer a hand in return.

ॐ ॐ ॐ

I SEND A FORGIVENESS CARD TO SOMEONE WHOM I'D LIKE BACK IN MY LIFE.

"Do not lose your inward peace for anything whatsoever, even if your whole world seems upset."

— Saint Frances de Sales

DEVELOPING INNER PEACE

Your days may be filled with stress, hectic activities, seemingly endless frustration, and interactions with tense people. But you can remain emotionally calm and physically serene in the face of any crisis. Here are two simple techniques for quelling tension:

- Practice a breath-counting meditation. Go to a quiet place, settle in a comfortable position, close your eyes, and begin to breathe slowly and deeply. When you feel yourself relaxing, picture in your mind a series of stairs that lead away from tension to a peaceful place. Begin walking up the stairs. Breathe in and count "one" as you step onto the first stair, then exhale. Breathe in and count "two" as you step onto the second stair, then exhale. Continue counting to ten as you slowly "walk" up the stairs toward your inner peace—and away from outer tension.

- Use Jin Shin Jyutsu, a gentle form of bodywork that uses pressure points used in acupuncture. In this exercise, take a lesson from babies who suck their thumbs when they're worried. Gently hold the thumb of one hand with the thumb and fingers of the other. "A harmonizing action occurs when you hold your thumb," says Jin Shin teacher Wayne Hackett. "Keep holding on until you feel your body start to relax. A big exhaling sigh is usually the clue. You can feel yourself letting go physically, emotionally, and spiritually."

ॐ ॐ ॐ

I DEVELOP A STRONG SENSE OF INNER PEACE.

*"He was in the grip of that most trying form of depression—
the melancholy of enforced inaction."*
— from *Down Among the Dead Men*, by Patricia Moyes

EXERCISING YOUR FATIGUE

One of the symptoms of depression that can be most frustrating is the feeling of fatigue and decreased energy. Many depressed people say, "I feel totally exhausted. It's like I have to drag myself through the day. And sleeping doesn't help. If I take a nap, I usually feel even more tired when I wake up."

It may seem contradictory, but physical exertion is the most natural answer for healing your body—even when it's in such a drained state. As Aaron Sussman says, "Walking is an excellent technique to drain off panic and dangerous impulses...." After 15 to 20 minutes of vigorous exercise, neurochemicals called catecholamines are secreted into your brain and endorphins are released into your bloodstream. Catecholamines help fight depression and encourage creativity, while endorphins are natural pain killers and mood elevators. So after exercise, when your body returns to its normal equilibrium, you feel relaxed, refreshed, and more energized.

As you begin your exercise workout, put aside all thoughts of how tired you feel. Concentrate on your stride or pace, your surroundings, and the sound of your breathing. Keep your body in motion, then let your mind begin to wander. What you may find is that your thoughts are no longer focused on how tired you are but on other activities you'd like to do when you finish your workout.

❧ ❧ ❧

I CURE MY FATIGUE WITH EXERCISE.

*"Make it a rule of life never to regret and never to look
back. Regret is an appalling waste of energy; you can't
build on it; it's only good for wallowing in."*
— Katherine Mansfield

GOING WITH THE FLOW

Life is dynamic—an incredible flow of energy that has a strong,
determined current. Like a river, it constantly flows, its currents
forming new patterns based on change. If you live your life as a dynamic person, then you aren't afraid to travel on the river of life.
You go wherever its flow takes you. You remain motionless when
its waters run calm; you race along when its waters rush; you make
twists and turns when the water forges its path. As the pattern of
the river of life changes, so does the way you move through it.

But when you live your life holding on to the past—by remembering the pains of childhood or by reminiscing over "glory days"
gone by—then you're not able to flow with the river. Instead, you
watch the river go by or fight wherever the river wants to take you.
Your regrets keep you from enjoying your travels down the river.

Many people resist enjoying their river journey or looking for-
ward to where the waters of life take them. But there's an old
Chinese adage that says, "Flowing water does not decay." When
you go with the flow, you move. When you don't, you stagnate.
From now on, get into motion. Move your mind, body, and spirit.
Do something new, different, exciting, and challenging. Be like
Huckleberry Finn. Build your raft and journey to wherever the river
of life takes you.

ໃ ໃ ໃ

I GO WITH THE FLOW OF LIFE'S CURRENT.

*"I have my own particular sorrows, loves, delights; and you
have yours. But sorrows, gladness, yearning, hope, love
belong to all of us, in all times and in all places."*
— H.A. Overstreet

SELF-FOCUS

When you were a child, did you want to emulate your favorite
heroes, wishing you could be as strong, as smart, or as self-
sufficient as they were? Do you still sometimes put people up on
pedestals and wish you could be just like them?

Mood disorders can lower your self-esteem to the extent that
you see yourself as quite different—and quite defective—when
compared to others. Because you can't trust your own perceptions,
feel different from others, and believe that you're not as good as
everyone else, you may strive to imitate those you think have it all
together. But in doing so, you neglect your own uniqueness. By
looking around you at what everyone else has, you ignore what you
have. By focusing your energy and attention on others rather
than on yourself, you hinder your ability to discover your own talents and skills.

Why not discover your own unique qualities and talents that
make you who you are? Create a "victory list"—a compilation of
your successes and the things you've done in your life that have
given you great satisfaction. A victory could be major, such as leaving a bad marriage or changing jobs, or it could be a daily
achievement such as taking time to meditate or calling a supportive
friend. It doesn't matter whether the victories are big or small or
how they compare to what others have done. What matters is how
they make you feel.

❧ ❧ ❧

I FOCUS ON MY OWN UNIQUE QUALITIES.

DECEMBER 1

"Some days confidence shrinks to the size of a pea, and the backbone feels like a feather. We want to be somewhere else, and don't know where—want to be someone else, and don't know who."

— Jean Hersey

SELF-DISCOVERY

Who are you? What do you like about yourself? What makes you happy? What are your strengths and talents?

These are certainly not easy questions to answer, particularly when you often feel down on yourself. At one time, when you were younger perhaps, you may have thought that you knew the answers to such questions. Now you may be confused, upset, disappointed, frustrated, ashamed, or angry with respect to who you believe you are.

You're not like anyone else in the world. You're not like your friends. Even if you dressed, walked, talked, and acted like them, you wouldn't be them. You're not like your siblings. Even if you're a twin, all you share is being a member of the same family. You're not like any other member of your profession, your support groups, your neighbors, or your class. No one is just like you.

You're an independent human being—emotionally, physically, and spiritually. That's why it's important to be true to yourself and your individuality even when you're not always happy with who you are. Self-growth as an individual is about standing on your own two feet and making your own decisions.

Today, revel in your independence from others. Celebrate your own separate thoughts, feelings, and actions.

🍃 🍃 🍃

I DISCOVER—AND LIKE—WHO I AM.

"Trials are medicines which our gracious and wise Physician prescribes, because we need them; and He proportions the frequency and weight of them to what the case requires. Let us trust His skill and thank Him for His prescription."
— John Newton

ANTIDEPRESSANT MEDICATION

Antidepressant medications have well-documented effectiveness in the treatment of biological depression as well as milder forms of depression that have biological symptoms (such as sleep problems, loss of appetite, fatigue). Antidepressants are a specific and unique class of medications which, when taken, don't produce a "high," but rather a "normalizing" effect. This means that they often make a depressed person control despondent feelings in the same way aspirin lowers a fever but won't lower normal body temperature.

The major antidepressant drugs—tricyclic antidepressants, monoamine oxidase inhibitors, the newer antidepressants (including Desyrel, Asendin, Prozac, Wellbutrin, and lithium)—aren't abused because they don't produce highs or elated feelings, even in "normal" people. Benefit can be derived from them over a long period of time because tolerance isn't built up. Because the symptoms of depression vary from one person to the other, there are those who can stop taking medication and remain at an even keel. But if you need to continue taking medication, remember that it's because you're still depressed—not because you're dependent upon the medication. Just as a person with high blood pressure needs medication for good health, so, too, must depression be treated to maintain a stable emotional state.

ßà ßà ßà

I AM GRATEFUL FOR THE BENEFITS DERIVED FROM MEDICATION.

DECEMBER 3

"Tell me, did you write the song, 'I'll Never Smile Again?'"
— Cary Grant to Deborah Kerr
in *An Affair to Remember*

COMMUNICATING YOUR NEEDS

When you're emotionally down, the last thing in the world you may want to hear are sarcastic, caustic, cutting, or critical comments about your "blue" mood. You're already well aware that you're down in the dumps, so well-meaning friends and family members who want you to get out of your depressed mood by ordering you to "Snap out of it!" or "Put on a happy face" are not helping you to feel any better.

How do you want to be treated when you're depressed? Several depressed people who participated in a study to explore ways out of their depression offered these suggestions about how they'd like others to respond to them when they're feeling low:

- I want someone to keep me safe or pray for me.
- I want people to remind me that this has happened before and I've gotten through it okay.
- I want someone to encourage me to take good care of myself or even help me to do so.
- I want people to be sympathetic to the pain I'm going through.
- I want someone to remind me not to be too hard on myself.
- I want people to be direct and ask if I need to talk.

Communicate what you'd like, need, or how you want to be treated when you're depressed. Receiving the support you desire is one way out of your depression.

ૐ ૐ ૐ

I ASK FOR WHAT I NEED.

"...the darkness was encumbering only because I relied upon my sight for everything I did, not knowing that another way was to let power be the guide."
— from a book by Carlos Castaneda

A SYMBOLIC CLEANSING

Traditions honoring the light and dark transitions of winter have been celebrated since the time that humans lived in tribes. Wise tribal heads, who understood the psychological need for renewal when darkness came early, created rituals for encouraging the return of the sun, letting go of the mistakes of the past, and creating possibilities for the future.

One ritual is called the Burning Bowl Ceremony, which you can do alone or with others. When you're indoors, use a wok or heavy pan near your kitchen sink; keep a tight-fitting lid handy. Outdoors, use a charcoal grill; a safe, contained bonfire; or a metal bowl set on a flat rock, away from dead leaves. Write a brief description of your emotions, attitudes, behaviors, or self-imposed limitations that you want to let go of on a piece of paper. Light a candle, then touch the flame to the paper and toss it into your "burning bowl." As you watch the paper burn, think of ways to replace what you're releasing. Pray to God or a Higher Power. Ask what needs to be realized in your life, what new strengths you can develop, what changes can benefit you, or what goals you can set.

As Gay and David Williamson describe in *Transformative Rituals: Celebration for Personal Growth*: "The fire takes the paper and changes it from one form to another. Likewise in our lives we will take these blocks, fears, old hurts, mistakes, and burn them. This releases our personal power, freeing it up to work in our lives in a more constructive way."

🌿 🌿 🌿

I LIGHT A CANDLE AND ILLUMINATE MY LIFE.

DECEMBER 5

"Life is an operation which is done in a forward direction. One lives toward the future, because to live consists inexorably in doing, in each individual life making itself."
— Spanish essayist José Ortega Y Gasset

FORWARD PROGRESS

A man who had moved from the East Coast to Southern California had so much packing and re-adjusting to do that he missed the summer planting season. He finally had time in the late fall to go to the nursery to buy seeds so he could bring in a winter harvest.

When the nursery worker looked at the man's seed packets, she commented, "It's much too late for you to be planting beans and squash. You might want to plant your winter vegetables now." The man ignored her advice. He planted yellow squash and green beans and was soon rewarded when the plants sprang up through the soil. But it wasn't long before the plants withered and died, for they needed long, hot summer days in order to flower and bear their fruit.

The man who had to plant his summer vegetables wanted to make up for the time in the past when he was too busy to get his garden planted. Rather than work with the seasons and plan ahead for the most appropriate crop, he remained focused on what he hadn't been able to do.

When you spend your days looking back at what you didn't get, couldn't do, should've done, or what you lost, or when you focus your energy on trying to recapture what's over and done with, then you'll never find happiness and joy in the present. Living requires movement; you need to flow with the passage of time.

ॐ ॐ ॐ

I MAKE PROGRESS TOWARDS MY FUTURE.

"How heavy the days are. There is not a fire that can warm me, not a sun to laugh with me. Everything base. Everything cold and merciless. And even the beloved stars look desolately down."

— Hermann Hesse

WORKING OUT OF DEPRESSION

Depression is an illness that can rob you of the meaning of life. When you ask yourself or others questions such as: "Who cares?" "What does it matter?" "What's the point?" and "Why bother?," you know you've lost your enthusiasm, sense of well-being, and contact with life's purpose. Unfortunately, this very symptom of depression can keep you from seeking professional treatment or from taking steps to help yourself. It can become a vicious cycle: as your untreated depression worsens, you feel that life is less and less worthwhile; as this feeling intensifies, you're less likely to seek treatment or explore self-healing options.

When, as Maryellen Walsh said, depression "creeps in and claims the person who once laughed with you, who once hugged you, who once loved to be first on the hill to catch the new powder snow," it's time to deal with your feelings. One way is to ask for help from a qualified therapist or psychiatrist. But bear in mind that establishing a patient-client relationship either in a one-to-one or group counseling situation is just one way to restore positive, healing feelings. Getting outdoors during daylight hours or using full-spectrum lighting, maintaining a diet that's nutritionally beneficial, participating in an exercise program, and taking medication can all play important parts in creating wellness in your life.

ৡৈ ৡৈ ৡৈ

I WORK OUT OF MY DEPRESSION AND WORK BACK INTO LIFE.

"One would think that it would be a sad experience—life on a pediatric ward—but it was not. In fact, it is the cheeriest place in the world, because as children always do, they create fun for themselves; their business is to deal with their pain first, and then to get on with their real business, which is to find joy."

— Forrest, father of a child with cancer

LEARNING FROM CHILDREN

Experiencing a serious, life-threatening illness is bad enough. But when you continually focus on it, it can make you feel worse. Even though you can't make your illness go away, and although you may eventually die from this ailment or complications from it, there are some things you can control while you're alive. One is your attitude. How can you remain positive while facing such a negative situation?

Adults can learn a lot from other adults who handle their illness with a positive attitude. But perhaps the best resource is children, who seem to have an incredible knack for overcoming suffering, an ability to live one moment at a time, and a talent for remaining social when adults would want to hide under a rock. One woman with cancer tried to see her life through the eyes of a child. She tried to find beauty in the smallest detail—a fiery red male cardinal at a backyard feeder, patterns of frost on a window, or the sound of ice-coated tree branches clicking together in the wind.

In a book written and illustrated by the children at the Center for Attitudinal Healing in California, titled *There Is a Rainbow Behind Every Dark Cloud*, they declare: "You can learn to control your mind and decide to be happy 'inside' with a smiling heart, in spite of what happens to you on the 'outside.'"

฿ะ ฿ะ ฿ะ

I FACE MY ILLNESS WITH A CHILD'S LIGHTHEARTED ATTITUDE.

"There is something infinitely healing in the repeated refrains of nature—the assurance that dawn comes after night, and spring after the winter."

— Rachel Carson

TRUSTING IN TODAY

Time brings summer to a close, and winter to an end as well. Time ages the brilliant petals of flowers and also prepares the new buds. Time advances moments in order to bring about change. Time brings the end to a life, as well as the beginning to another. Because of this continuum, you can trust that time will bring the good to you, as well as take away the bad.

Yet sometimes it may seem as though time speeds up during the fun-filled, relaxing, enjoyable hours—your moments of inner peace—and slows down during times of boredom, misery, and pain—your times of depression, grief, and "the blues." But time always proceeds at its same, steady, unchanging pace. As a result, you can be assured that with every minute that passes there can be new hope. Trying times will end with the great healer: time.

Yesterday may have been difficult; you may believe that today will be equally challenging to get through. Each moment may seem filled with stress, tension, pain, heartache, loneliness, hopelessness, rejection, and dejection. But rest assured that you can get through today, tomorrow, and all the tomorrows thereafter. You can always trust in the constancy of this fact: time will always move forward, taking you away from the old, and gently guiding you towards the new. Time is always on your side, taking you ever closer to new moments that are fresh and untouched.

🐚 🐚 🐚

I TRUST IN TODAY AS WELL AS TOMORROW.

"The death of a dear friend, wife, brother, lover, which seemed nothing but privation, somewhat later assumes the aspect of a guide or genius; for it commonly operates revolutions in our way of life, terminates an epoch of infancy or of youth which was waiting to be closed...and allows the formation of new ones more friendly to the growth of character."

— Ralph Waldo Emerson

BEING STRONG

Do you believe that because of illness, relocation, or a forced separation, this may be the last holiday season you'll share with your life partner, your family, or your friends? Whether you or someone else will be going away, the pain you may feel about the upcoming separation or anticipated loss can seem insurmountable. You may spend every minute of every day fearfully focusing on the time when that special person or people will be far away from you or no longer in your life. You may long to freeze time or just wish your pain would go away.

But your sorrows will pass, just as your happiness sometimes does. Your pain will ease up, just as your pleasure sometimes does. Nothing ever really stays the same. Nothing ever stands still. Nothing remains unchanged. Life is all about change—about tides coming in and out, and about people, places, and things moving in and out of your life.

What you need to do right now is take a deep breath and endure the present moment. Keep in mind the words, "And this, too, shall pass away." This present hour will not endure; time passes, and so will the pain.

 youtube youtube youtube

I AM STRONG AND WILL GET THROUGH EACH MOMENT TODAY.

"The first three times you came with the same story [they] would listen and try to help. But if you showed up a fourth time and it was the same old tired things, the others in the circle would just get up and move...it was time you did something about it."

— Anne Cameron

MAKING AN ACTION PLAN

Do you ever rehash the same situations or feelings all the time, but never do anything about them? You may hold fast to something—a fear, a past relationship, a miserable childhood, the death of a loved one, or your way of doing things—and thus hold yourself back, preventing forward motion as well as your growth. Instead of taking a risk, trying something new, getting on with your life, or accepting your limitations, you may remain mired in some internal conflict or your feelings of hopelessness. Like an old tree that has to remain rooted in one spot, you become unbending, rigid, and inflexible.

For centuries, Chinese calligraphers have painted bamboo as a symbol that shows how to harmonize with change and growth. Bamboo is thick on the outside, but hollow inside, so it's open to new possibilities; it's strong on the outside, but bends with the wind and doesn't break, so it's capable of being yielding.

You, too, can be more like bamboo. Remember that it's one thing to ask, "What would I really like to do about this?" and another to say, "Here's what I can do about this." Whenever you're faced with a dilemma in your life, stop talking and start doing. Come up with at least three alternatives that can help you get on with your life.

☙ ☙ ☙

I MAKE AN ACTION PLAN FOR EFFECTING CHANGE.

"Adversity draws men together and produces beauty and harmony in life's relationships, just as the cold of winter produces ice-flowers on the window-panes, which vanish with the warmth."
— Danish philosopher Sören Kierkegaard

FAMILY SUPPORT

Do you have other family members who experience mood swings or who are mutually grieving the loss of a loved one? Discussing your problems together, encouraging each other, providing mutual understanding and support, educating each other, building each other up, increasing your communication, offering unconditional love, advocating appropriate treatment, and providing mutual help in monitoring and recognizing symptoms are just a few of the ways you can work with other family members through mood swings and the grieving process. Also, involving family members who may not share in your feelings or symptoms but who can be understanding and supportive can also be helpful to your healing and recovery. By being open and honest about how you feel, you may be pleasantly surprised by the interest your family expresses in knowing more about your mood swings and treatment. They may even wish to attend support group meetings with you or a counseling session.

Mary Ellen Copeland, author of *The Depression Workbook*, stresses how important and helpful her family was during her most difficult times—and still are today: "The support of my grown children, their partners, my partner, and my mother was, and continues to be, essential to my own level of wellness....Their belief in me, and love for me, sustained me through my darkest hours."

ᢒᢇ ᢒᢇ ᢒᢇ

I REACH OUT TO A FAMILY MEMBER FOR SUPPORT.

"It usually happened...particularly at the beginning of a holiday. Then, when I was hoping for nothing but sleep and peace, the chattering echoes of recent concerns would race through my head, and the more I sought rest the more I could not find it."

— author Joanne Field

HOLIDAY STRESS

Depression and anxiety are especially dominant before and during the holidays. The upcoming family events, shopping, cooking, preparing for guests, and the scheduling of activities may seem to take precedence over everything else in your life—sleep included—as you nervously rush through your day or lie awake at night, your body physically exhausted but your mind restlessly processing, causing you to toss and turn in worry and anticipation.

Yet, there are ways to seek out calmness, peace, and serenity amidst all the emotional ups and downs and the hustle and bustle so common at this time of year. Instead of emotionally shutting down during the day or lying in bed at night focusing on all the things that put pressure on you, focus instead on things that are positive and hold enjoyment for you about the upcoming holidays. You might think, "I'm looking forward to eating a great meal with all my favorite dishes," "I can hardly wait for time off from work," "It'll be great to see my cousins again," or "I especially like watching the parades, old movies, and football games on TV."

With such positive images in mind, pick up a book you've been meaning to read or rent one of your favorite holiday videos. By putting holiday enjoyment first in your mind, you can get the physical, mental, and spiritual rest and relaxation you need.

🍂 🍂 🍂

I PUT THE STRESS OF THE HOLIDAY SEASON OUT OF MY MIND.

"I reached for sleep and drew it round me like a blanket muffling pain and thought together in the merciful dark."
— from *The Hollow Hills*, by Mary Stewart

SLEEP DISORDERS

Most people who are depressed also suffer from sleep disorders. The most common sleep disorder is insomnia—the inability to fall asleep and stay asleep. That's why people suffering from depression often say, "I can't remember the last time I had a good night's sleep." When you have difficulty falling asleep, a problem staying asleep because you awaken several times during the night, or when you experience early-morning awakenings at three or four o'clock in the morning and then can't get back to sleep, you're losing precious time to rest and relax your body and restore your mental concentration.

As Percy Knauth said, "As the lack of sleep wore me down, a sense of hopelessness enveloped me....I was convinced I was laboring under some kind of curse so that any efforts of my own to fight this situation were foredoomed to failure."

At the other end of the spectrum of sleep disorders is hypersomnia. People with hypersomnia can sleep 10, 12, or even 14 hours at a stretch and then still take naps during the day. Yet hypersomniacs also report feelings of exhaustion despite all the sleep they're getting.

The treatment for insomnia is not alcohol or sleeping pills; the treatment for hypersomnia is not caffeine or amphetamines. Focusing on the symptoms of depression won't make the depression go away. The best help you can get is to discuss your symptoms and a possible link with depression with your physician.

ॐ ॐ ॐ

I SEEK HELP FOR MY SLEEP DISORDER.

"It is a time when one's spirit is subdued and sad, one knows not why; when the past seems a storm-swept desolation, life a vanity and a burden, and the future but a way to death."

— Mark Twain

HOLIDAY PLANNING

Seasonal activities often trigger suicidal thoughts, behaviors, or actions. The holidays—when it seems that everyone is having such a great time planning for upcoming events, attending parties, and experiencing the joys of togetherness—can be the worst time of year for you if you're depressed, alone, or have recently lost a loved one. Couple these feelings with the reduced daylight hours during the winter season, and you have the recipe for suicidal thoughts. Anyone who has ever worked on a suicide hotline knows that the Christmas holidays inspire the greatest number of suicide attempts in this country.

However, there are things you can do to make the holiday season less stressful. Be selective about the parties and gatherings you'd like to attend; maybe choose to go to one or two, rather than several. Try not to overextend yourself by taking on too many activities. Keep a close watch on your checkbook and credit cards so you only spend what you can afford. Call on members of your support network, or attend as many meetings of your support groups as possible. Plan simple but pleasant times with people who know you well and can be understanding of your moods at this time of year. By breaking this holiday season down into manageable steps, you may discover that there are some things in life that you can enjoy.

🍂 🍂 🍂

I MAKE A LIFE-SAVING PLAN FOR THIS HOLIDAY SEASON.

"Heavy thoughts bring on physical maladies."
— Martin Luther

DEPRESSION AND ADDICTION

Depression is the number-one cause of alcoholism, drug abuse, and other addictions. Since being depressed can be such an intense emotional, physical, and spiritual source of misery, it's not uncommon to seek immediate solace from the pain. Almost any drug or distraction will do—both positive and negative panaceas can be abused in an effort to self-medicate the symptoms of depression. Self-medications need not be chemical; you can abuse just about anything in an effort to distract yourself from an untreated depression: sex, TV, gambling, work, relationships, and even religion.

But chemicals are usually the most common choice, for they have the greatest impact. Alcohol is the most commonly self-prescribed painkiller for depression; it's readily available, affordable, and socially acceptable. Unfortunately, alcohol is also a chemical depressant. After its brief euphoric effects wear off, your depression will only worsen. Drugs of all kinds—legal, illegal, over-the-counter, or prescription—are sometimes used inappropriately for numbing specific symptoms. Unfortunately, such drugs don't treat the underlying cause of the discomfort. Depression may also contribute to eating disorders; likewise, eating disorders may contribute to depression. Anorexia nervosa (self-starvation), bulimia (binge-eating followed by purging), and overeating are part of the downward spiral of depression.

If you feel you may have one of these "bad habits," then get help.

❧ ❧ ❧

I DEAL WITH MY PAIN RATHER THAN NUMB IT.

"The greater the obstacle, the greater the glory we have in overcoming it."

— Molière

PROGRESSIVE RELAXATION

Relaxation techniques can be a valuable resource in helping you work through difficult times and despondent moods. You can use the following calming meditation during a stressful time or crisis; have a partner read this passage to you, or record it yourself and then play it back as you listen to relaxing music:

Get in a very comfortable position, sitting in a chair or lying on a carpeted floor, couch, or bed. Stare at a spot directly in front of you or, if you're lying down, directly above you on the ceiling. Slowly take a deep breath to the count of eight, hold it for a count of four, then let it out for a count of eight. Do this a few times, then close your eyes and repeat the process as you focus on the muscle groups in each part of your body. Begin by focusing on your feet. Breathe in, hold, and then breathe out, allowing your feet to completely relax. Move your focus slowly up your legs, through your calves, then to your knees and your thighs as you continue your relaxed breathing.

Let these feelings of relaxation move slowly through your buttocks as you breathe, then focus on your lower abdomen and your lower back. Move the relaxed feeling slowly up your spine and through your abdomen. Continue breathing as you extend relaxation to your chest and upper back. Let this feeling flow into your shoulders, down your arms, through your elbows and wrists, and into your hands and finger. Breathe relaxation into your throat and your neck. Finally, focus on your face; breath into your jaw and cheek muscles, your eyes, your forehead, and your scalp. Your body is now completely relaxed.

❦ ❦ ❦

I RELAX EVERY MUSCLE AND CELL OF MY BODY.

"Sing away sorrow, cast away care."

— Cervantes

APPRECIATING MUSIC

Music can soothe, stimulate, or enhance almost any activity, emotion, or mood—from crying to dancing to having mystical visions. Carefully selected music can elicit positive, uplifting feelings. As William Congreve wrote in 1697, "Music has charms to soothe a savage breast, To soften rocks, or to bend a knotted oak." In what ways can you or do you use music to help ease your grief or keep you from singing "the blues"?

Music you find soothing can make an excellent accompaniment to a guided meditation or can even become a relaxing meditation by itself. Music you find stimulating can encourage you to become more active—it can make you want to dance, engage in a vigorous workout, sing along, or get up off your couch and do something. Music and musicians you enjoy can entice you out of the home, to concerts and coffeehouses. Appreciating music can be an activity that eases isolation as you share your musical interests with another.

Music can have its greatest healing effect upon you when it's not in the background, but when you're focused on it—truly hearing it, spending time with it, savoring it. As T.S. Eliot wrote, "Music heard so deeply that it is not heard at all, but you are the music/While the music lasts." Music is language. Music is affection. Music is communication. Music is a splendid, spectacular manifestation of creativity that can take you to a magical healing place in which you can sing away your sorrows and forget your woes.

ॐ ॐ ॐ

I APPRECIATE THE HEALING POWERS OF MUSIC TODAY.

"Use what talents you have; the woods would have little music if no birds sang their song except those who sang best."

— Rev. Oliver G. Wilson

USING YOUR CREATIVITY

When you're feeling down and lose confidence in yourself, it may be easy to doubt that you're good at anything. As a result, you may have no desire to discover your hidden talents or creativity. Instead, you may tell yourself, "If I can't do something better than someone else, then I'm not going to try at all."

This decision can serve to level some pretty harsh criticism in your direction. As you look over photographs you've taken, you may think, "I'm no Ansel Adams." As you reread a poem you've written, you may determine, "I'm no Emily Dickenson." As you assess your current position in business, you may say, "I'm no Lee Iacocca." Or you may tell the parent in you, "You're no Dr. Spock."

Such critical messages have an uncanny way of making you feel inferior before you even attempt something. They can also hurt or damage your attitude about your creativity and talents so you give up even trying. "After all," you might think, "I'll never be that good!"

But how do you know you won't be any good? It doesn't matter whether you become famous or successful. What does matter is that with talent, determination, and effort, you give yourself a chance to achieve splendid things.

Today, ignore the critical, negative messages you give yourself. Be curious about, and accepting of, what you can do. Let your creativity flow!

❦ ❦ ❦

I POSITIVELY EXPRESS MY TALENTS AND CREATIVITY.

"Question: I have so much on my mind as the holidays approach that my stomach is clenched. I feel mean and cranky. I wish I knew some simple, natural ways to deal with all this anxiety."

— journalist Jean Callahan

NATURAL HEALING

Depending on the form your anxiety takes, there are a variety of homeopathic self-treatments recommended for calming. *Gelsemium* is beneficial for fear-based anxiety; *Chamomilla* or *Pulsatilla* is used for irritability and anger; *Passiflora* is great for general anxiety; and *Ignatia* is best for anxiety associated with sadness or loss.

Herbal massages can also be quite soothing. You can make your own massage oil from high-quality olive oil or almond oil and a variety of herbal ingredients, available at health food stores. Begin with two ounces of oil, then add one ounce of cramp bark tincture, one-half ounce of lobelia tincture, and one-quarter ounce of wintergreen oil. If you can't find the particular tinctures, you can use lavender, rosemary, ylang-ylang, or pine oil to add a refreshing scent—whatever fragrance you find most relaxing.

Aromatherapy can also be used for bedtime soothers. Take a bath in essential oils—add only a drop or two to an entire tubful of water—for peaceful sleep. You can also make an herbal pillow with your favorite herbal scents. Fill a small pillow or cloth pouch with fresh herbs or fresh-dried herbs, then sleep with it close to your face.

Finally, in place of a nightcap, you can brew a packaged herbal tea such as chamomile or lemon balm.

ॐ ॐ ॐ

I EXPLORE NATURAL WAYS TO CALM MYSELF.

"...my relationship with Phil suffered from a kind of profound neglect. We'd see each other just a few times a year, usually on holidays, virtually always in a crowd. Worse, whenever Phil and I did find ourselves alone, a painful unease set in. We were like strangers at a party who ran out of conversation too quickly and rushed to refill our drinks before the silences became too obvious."

— author Marian Sandmaier

SIBLING RELATIONSHIPS

It took two major events in Marian Sandmaier's life to make her want to reconnect with her siblings. First, her brother Bob died of an accidental drug overdose, taking too much prescription codeine to treat his bad back; two years after that, almost to the exact day, her father died. She realized in her grief that her family was shrinking and became more powerfully conscious of those still around her. But how could she reconnect with her only other brother, Phil, who lived only 15 minutes from her and who had built a deck on his house that she didn't even know about until she stood on it three years later?

Because your brothers and sisters were there with you growing up, witnessing and participating in the family drama that shaped you, reconnecting with them can help you piece together the adulthood puzzle of yourself. But you can't reconnect with them until you let go of residual feelings that can get in the way of establishing new beginnings in your relationship. You need to release your anger over your sibling not being the first to try to reconnect, feel your sadness over the "lost years" you missed out on, and accept that your overtures of friendliness may be rebuffed.

ॐ ॐ ॐ

I RECONCILE WITH A SIBLING AND BEGIN ANEW.

> *"And I saw darkness for weeks. It never dawned on me that I could come out of it, but you heal. Nature heals you, and you do come out of it. All of a sudden I saw a crack of light...then all of a sudden I saw another crack of light.. And I recognized that there was no darkness, that in darkness there'll always be light."*
>
> — from *Dawns + Dusks*, by Louise Nevelson

HOLIDAY DARKNESS

"The blues" you feel over the holiday season may have a lot to do with the darkness outside you as well as the darkness inside you. It's not as if you're unaware of how you're feeling or behaving. You may be familiar with your argumentativeness, how you pick away at or obsess about issues, your oversensitivity, your ability to deliver cutting or biting remarks to those who care the most, your sudden outbursts into tears for no apparent reason, and your sullen silence and unresponsive brooding. But being aware of such behaviors doesn't mean they'll go away. Rather, being cognizant of them may make you feel worse: you feel sorry, embarrassed, guilty, and ashamed.

Christmas can, unfortunately, be the ultimate test for you. You know you're supposed to be joyous and happy. You know you're supposed to be decking the halls and "fa-la-la"-ing. You know you're supposed to wish everyone around you merry, happy holidays—and mean it. So you paste a smile on your face and really try to pull it off. But inside, you're absolutely blue.

Getting out in the light or gazing at bright lights is the best cure for a "Blue Christmas." Also, keep in mind that you're living in the darkest time of the year; the days will now begin to get progressively longer and lighter.

ℬ℘ ℬ℘ ℬ℘

I KEEP THE DARKNESS OUTSIDE ME—NOT INSIDE ME.

"As we struggle with shopping lists and invitations, compounded by December's bad weather, it is good to be reminded that there are people in our lives who are worth this aggravation, and people to whom we are worth the same."
— author Donald E. Westlake

THE SPIRIT OF GIVING

Perhaps the most wondrous gift is that given to a child so young that it only knows the pure joy of receiving. The child isn't bothered by knowing who gave the gift, why it was given, or whether something needs to be given in return. How can you capture that genuine spirit of giving with those who have supported you throughout the year?

As you work hard to overcome your depression, grief, or "blues," you may find that your healing is enhanced by giving to others. What can you give to others? You can give what you now have—knowledge about why you feel the way you do, self-help techniques that work for you, and treatment and support groups that you've found helpful. You can share this information with others who are just starting out on their road to recovery or remind others about it when they go through tough times. As Thomas Moore says, "[To] take something from yourself, to give to another, that is humane and gentle and never takes away as much comfort as it brings again."

This holiday season, perhaps your greatest gift can be a gift that comes from your heart, not your wallet. Ask a member of your support group out for coffee, organize a household donation to a worthwhile charity, provide a home for an animal from a shelter, or tell your story of hope to someone who feels down.

🌿 🌿 🌿

I GIVE GIFTS FROM THE HEART.

"Evidently Christmas was an unmitigated joy only for the people who inhabited department-store brochures and seasonal television specials. For everyone else the day seemed to be a trip across a mine field seeded with resurrected family feuds, exacerbated loneliness, emotional excess..."
— from *The Cracker Factory*, by Joyce Rebeta-Burditt

CONTROLLING MANIA

You may note that there's a seasonal pattern to your manic depression, and it may be in full swing today. Here are some things you can do when you're getting manic:

- Seek help before things get out of hand. Use your support system. Let these individuals know how you're feeling.
- As much as possible, reduce the stress in your environment. Stay home or in familiar surroundings, away from stimulating environments such as bars, dances, or office parties. It may help to take a hot bath, listen to soothing music, or use a relaxation technique.
- Make a list of things you can do to use up excess energy in positive ways. You can do the laundry, clean the house, reorganize your photo album, or clean out a closet.
- Avoid spending money Give your credit cards and money to a trusted friend or family member.
- Avoid sugar, caffeine, and alcohol. Eat regular meals.
- Take several breaks throughout the day and practice deep breathing.

%a %a %a

I BRING MY MANIA UNDER CONTROL.

*"While you have a thing it can be taken from you...but
when you give it, you have given it. No robber can take it
from you. It is yours then for ever when you have given it.
It will be yours always. That is to give."*

— James Joyce

SELFLESS GIVING

When you finish eating your filling holiday meals or exchanging
presents with family, co-workers, and friends, do you feel that
your hunger is truly satisfied? Or are you left with an empty sensation inside—a restless, unsettled feeling that may come from trying to fill your emptiness with consumable goods rather than by
selfless giving to others?

On Christmas Eve, you can celebrate the holiday in ways that
can satisfy your physical hunger as well as your spiritual hunger.
Call an old school chum you haven't seen for years and reminisce
about old times. Take the weekend off from work and home responsibilities and, with friends or family, explore the city you live
in. Approach the city as you would if you were a visitor: go to a
museum, walk through a park, explore some unique stores, and
sample the nightlife.

Contact friends and relatives you know who will be alone tomorrow or on New Year's Eve and invite them to spend the holidays with you. Organize an event for senior citizens at a local
nursing home. Arrange in advance to donate a portion of your holiday meal to a local homeless shelter. And, before you go to sleep
tonight, communicate with your Higher Power about how thankful
you are for all you've been given. By giving freely to others, you
can be more at peace with yourself and in your world.

❦ ❦ ❦

I GIVE TO OTHERS AND SO, TOO, GIVE TO MYSELF.

"Intimacy happens in moments. The mistake we make is in wanting it all the time."

— JoAnn Magdoff

INTIMATE MOMENTS

Wouldn't it be nice if the warm glow, loving feelings, nurturing acceptance, and laughter and lightness you feel with your loved ones today was like an eternal flame? That would mean, from this moment on, no matter what circumstances occurred, how difficult times became, or how much time passed, the flame of intimacy would always burn bright.

Close your eyes and think about how your loved ones can interact on this day. See them gathered together in peace and harmony, but keep this thought in mind: "This is what holidays are all about." That doesn't mean that from now on, conflicts will be easier to handle, loving feelings will predominate, or loved ones will now understand your depression or despondent moods and be able to support you in times of need. What it does mean is that for one day, there's a respite from the tension of the day-to-day or year-to-year struggle to get along. And that respite can be enjoyed for as long as it lasts and then released, without a struggle, when—or if—it ends.

You can delight in the shared laughter, relax with the ease of casual chatter, and be excited by a physical touch or embrace. Enjoy each intimate moment as it occurs, but remember that intimacy, like everything else, changes. Rather than strive to light an eternal flame from this evening's intimate moments, seek out the glow of a simple candle. Although from time to time the glow may be extinguished, it can always be relit.

❧ ❧ ❧

I ENJOY HOLIDAY MOMENTS OF PEACE AND INTIMACY.

"Life is pain and the enjoyment of love is an anesthetic."
— author Cesare Pavese

EXPRESSING LOVE

Love isn't a word you say or write. Love is the way you present yourself to the world—the face you put on, the clothes you wear, the way you walk and move—your very heart and soul. If you're not made up of love, you'll reflect this feeling to others and experience it within yourself. Inside your chest will be a heart, but one that's heavy and cold and made of stone.

Love isn't just a feeling. Love is a truth filled with forgiveness and kindness. It's a gift that's bursting with generosity and honesty. Love is the willingness to serve and protect, to cherish and respect, to honor and be strong. You don't have to be in love to feel love; you simply need to embody it. That means that while you might not have feelings of love for everyone you meet, you can love them, nonetheless.

Thomas À. Kempis described love in this way: "Love is a great thing, a good above all others, which alone maketh every burden light. Love is watchful, and whilst sleeping, still keeps watch; though fatigued, it is not weary; though pressed, it is not forced."

Have you loved those around you? Have you shown them that you accept them and care for them just the way they are? Have you given this love freely and willingly, with no expectations of anything being returned in kind? Do you acknowledge the goodness, wisdom, beauty, and love in others in the same way you'd like them to acknowledge such things in you?

ॐ ॐ ॐ

I EXPRESS LOVE TO OTHERS AND SO, LOVE MYSELF.

"This is my 'depressed stance.' When you're depressed, it makes a lot of difference how you stand. The worst thing you can do is straighten up and hold your head high because then you'll start to feel better. If you're going to get any joy out of being depressed, you've got to stand like this."

— "Charlie Brown," from *Peanuts*, by Charles Schulz

STANDING TALL, BREATHING DEEP

The classic "depressed stance" is one in which you're stooped over, head down, shoulders rounded. When you adopt such a posture, you convey to everyone around you that you're carrying the weight of the world on your shoulders. With your head hanging down, you can't change your scenery or be distracted by or involved with all the people and activity around you. With your shoulders rounded, you hold yourself as much as possible in a tight ball, as if protecting yourself from further exposure to other hurt, pain, and misfortune.

Consciously changing your posture can really alter your depressed mood. This effort might not make your despondent feelings completely disappear, but with your head held up and shoulders back, you *will* feel better. Give yourself the military commands that will snap you to attention and out of your depressed mood: "Straighten up! Head up! Shoulders back! Eyes forward!" By being able to look around you and see the world face-to-face, you might discover that it's not as scary, as overwhelming, or as draining as you had thought it to be. By not slouching, you're also able to concentrate more on deep breathing to increase your supply of oxygen. Take slow, deep breaths, expanding your chest as well as your abdomen as you walk tall and proud.

ꝋꝋ ꝋꝋ ꝋꝋ

I HOLD MY HEAD HIGH AND WALK WITH ASSURANCE.

"We forge gradually our greatest instrument for understanding the world—introspection."

— Walter Lippmann, U.S. journalist

THE BENEFITS OF MEDITATION

Meditation is a time you can spend with your "self." It's an activity that helps you to focus your attention outside yourself; in so doing, you learn to transcend your problems and, over time, can learn how to transform them in positive, healing ways.

It can be helpful before meditating to move into a quieter frame of mind by reading an inspiring passage from a book, listening to soothing music, lighting candles or incense, or gazing at a favorite picture or object. Then begin your meditation:

- Select a position that's comfortable for you. You may like to sit in a chair, sit cross-legged on the floor, kneel on a cushion, or lie down.
- Spend several minutes getting in touch with yourself. Close your eyes and focus first on each part of your body. Notice where your body touches the chair, cushion, floor, or bed. Pay attention to how your muscles feel. Be aware of your heartbeat. Cover yourself with a blanket if you're feeling chilled.
- Take several deep breaths and notice your breathing. Breathe slowly and deeply into your abdomen, then slowly release each breath. Practice "moving" your breath from one part of your body to another, relaxing your muscles as you do.
- Allow all thoughts to drift through your mind. Remember that you may have intrusive thoughts while you meditate. Just let them drift through your consciousness like puffy white clouds as you maintain your inner peace.

ֆа ֆа ֆа

I PRACTICE MEDITATION EACH DAY.

"To be happy is to be able to become aware of oneself without fright."

— German philosopher Walter Benjamin

SELF-AFFIRMATIONS

After the social whirl of the holidays, you might need some time on your own to settle down, reflect, and re-establish the balance and healing you were working hard to establish before being distracted by the holidays.

One way to do this—and to get a head start on the new year—is to think about, write down in a journal, or share with a supportive friend or family member self-affirmations: statements that affirm the good things you're doing for yourself. You can create affirmations such as:

- I envision what the "healed me" is.
- I flow with the ups and downs of my recovery.
- I seek the support of others.
- I am gentle with myself and ask myself for support.
- I view my problems as creative challenges.
- I enjoy the good that comes my way.
- I treat myself well.
- I praise myself for my courage to learn, risk, and grow.
- I make peace with depression, grief, or "the blues."
- I am patient with myself and the process of healing.

As Confucius said, "It does not matter how slowly you go as long as you do not stop."

やる やる やる

I AFFIRM MY MIND, BODY, AND SPIRITUAL HEALING.

*"You see, George, you've really had a wonderful life. Don't
you see what a mistake it would be to throw it away?"*
— "Angel" talking James Stewart out of suicide
in *It's a Wonderful Life*

AN ATTITUDE OF GRATITUDE

You have so much to be grateful for, and yet depression can rob
you of your gratitude; grief can prevent you from seeing the
good in your loss. Sometimes not being able to be grateful for what
you have denies you the ability to be happy. Whether your despondent moods have led to ingratitude, or being ungrateful has inspired your feelings of depression isn't important. For, as Randall
Miller pointed out, "You can't be depressed and grateful at the
same time." So you have a choice—to be grateful or not.

In any moment, there's something to be grateful for. Look
around you. Focus on one object. Actually, say a statement to yourself such as, "I'm grateful for my lamp." Then find a reason why
you're grateful for that object: "I'm grateful for my lamp because it
provides me with light so I can read." Then move on to another object and feel gratitude for it. Be grateful for all things—what you
can see, hear, taste, touch, and smell.

Share your gratitude with others by expressing your appreciation
and compliments honestly and freely: "You look nice in that outfit,"
"I'm really thankful that you're there for me," and "I like your taste
in music" are just a few examples.

But be sure to be grateful now for the things in your life. As
Colette once wrote: "What a wonderful life I've had! I only wish I'd
realized it sooner."

ॐ ॐ ॐ

I AM GRATEFUL FOR ALL THE PEOPLE AND THINGS IN MY LIFE.

"Together, this collage of thoughts, feelings, and desires forms a visual Inner Map, leading us deep into our hearts and souls—to our very essence."
— authors Gay and David Williamson

CREATING AN INNER MAP

You traditionally look forward to a fresh start—a clean slate—at the beginning of a new year. But the majority of the resolutions you make on New Year's Eve can be punitive rather than positive, or they may focus on what you think is "wrong" rather than on what you think is right. After all, how many of your resolutions begin with "I will not..." "I should..." or "I've got to..."?

Gay and David Williamson suggest an end-of-the-year exercise that encourages you to create an Inner Map—a sort of visual New Year's resolution that allows you to focus on your hopes and dreams rather than on your mistakes or regrets. You'll need scissors, colored paper, glue, old magazines, old greeting cards or postcards, dried flowers and herbs, small beads, glitter—anything suitable to create a collage. Reflect on an aspect of your life you'd like to improve, such as your diet, your moods, and so on. Begin to assemble a collage of images and words that reflects your deepest thoughts on this aspect. Refrain from forcing your design; rather, let your creativity flow.

Then, when your piece is finished, examine it for messages and guidance as a way to get in touch with your deepest needs. Or share this New Year's Eve activity with a supportive friend or family member or members of your support group so you can build communication and closeness.

❧ ❧ ❧

I CREATE AN INNER MAP FOR THE NEW YEAR.

INDEX

ชช ชช ชช

We hope you enjoyed this Hay House book.
If you would like to receive a free catalog
featuring additional Hay House books and products,
or if you would like information about the
Hay Foundation, please write to:

Hay House, Inc., 1154 E. Dominguez St.
P.O. Box 6204, Carson, CA 90749-6204

or call:

(800) 654-5126

ชช ชช ชช